Programming Pig

Alan Gates

Beijing · Cambridge · Farnham · Köln · Sebastopol · Tokyo

Programming Pig
by Alan Gates

Published by O'Reilly Media, Inc., 1005 Gravenstein Highway North, Sebastopol, CA 95472.

O'Reilly books may be purchased for educational, business, or sales promotional use. Online editions are also available for most titles (*http://my.safaribooksonline.com*). For more information, contact our corporate/institutional sales department: (800) 998-9938 or *corporate@oreilly.com*.

Editors: Mike Loukides and Meghan Blanchette	**Indexer:** Jay Marchand
Production Editor: Adam Zaremba	**Cover Designer:** Karen Montgomery
Copyeditor: Genevieve d'Entremont	**Interior Designer:** David Futato
Proofreader: Marlowe Shaeffer	**Illustrator:** Robert Romano

October 2011:   First Edition.

Revision History for the First Edition:
     2011-09-27   First release
See *http://oreilly.com/catalog/errata.csp?isbn=9781449302641* for release details.

ISBN: 978-1-449-30264-1

[LSI]

1317137097

To my wife, Barbara, and our boys, Adam and Joel. Their support, encouragement, and sacrificed Saturdays have made this book possible.

Table of Contents

Preface

Data Addiction

Data is addictive. Our ability to collect and store data has grown massively in the last several decades. Yet our appetite for ever more data shows no sign of being satiated. Scientists want to be able to store more data in order to build better mathematical models of the world. Marketers want better data to understand their customers' desires and buying habits. Financial analysts want to better understand the workings of their markets. And everybody wants to keep all their digital photographs, movies, emails, etc.

The computer and Internet revolutions have greatly increased our ability to collect and store data. Before these revolutions, the US Library of Congress was one of the largest collections of data in the world. It is estimated that its printed collections contain approximately 10 terabytes (TB) of information (*http://www2.sims.berkeley.edu/research/projects/how-much-info/datapowers.html*). Today large Internet companies collect that much data on a daily basis. And it is not just Internet applications that are producing data at prodigious rates. For example, the Large Synoptic Survey Telescope (LSST) planned for construction in Chile is expected to produce 20 TB of data every day (*http://www.symmetrymagazine.org/breaking/2010/10/18/astronomical-computing*).

Part of the reason for this massive growth in data is our ability to collect much more data. Every time someone clicks on a website's links, the web server can record information about what page the user was on and which link he clicked. Every time a car drives over a sensor in the highway, its speed can be recorded. But much of the reason is also our ability to store that data. Ten years ago, telescopes took pictures of the sky every night. But they could not store it at the same detail level that will be possible when the LSST is operational. The extra data was being thrown away because there was nowhere to put it. The ability to collect and store vast quantities of data only feeds our data addiction.

One of the most commonly used tools for storing and processing data in computer systems over the last few decades has been the relational database management system (RDBMS). But as data sets have grown large, only the more sophisticated (and hence more expensive) RDBMSs have been able to reach the scale many users now desire. At the same time, many engineers and scientists involved in processing the data have realized that they do not need everything offered by an RDBMS. These systems are powerful and have many features, but many data owners who need to process terabytes or petabytes of data need only a subset of those features.

The high cost and unneeded features of RDBMSs have led to the development of many alternative data-processing systems. One such alternative system is Apache *Hadoop*. Hadoop is an open source project (*http://hadoop.apache.org*) started by Doug Cutting. Over the past several years, Yahoo! and a number of other web companies have driven the development of Hadoop, which was based on papers published by Google describing how their engineers were dealing with the challenge of storing (*http://labs.google .com/papers/gfs.html*) and processing (*http://labs.google.com/papers/mapreduce.html*) the massive amounts of data they were collecting. For a history of Hadoop, see *Hadoop: The Definitive Guide* (*http://oreilly.com/catalog/9781449389734*), by Tom White (O'Reilly). Hadoop is installed on a cluster of machines and provides a means to tie together storage and processing in that cluster.

The development of new data-processing systems such as Hadoop has spurred the porting of existing tools and languages and the construction of new tools, such as Apache *Pig*. Tools like Pig provide a higher level of abstraction for data users, giving them access to the power and flexibility of Hadoop without requiring them to write extensive data-processing applications in low-level Java code.

Who Should Read This Book

This book is intended for Pig programmers, new and old. Those who have never used Pig will find introductory material on how to run Pig and to get them started writing Pig Latin scripts. For seasoned Pig users, this book covers almost every feature of Pig: different modes it can be run in, complete coverage of the Pig Latin language, and how to extend Pig with your own User Defined Functions (UDFs). Even those who have been using Pig for a long time are likely to discover features they have not used before.

Being a relatively young project, Pig has changed and grown significantly over the last four years. In that time we have released versions 0.1 through 0.9. This book assumes Pig 0.7 as the base version. Wherever features are only in versions 0.8 or 0.9, this is called out. The biggest change from 0.6 to 0.7 is that load and store function interfaces were rewritten, so Chapter 11 will not be usable by those on 0.6 or earlier versions. However, the rest of the book will still be applicable.

Some knowledge of Hadoop will be useful for readers and Pig users. Appendix B provides an introduction to Hadoop and how it works. "Pig on Hadoop" on page 1 walks through a very simple example of a Hadoop job. These sections will be helpful for those not already familiar with Hadoop.

Small snippets of Java, Python, and SQL are used in parts of this book. Knowledge of these languages is not required to use Pig, but knowledge of Python and Java will be necessary for some of the more advanced features. Those with a SQL background may find "Comparing query and dataflow languages" on page 4 to be a helpful starting point in understanding the similarities and differences between Pig Latin and SQL.

Conventions Used in This Book

The following typographical conventions are used in this book:

Italic
: Indicates new terms, URLs, email addresses, filenames, and file extensions.

`Constant width`
: Used for program listings, as well as within paragraphs to refer to program elements such as variable or function names, databases, data types, environment variables, statements, and keywords.

`Constant width bold`
: Shows commands or other text that should be typed literally by the user.

`Constant width italic`
: Shows text that should be replaced with user-supplied values or by values determined by context.

 This icon signifies a tip, suggestion, or general note.

 This icon indicates a warning or caution.

Code Examples in This Book

Many of the example scripts, User Defined Functions (UDFs), and data used in this book are available for download from my GitHub repository (*https://github.com/alanf gates/programmingpig*). *README* files are included to help you get the UDFs built and to understand the contents of the datafiles. Each example script in the text that is available on GitHub has a comment at the beginning that gives the filename. Pig Latin and Python script examples are organized by chapter in the *examples* directory. UDFs, both Java and Python, are in a separate directory, *udfs*. All data sets are in the *data* directory.

For brevity, each script is written assuming that the input and output are in the local directory. Therefore, when in local mode, you should run Pig in the directory that the input data is in. When running on a cluster, you should place the data in your home directory on the cluster.

Example scripts were tested against Pig 0.8.0 or 0.8.1, except those scripts that use functionality newly introduced in version 0.9. These were run against builds from the 0.9 branch because 0.9 was not released until much of the book had been written.

The three data sets used in the examples are real data sets, though quite small. The file *baseball* contains baseball player statistics. A second set contains New York Stock Exchange data in two files: *NYSE_daily* and *NYSE_dividends*. This data was trimmed to include only stock symbols, starting with C from the year 2009, to make the data small enough to download easily. However, the schema of the data has not changed. If you want to download the entire data set and place it on a cluster (only a few nodes would be necessary), it would be a more realistic demonstration of Pig and Hadoop. Instructions on how to download the data are in the *README* files. The third data set is a very brief web crawl started from Pig's web page.

Using Code Examples

This book is here to help you get your job done. In general, you may use the code in this book in your programs and documentation. You do not need to contact us for permission unless you're reproducing a significant portion of the code. For example, writing a program that uses several chunks of code from this book does not require permission. Selling or distributing a CD-ROM of examples from O'Reilly books does require permission. Answering a question by citing this book and quoting example code does not require permission. Incorporating a significant amount of example code from this book into your product's documentation does require permission.

We appreciate, but do not require, attribution. An attribution usually includes the title, author, publisher, and ISBN. For example: "*Programming Pig* by Alan Gates (O'Reilly). Copyright 2011 Yahoo!, Inc., 978-1-449-30264-1."

If you feel your use of code examples falls outside fair use or the permission given above, feel free to contact us at *permissions@oreilly.com*.

Safari® Books Online

Safari Books Online is an on-demand digital library that lets you easily search over 7,500 technology and creative reference books and videos to find the answers you need quickly.

With a subscription, you can read any page and watch any video from our library online. Read books on your cell phone and mobile devices. Access new titles before they are available for print, and get exclusive access to manuscripts in development and post feedback for the authors. Copy and paste code samples, organize your favorites, download chapters, bookmark key sections, create notes, print out pages, and benefit from tons of other time-saving features.

O'Reilly Media has uploaded this book to the Safari Books Online service. To have full digital access to this book and others on similar topics from O'Reilly and other publishers, sign up for free at *http://my.safaribooksonline.com*.

How to Contact Us

Please address comments and questions concerning this book to the publisher:

O'Reilly Media, Inc.
1005 Gravenstein Highway North
Sebastopol, CA 95472
800-998-9938 (in the United States or Canada)
707-829-0515 (international or local)
707-829-0104 (fax)

We have a web page for this book, where we list errata, examples, and any additional information. You can access this page at:

http://shop.oreilly.com/product/0636920018087.do

To comment or ask technical questions about this book, send email to:

bookquestions@oreilly.com

For more information about our books, conferences, Resource Centers, and the O'Reilly Network, see our website at:

http://www.oreilly.com

Acknowledgments

A book is like a professional football team. Much of the glory goes to the quarterback or a running back. But if the team has a bad offensive line, the quarterback never gets the chance to throw the ball. Receivers must be able to catch, and the defense must be able to prevent the other team from scoring. In short, the whole team must play well in order to win. And behind those on the field there is an array of coaches, trainers, and managers who prepare and guide the team. So it is with this book. My name goes on the cover. But without the amazing group of developers, researchers, testers, documentation writers, and users that contribute to the Pig project, there would be nothing worth writing about.

In particular, I would like to acknowledge Pig contributors and users for their contributions and feedback on this book. Chris Olston, Ben Reed, Richard Ding, Olga Natkovitch, Thejas Nair, Daniel Dai, and Dmitriy Ryaboy all provided helpful feedback on draft after draft. Julien Le Dem provided the example code for embedding Pig in Python. Jeremy Hanna wrote the section for Pig and Cassandra. Corrine Chandel deserves special mention for reviewing the entire book. Her feedback has added greatly to the book's clarity and correctness.

Thanks go to Tom White for encouraging me in my aspiration to write this book, and for the sober warnings concerning the amount of time and effort it would require. Chris Douglas of the Hadoop project provided me with very helpful feedback on the sections covering Hadoop and MapReduce.

I would also like to thank Mike Loukides and the entire team at O'Reilly. They have made writing my first book an enjoyable and exhilarating experience. Finally, thanks to Yahoo! for nurturing Pig and dedicating more than 25 engineering years (and still counting) of effort to it, and for graciously giving me the time to write this book.

## CHAPTER 1

Introduction

What Is Pig?

Pig provides an engine for executing data flows in parallel on Hadoop. It includes a language, *Pig Latin*, for expressing these data flows. Pig Latin includes operators for many of the traditional data operations (join, sort, filter, etc.), as well as the ability for users to develop their own functions for reading, processing, and writing data.

Pig is an Apache open source project (*http://pig.apache.org*). This means users are free to download it as source or binary, use it for themselves, contribute to it, and—under the terms of the Apache License—use it in their products and change it as they see fit.

Pig on Hadoop

Pig runs on Hadoop. It makes use of both the Hadoop Distributed File System, *HDFS*, and Hadoop's processing system, *MapReduce*.

HDFS is a distributed filesystem that stores files across all of the nodes in a Hadoop cluster. It handles breaking the files into large blocks and distributing them across different machines, including making multiple copies of each block so that if any one machine fails no data is lost. It presents a POSIX-like interface to users. By default, Pig reads input files from HDFS, uses HDFS to store intermediate data between MapReduce jobs, and writes its output to HDFS. As you will see in Chapter 11, it can also read input from and write output to sources other than HDFS.

MapReduce is a simple but powerful parallel data-processing paradigm. Every job in MapReduce consists of three main phases: map, shuffle, and reduce. In the map phase, the application has the opportunity to operate on each record in the input separately. Many maps are started at once so that while the input may be gigabytes or terabytes in size, given enough machines, the map phase can usually be completed in under one minute.

Part of the specification of a MapReduce job is the key on which data will be collected. For example, if you were processing web server logs for a website that required users to log in, you might choose the user ID to be your key so that you could see everything done by each user on your website. In the shuffle phase, which happens after the map phase, data is collected together by the key the user has chosen and distributed to different machines for the reduce phase. Every record for a given key will go to the same reducer.

In the reduce phase, the application is presented each key, together with all of the records containing that key. Again this is done in parallel on many machines. After processing each group, the reducer can write its output. See the next section for a walkthrough of a simple MapReduce program. For more details on how MapReduce works, see "MapReduce" on page 189.

MapReduce's hello world

Consider a simple MapReduce application that counts the number of times each word appears in a given text. This is the "hello world" program of MapReduce. In this example the map phase will read each line in the text, one at a time. It will then split out each word into a separate string, and, for each word, it will output the word and a 1 to indicate it has seen the word one time. The shuffle phase will use the word as the key, hashing the records to reducers. The reduce phase will then sum up the number of times each word was seen and write that together with the word as output. Let's consider the case of the nursery rhyme "Mary Had a Little Lamb." Our input will be:

```
Mary had a little lamb
its fleece was white as snow
and everywhere that Mary went
the lamb was sure to go.
```

Let's assume that each line is sent to a different map task. In reality, each map is assigned much more data than this, but it makes the example easier to follow. The data flow through MapReduce is shown in Figure 1-1.

Once the map phase is complete, the shuffle phase will collect all records with the same word onto the same reducer. For this example we assume that there are two reducers: all words that start with A-L are sent to the first reducer, and M-Z are sent to the second reducer. The reducers will then output the summed counts for each word.

Pig uses MapReduce to execute all of its data processing. It compiles the Pig Latin scripts that users write into a series of one or more MapReduce jobs that it then executes. See Example 1-1 for a Pig Latin script that will do a word count of "Mary Had a Little Lamb."

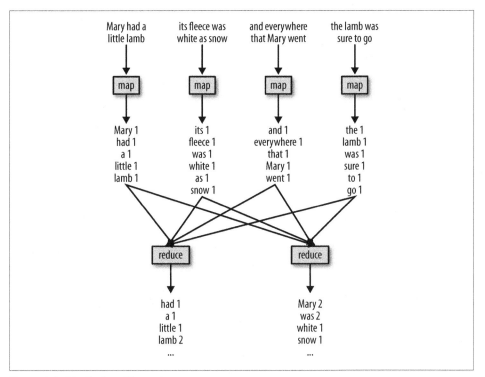

Figure 1-1. MapReduce illustration

Example 1-1. Pig counts Mary and her lamb

```
-- Load input from the file named Mary, and call the single
-- field in the record 'line'.
input = load 'mary' as (line);

-- TOKENIZE splits the line into a field for each word.
-- flatten will take the collection of records returned by
-- TOKENIZE and produce a separate record for each one, calling the single
-- field in the record word.
words = foreach input generate flatten(TOKENIZE(line)) as word;

-- Now group them together by each word.
grpd  = group words by word;

-- Count them.
cntd  = foreach grpd generate group, COUNT(words);
-- Print out the results.
dump cntd;
```

There is no need to be concerned with map, shuffle, and reduce phases when using Pig. It will manage decomposing the operators in your script into the appropriate MapReduce phases.

Pig Latin, a Parallel Dataflow Language

Pig Latin is a dataflow language. This means it allows users to describe how data from one or more inputs should be read, processed, and then stored to one or more outputs in parallel. These data flows can be simple linear flows like the word count example given previously. They can also be complex workflows that include points where multiple inputs are joined, and where data is split into multiple streams to be processed by different operators. To be mathematically precise, a Pig Latin script describes a *directed acyclic graph* (DAG), where the edges are data flows and the nodes are operators that process the data.

This means that Pig Latin looks different from many of the programming languages you have seen. There are no if statements or for loops in Pig Latin. This is because traditional procedural and object-oriented programming languages describe control flow, and data flow is a side effect of the program. Pig Latin instead focuses on data flow. For information on how to integrate the data flow described by a Pig Latin script with control flow, see Chapter 9.

Comparing query and dataflow languages

After a cursory look, people often say that Pig Latin is a procedural version of SQL. Although there are certainly similarities, there are more differences. SQL is a query language. Its focus is to allow users to form queries. It allows users to describe what question they want answered, but not how they want it answered. In Pig Latin, on the other hand, the user describes exactly how to process the input data.

Another major difference is that SQL is oriented around answering one question. When users want to do several data operations together, they must either write separate queries, storing the intermediate data into temporary tables, or write it in one query using subqueries inside that query to do the earlier steps of the processing. However, many SQL users find subqueries confusing and difficult to form properly. Also, using subqueries creates an inside-out design where the first step in the data pipeline is the innermost query.

Pig, however, is designed with a long series of data operations in mind, so there is no need to write the data pipeline in an inverted set of subqueries or to worry about storing data in temporary tables. This is illustrated in Examples 1-2 and 1-3.

Consider a case where a user wants to group one table on a key and then join it with a second table. Because joins happen before grouping in a SQL query, this must be expressed either as a subquery or as two queries with the results stored in a temporary table. Example 1-3 will use a temporary table, as that is more readable.

Example 1-2. Group then join in SQL

```
CREATE TEMP TABLE t1 AS
SELECT customer, sum(purchase) AS total_purchases
FROM transactions
GROUP BY customer;

SELECT customer, total_purchases, zipcode
FROM t1, customer_profile
WHERE t1.customer = customer_profile.customer;
```

In Pig Latin, on the other hand, this looks like Example 1-3.

Example 1-3. Group then join in Pig Latin

```
-- Load the transactions file, group it by customer, and sum their total purchases
txns    = load 'transactions' as (customer, purchase);
grouped = group txns by customer;
total   = foreach grouped generate group, SUM(txns.purchase) as tp;
-- Load the customer_profile file
profile = load 'customer_profile' as (customer, zipcode);
-- join the grouped and summed transactions and customer_profile data
answer  = join total by group, profile by customer;
-- Write the results to the screen
dump answer;
```

Furthermore, each was designed to live in a different environment. SQL is designed for the RDBMS environment, where data is normalized and schemas and proper constraints are enforced (that is, there are no nulls in places they do not belong, etc.). Pig is designed for the Hadoop data-processing environment, where schemas are sometimes unknown or inconsistent. Data may not be properly constrained, and it is rarely normalized. As a result of these differences, Pig does not require data to be loaded into tables first. It can operate on data as soon as it is copied into HDFS.

An analogy with human languages and cultures might help. My wife and I have been to France together a couple of times. I speak very little French. But because English is the language of commerce (and probably because Americans and the British like to vacation in France), there is enough English spoken in France for me to get by. My wife, on the other hand, speaks French. She has friends there to visit. She can talk to people we meet. She can explore the parts of France that are not on the common tourist itinerary. Her experience of France is much deeper than mine because she can speak the native language.

SQL is the English of data processing. It has the nice feature that everyone and every tool knows it, which means the barrier to adoption is very low. Our goal is to make Pig Latin the native language of parallel data-processing systems such as Hadoop. It may take some learning, but it will allow users to utilize the power of Hadoop much more fully.

How Pig differs from MapReduce

I have just made the claim that a goal of the Pig team is to make Pig Latin the native language of parallel data-processing environments such as Hadoop. But does MapReduce not provide enough? Why is Pig necessary?

Pig provides users with several advantages over using MapReduce directly. Pig Latin provides all of the standard data-processing operations, such as join, filter, group by, order by, union, etc. MapReduce provides the group by operation directly (that is what the shuffle plus reduce phases are), and it provides the order by operation indirectly through the way it implements the grouping. Filter and projection can be implemented trivially in the map phase. But other operators, particularly join, are not provided and must instead be written by the user.

Pig provides some complex, nontrivial implementations of these standard data operations. For example, because the number of records per key in a dataset is rarely evenly distributed, the data sent to the reducers is often skewed. That is, one reducer will get 10 or more times the data than other reducers. Pig has join and order by operators that will handle this case and (in some cases) rebalance the reducers. But these took the Pig team months to write, and rewriting these in MapReduce would be time consuming.

In MapReduce, the data processing inside the map and reduce phases is opaque to the system. This means that MapReduce has no opportunity to optimize or check the user's code. Pig, on the other hand, can analyze a Pig Latin script and understand the data flow that the user is describing. That means it can do early error checking (did the user try to add a string field to an integer field?) and optimizations (can these two grouping operations be combined?).

MapReduce does not have a type system. This is intentional, and it gives users the flexibility to use their own data types and serialization frameworks. But the downside is that this further limits the system's ability to check users' code for errors both before and during runtime.

All of these points mean that Pig Latin is much lower cost to write and maintain than Java code for MapReduce. In one very unscientific experiment, I wrote the same operation in Pig Latin and MapReduce. Given one file with user data and one with click data for a website, the Pig Latin script in Example 1-4 will find the five pages most visited by users between the ages of 18 and 25.

Example 1-4. Finding the top five URLs

```
Users = load 'users' as (name, age);
Fltrd = filter Users by age >= 18 and age <= 25;
Pages = load 'pages' as (user, url);
Jnd   = join Fltrd by name, Pages by user;
Grpd  = group Jnd by url;
Smmd  = foreach Grpd generate group, COUNT(Jnd) as clicks;
Srtd  = order Smmd by clicks desc;
Top5  = limit Srtd 5;
store Top5 into 'top5sites';
```

The first line of this program loads the file *users* and declares that this data has two fields: name and age. It assigns the name of Users to the input. The second line applies a filter to Users that passes through records with an age between 18 and 25, inclusive. All other records are discarded. Now the data has only records of users in the age range we are interested in. The results of this filter are named Fltrd.

The second load statement loads *pages* and names it Pages. It declares its schema to have two fields, user and url.

The line Jnd = join joins together Fltrd and Pages using Fltrd.name and Pages.user as the key. After this join we have found all the URLs each user has visited.

The line Grpd = group collects records together by URL. So for each value of url, such as pignews.com/frontpage, there will be one record with a collection of all records that have that value in the url field. The next line then counts how many records are collected together for each URL. So after this line we now know, for each URL, how many times it was visited by users aged 18–25.

The next thing to do is to sort this from most visits to least. The line Srtd = order sorts on the count value from the previous line and places it in desc (descending) order. Thus the largest value will be first. Finally, we need only the top five pages, so the last line limits the sorted results to only five records. The results of this are then stored back to HDFS in the file *top5sites*.

In Pig Latin this comes to nine lines of code and took about 15 minutes to write and debug. The same code in MapReduce (omitted here for brevity) came out to about 170 lines of code and took me four hours to get working. The Pig Latin will similarly be easier to maintain, as future developers can easily understand and modify this code.

There is, of course, a cost to all this. It is possible to develop algorithms in MapReduce that cannot be done easily in Pig. And the developer gives up a level of control. A good engineer can always, given enough time, write code that will out perform a generic system. So for less common algorithms or extremely performance-sensitive ones, Map-Reduce is still the right choice. Basically this is the same situation as choosing to code in Java versus a scripting language such as Python. Java has more power, but due to its lower-level nature, it requires more development time than scripting languages. Developers will need to choose the right tool for each job.

What Is Pig Useful For?

In my experience, Pig Latin use cases tend to fall into three separate categories: traditional extract transform load (ETL) data pipelines, research on raw data, and iterative processing.

The largest use case is data pipelines. A common example is web companies bringing in logs from their web servers, cleansing the data, and precomputing common aggregates before loading it into their data warehouse. In this case, the data is loaded onto the grid, and then Pig is used to clean out records from bots and records with corrupt data. It is also used to join web event data against user databases so that user cookies can be connected with known user information.

Another example of data pipelines is using Pig offline to build behavior prediction models. Pig is used to scan through all the user interactions with a website and split the users into various segments. Then, for each segment, a mathematical model is produced that predicts how members of that segment will respond to types of advertisements or news articles. In this way the website can show ads that are more likely to get clicked on, or offer news stories that are more likely to engage users and keep them coming back to the site.

Traditionally, ad-hoc queries are done in languages such as SQL that make it easy to quickly form a question for the data to answer. However, for research on raw data, some users prefer Pig Latin. Because Pig can operate in situations where the schema is unknown, incomplete, or inconsistent, and because it can easily manage nested data, researchers who want to work on data before it has been cleaned and loaded into the warehouse often prefer Pig. Researchers who work with large data sets often use scripting languages such as Perl or Python to do their processing. Users with these backgrounds often prefer the dataflow paradigm of Pig over the declarative query paradigm of SQL.

Users building iterative processing models are also starting to use Pig. Consider a news website that keeps a graph of all news stories on the Web that it is tracking. In this graph each news story is a node, and edges indicate relationships between the stories. For example, all stories about an upcoming election are linked together. Every five minutes a new set of stories comes in, and the data-processing engine must integrate them into the graph. Some of these stories are new, some are updates of existing stories, and some supersede existing stories. Some data-processing steps need to operate on this entire graph of stories. For example, a process that builds a behavioral targeting model needs to join user data against this entire graph of stories. Rerunning the entire join every five minutes is not feasible because it cannot be completed in five minutes with a reasonable amount of hardware. But the model builders do not want to update these models only on a daily basis, as that means an entire day of missed serving opportunities.

To cope with this problem, it is possible to first do a join against the entire graph on a regular basis, for example, daily. Then, as new data comes in every five minutes, a join can be done with just the new incoming data, and these results can be combined with the results of the join against the whole graph. This combination step takes some care, as the five-minute data contains the equivalent of inserts, updates, and deletes on the entire graph. It is possible and reasonably convenient to express this combination in Pig Latin.

One point that is implicit in everything I have said so far is that Pig (like MapReduce) is oriented around the batch processing of data. If you need to process gigabytes or terabytes of data, Pig is a good choice. But it expects to read all the records of a file and write all of its output sequentially. For workloads that require writing single or small groups of records, or looking up many different records in random order, Pig (like MapReduce) is not a good choice. See "NoSQL Databases" on page 166 for a discussion of applications that are good for these use cases.

Pig Philosophy

Early on, people who came to the Pig project as potential contributors did not always understand what the project was about. They were not sure how to best contribute or which contributions would be accepted and which would not. So, the Pig team produced a statement of the project's philosophy (*http://pig.apache.org/philosophy.html*) that summarizes what Pig aspires to be:

Pigs eat anything
> Pig can operate on data whether it has metadata or not. It can operate on data that is relational, nested, or unstructured. And it can easily be extended to operate on data beyond files, including key/value stores, databases, etc.

Pigs live anywhere
> Pig is intended to be a language for parallel data processing. It is not tied to one particular parallel framework. It has been implemented first on Hadoop, but we do not intend that to be only on Hadoop.

Pigs are domestic animals
> Pig is designed to be easily controlled and modified by its users.
>
> Pig allows integration of user code wherever possible, so it currently supports user defined field transformation functions, user defined aggregates, and user defined conditionals. These functions can be written in Java or in scripting languages that can compile down to Java (e.g., Jython). Pig supports user provided load and store functions. It supports external executables via its `stream` command and MapReduce JARs via its `mapreduce` command. It allows users to provide a custom partitioner for their jobs in some circumstances, and to set the level of reduce parallelism for their jobs.
>
> Pig has an optimizer that rearranges some operations in Pig Latin scripts to give better performance, combines MapReduce jobs together, etc. However, users can easily turn this optimizer off to prevent it from making changes that do not make sense in their situation.

Pigs fly
> Pig processes data quickly. We want to consistently improve performance, and not implement features in ways that weigh Pig down so it can't fly.

Pig's History

Pig started out as a research project in Yahoo! Research, where Yahoo! scientists designed it and produced an initial implementation. As explained in a paper presented at SIGMOD in 2008,[*] the researchers felt that the MapReduce paradigm presented by Hadoop "is too low-level and rigid, and leads to a great deal of custom user code that is hard to maintain and reuse." At the same time they observed that many MapReduce users were not comfortable with declarative languages such as SQL. Thus they set out to produce "a new language called Pig Latin that we have designed to fit in a sweet spot between the declarative style of SQL, and the low-level, procedural style of MapReduce."

Yahoo! Hadoop users started to adopt Pig. So, a team of development engineers was assembled to take the research prototype and build it into a production-quality product. About this same time, in fall 2007, Pig was open sourced via the Apache Incubator. The first Pig release came a year later in September 2008. Later that same year, Pig graduated from the Incubator and became a subproject of Apache Hadoop.

Early in 2009 other companies started to use Pig for their data processing. Amazon also added Pig as part of its Elastic MapReduce service. By the end of 2009 about half of Hadoop jobs at Yahoo! were Pig jobs. In 2010, Pig adoption continued to grow, and Pig graduated from a Hadoop subproject, becoming its own top-level Apache project.

Why Is It Called Pig?

One question that is frequently asked is, "Why is it named Pig?" People also want to know whether Pig is an acronym. It is not. The story goes that the researchers working on the project initially referred to it simply as "the language." Eventually they needed to call it something. Off the top of his head, one researcher suggested Pig, and the name stuck. It is quirky yet memorable and easy to spell. While some have hinted that the name sounds coy or silly, it has provided us with an entertaining nomenclature, such as Pig Latin for a language, Grunt for a shell, and Piggybank for a CPAN-like shared repository.

---

[*] Christopher Olston et al, "Pig Latin: A Not-So-Foreign Language for Data Processing," available at *http://portal.acm.org/citation.cfm?id=1376726*.

## CHAPTER 2

Installing and Running Pig

Downloading and Installing Pig

Before you can run Pig on your machine or your Hadoop cluster, you will need to download and install it. If someone else has taken care of this, you can skip ahead to "Running Pig" on page 13.

You can download Pig as a complete package or as source code that you build. You can also get it as part of a Hadoop distribution.

Downloading the Pig Package from Apache

This is the official version of Apache Pig. It comes packaged with all of the JAR files needed to run Pig. It can be downloaded by going to Pig's release page (*http://pig.apache .org/releases.html*).

Pig does not need to be installed on your Hadoop cluster. It runs on the machine from which you launch Hadoop jobs. Though you can run Pig from your laptop or desktop, in practice, most cluster owners set up one or more machines that have access to their Hadoop cluster but are not part of the cluster (that is, they are not data nodes or task nodes). This makes it easier for administrators to update Pig and associated tools, as well as to secure access to the clusters. These machines are called *gateway machines* or *edge machines*. In this book I use the term gateway machine.

You will need to install Pig on these gateway machines. If your Hadoop cluster is accessible from your desktop or laptop, you can install Pig there as well. Also, you can install Pig on your local machine if you plan to use Pig in local mode.

The core of Pig is written in Java and is thus portable across operating systems. The shell script that starts Pig is a bash script, so it requires a Unix environment. Hadoop, which Pig depends on, even in local mode, also requires a Unix environment for its filesystem operations. In practice, most Hadoop clusters run a flavor of Linux. Many Pig developers develop and test Pig on Mac OS X.

Pig requires Java 1.6, and Pig versions 0.5 through 0.9 require Hadoop 0.20. For future versions, check the download page for information on what version(s) of Hadoop they require. The correct version of Hadoop is included with the Pig download. If you plan to use Pig in local mode or install it on a gateway machine where Hadoop is not currently installed, there is no need to download Hadoop separately.

Once you have downloaded Pig, you can place it anywhere you like on your machine, as it does not depend on being in a certain location. To install it, place the tarball in the directory of your choosing and type:

```
tar xzf filename
```

where *filename* is the TAR file you downloaded.

The only other setup in preparation for running Pig is making sure that the environment variable JAVA_HOME is set to the directory that contains your Java distribution. Pig will fail immediately if this value is not in the environment. You can set this in your shell, specify it on the command line when you invoke Pig, or set it explicitly in your copy of the Pig script pig, located in the *bin* directory that you just unpacked. You can find the appropriate value for JAVA_HOME by executing which java and stripping the bin/java from the end of the result.

Downloading Pig from Cloudera

In addition to the official Apache version, there are companies that repackage and distribute Hadoop and associated tools. Currently the most popular of these is Cloudera, which produces RPMs for Red Hat–based systems and packages for use with APT on Debian systems. It also provides tarballs for other systems that cannot use one of these package managers.

The upside of using a distribution like Cloudera's is that all of the tools are packaged and tested together. Also, if you need professional support, it is available. The downside is that you are constrained to move at the speed of your distribution provider. There is a delay between an Apache release of Pig and its availability in various distributions.

For complete instructions on downloading and installing Hadoop and Pig from Cloudera, see Cloudera's download site (*http://www.cloudera.com/downloads*). Note that you have to download Pig separately; it is not part of the Hadoop package.

Downloading Pig Artifacts from Maven

In addition to the official release available from Pig's Apache site, it is possible to download Pig from Apache's Maven repository (*https://repository.apache.org/content/repositories/releases/org/apache/pig/pig*). This site includes JAR files for Pig, for the source code, and for the Javadocs, as well as the POM file that defines Pig's dependencies. Development tools that are Maven-aware can use this to pull down Pig's source and Javadoc. If you use maven or ant in your build process, you can also pull the Pig JAR from this repository automatically.

Downloading the Source

When you download Pig from Apache, you also get the Pig source code. This enables you to debug your version of Pig or just peruse the code to see how it works. But if you want to live on the edge and try out a feature or a bug fix before it is available in a release, you can download the source from Apache's Subversion repository. You can also apply patches that have been uploaded to Pig's issue-tracking system (*http://issues .apache.org/jira/browse/PIG*) but that are not yet checked into the code repository. Information on checking out Pig using svn or cloning the repository via git is available on Pig's version control page (*http://pig.apache.org/version_control.html*).

Running Pig

You can run Pig locally on your machine or on your grid. You can also run Pig as part of Amazon's Elastic MapReduce service.

Running Pig Locally on Your Machine

Running Pig locally on your machine is referred to in Pig parlance as *local mode*. Local mode is useful for prototyping and debugging your Pig Latin scripts. Some people also use it for small data when they want to apply the same processing to large data—so that their data pipeline is consistent across data of different sizes—but they do not want to waste cluster resources on small files and small jobs.

In versions 0.6 and earlier, Pig executed scripts in local mode itself. Starting with version 0.7, it uses the Hadoop class LocalJobRunner that reads from the local filesystem and executes MapReduce jobs locally. This has the nice property that Pig jobs run locally in the same way as they will on your cluster, and they all run in one process, making debugging much easier. The downside is that it is slow. Setting up a local instance of Hadoop has approximately a 20-second overhead, so even tiny jobs take at least that long.[*]

Let's run a Pig Latin script in local mode. See "Code Examples in This Book" on page xi for how to download the data and Pig Latin for this example. The simple script in Example 2-1 loads the file *NYSE_dividends*, groups the file's rows by stock ticker symbol, and then calculates the average dividend for each symbol.

---

[*] Another reason for switching to MapReduce for local mode was that as Pig added features that took advantage of more advanced MapReduce features, it became difficult or impossible to replicate those features in local mode. Thus local mode and MapReduce mode were diverging in their feature set.

Example 2-1. Running Pig in local mode

```
--average_dividend.pig
-- load data from NYSE_dividends, declaring the schema to have 4 fields
dividends = load 'NYSE_dividends' as (exchange, symbol, date, dividend);
-- group rows together by stock ticker symbol
grouped   = group dividends by symbol;
-- calculate the average dividend per symbol
avg       = foreach grouped generate group, AVG(dividends.dividend);
-- store the results to average_dividend
store avg into 'average_dividend';
```

If you use head -5 to look at the *NYSE_dividends* file, you will see:

```
NYSE    CPO 2009-12-30  0.14
NYSE    CPO 2009-09-28  0.14
NYSE    CPO 2009-06-26  0.14
NYSE    CPO 2009-03-27  0.14
NYSE    CPO 2009-01-06  0.14
```

This matches the schema we declared in our Pig Latin script. The first field is the exchange this stock is traded on, the second field is the stock ticker symbol, the third is the date the dividend was paid, and the fourth is the amount of the dividend.

> Remember that to run Pig you will need to set the JAVA_HOME environment variable to the directory that contains your Java distribution.

Switch to the directory where *NYSE_dividends* is located. You can then run this example on your local machine by entering:

```
pig_path/bin/pig -x local average_dividend.pig
```

where *pig_path* is the path to the Pig installation on your local machine.

The result should be a lot of output on your screen. Much of this is MapReduce's LocalJobRunner generating logs. But some of it is Pig telling you how it will execute the script, giving you the status as it executes, etc. Near the bottom of the output you should see the simple message Success!. This means all went well. The script stores its output to *average_dividend*, so you might expect to find a file by that name in your local directory. Instead you will find a directory named *average_dividend* that contains a file named *part-r-00000*. Because Hadoop is a distributed system and usually processes data in parallel, when it outputs data to a "file" it creates a directory with the file's name, and each writer creates a separate *part file* in that directory. In this case we had one writer, so we have one part file. We can look in that part file for the results by entering:

```
cat average_dividend/part-r-00000 | head -5
```

which returns:

```
CA    0.04
CB    0.35
CE    0.04
CF    0.1
CI    0.04
```

Running Pig on Your Hadoop Cluster

Most of the time you will be running Pig on your Hadoop cluster. As was covered in "Downloading and Installing Pig" on page 11, Pig runs locally on your machine or your gateway machine. All of the parsing, checking, and planning is done locally. Pig then executes MapReduce jobs in your cluster.

 When I say "your gateway machine," I mean the machine from which you are launching Pig jobs. Usually this will be one or more machines that have access to your Hadoop cluster. However, depending on your configuration, it could be your local machine as well.

The only thing Pig needs to know to run on your cluster is the location of your cluster's *NameNode* and *JobTracker*. The NameNode is the manager of HDFS, and the Job-Tracker coordinates MapReduce jobs. In Hadoop 0.18 and earlier, these locations are found in your *hadoop-site.xml* file. In Hadoop 0.20 and later, they are in three separate files: *core-site.xml*, *hdfs-site.xml*, and *mapred-site.xml*.

If you are already running Hadoop jobs from your gateway machine via MapReduce or another tool, you most likely have these files present. If not, the best course is to copy these files from nodes in your cluster to a location on your gateway machine. This guarantees that you get the proper addresses plus any site-specific settings.

If, for whatever reason, it is not possible to copy the appropriate files from your cluster, you can create a *hadoop-site.xml* file yourself. It will look like the following:

```
<configuration>
<property>
  <name>fs.default.name</name>
  <value>namenode_hostname:port</value>
</property>

<property>
  <name>mapred.job.tracker</name>
  <value>jobtrack_hostname:port</value>
</property>
</configuration>
```

You will need to find the names and ports for your NameNode and JobTracker from your cluster administrator.

Once you have located, copied, or created these files, you will need to tell Pig the directory they are in by setting the PIG_CLASSPATH environment variable to that directory. Note that this must point to the *directory* that the XML file is in, not the file itself. Pig will read all XML and properties files in that directory.

Let's run the same script on your cluster that we ran in the local mode example (Example 2-1). If you are running on a Hadoop cluster you have never used before, you will most likely need to create a home directory. Pig can do this for you:

```
PIG_CLASSPATH=hadoop_conf_dir pig_path/bin/pig -e fs -mkdir /user/username
```

where *hadoop_conf_dir* is the directory where your *hadoop-site.xml* or *core-site.xml*, *hdfs-site.xml*, and *mapred-site.xml* files are located; *pig_path* is the path to Pig on your gateway machine; and *username* is your username on the gateway machine. If you are using 0.5 or earlier, change fs -mkdir to mkdir.

 Remember, you need to set JAVA_HOME before executing any Pig commands. See "Downloading the Pig Package from Apache" on page 11 for details.

In order to run this example on your cluster, you first need to copy the data to your cluster:

```
PIG_CLASSPATH=hadoop_conf_dir pig_path/bin/pig -e fs -copyFromLocal NYSE_dividends
    NYSE_dividends
```

If you are running Pig 0.5 or earlier, change fs -copyFromLocal to copyFromLocal.

Now you are ready to run the Pig Latin script itself:

```
PIG_CLASSPATH=hadoop_conf_dir pig_path/bin/pig average_dividend.pig
```

The first few lines of output will tell you how Pig is connecting to your cluster. After that it will describe its progress in executing your script. It is important for you to verify that Pig is connecting to the appropriate filesystem and JobTracker by checking that these values match the values for your cluster. If the filesystem is listed as *file:///* or the JobTracker says localhost, Pig did not connect to your cluster. You will need to check that you entered the values properly in your configuration files and properly set PIG_CLASSPATH to the directory that contains those files.

Near the end of the output there should be a line saying Success!. This means that your execution succeeded. You can see the results by entering:

```
PIG_CLASSPATH=hadoop_conf_dir pig_path/bin/pig -e cat average_dividend
```

which should give you the same connection information and then dump all of the stock ticker symbols and their average dividends.

In Example 2-1 you may have noticed that I made a point to say that *average_dividend* is a directory, and thus you have to cat the part file contained in that directory.

However, in this example I ran `cat` directly on *average_dividend*. If you list *average_dividend*, you will see that it is still a directory in this example, but in Pig, `cat` can operate on directories. See Chapter 3 for a discussion of this.

Running Pig in the Cloud

Cloud computing[†] along with the *software as a service* (SaaS) model have taken off in recent years. This has been fortuitous for hardware-intensive applications such as Hadoop. Setting up and maintaining a Hadoop cluster is an expensive proposition in terms of hardware acquisition, facility costs, and maintenance and administration. Many users find that it is cheaper to rent the hardware they need instead.

Whether you or your organization decides to use Hadoop and Pig in the cloud or on owned and operated machines, the instructions for running Pig on your cluster are the same; see "Running Pig on Your Hadoop Cluster" on page 15.

However, Amazon's *Elastic MapReduce* (EMR) cloud offering is different. Rather than allowing customers to rent machines for any type of process (like Amazon's Elastic Cloud Computing [EC2] service and other cloud services), EMR allows users to rent virtual Hadoop clusters. These clusters read data from and write data to Amazon's Simple Storage Service (S3). This means users do not even need to set up their own Hadoop cluster, which they would have to do if they used EC2 or a similar service.

EMR users can access their rented Hadoop cluster via their browser, SSH, or a web services API. For information about EMR, visit *http://aws.amazon.com/elasticmapreduce*. However, I suggest beginning with this nice tutorial (*http://s3.amazonaws.com/awsVideos/AmazonElasticMapReduce/ElasticMapReduce-PigTutorial.html*), which will introduce you to the service.

Command-Line and Configuration Options

Pig has a number of command-line options that you can use with it. You can see the full list by entering `pig -h`. Most of these options will be discussed later, in the sections that cover the features these options control. In this section I discuss the remaining miscellaneous options:

-e *or* -execute
> Execute a single command in Pig. For example, `pig -e fs -ls` will list your home directory.

-h *or* -help
> List the available command-line options.

---

† Being the current flavor of the month, the term cloud computing is being used to describe just about anything that takes more than one computer and is not located on a person's desktop. In this chapter I use cloud computing to mean the ability to rent a cluster of computers and place software of your choosing on those computers.

`-h properties`
> List the properties that Pig will use if they are set by the user.

`-P` *or* `-propertyFile`
> Specify a property file that Pig should read.

`-version`
> Print the version of Pig.

Pig also uses a number of Java properties. The entire list can be printed out with `pig -h properties`. Specific properties are discussed later in sections that cover the features they control.

Hadoop also has a number of Java properties it uses to determine its behavior. For example, you can pass options to the JVM that runs your map and reduce tasks by setting `mapred.child.java.opts`. In Pig version 0.8 and later, these can be passed to Pig, and then Pig will pass them on to Hadoop when it invokes Hadoop. In earlier versions, the properties had to be in *hadoop-site.xml* so that the Hadoop client itself would pick them up.

Properties can be passed to Pig on the command line using `-D` in the same format as any Java property—for example, `bin/pig -D exectype=local`. When placed on the command line, these property definitions must come before any Pig-specific command-line options (such as `-x local`). They can also be specified in the *conf/pig.properties* file that is part of your Pig distribution. Finally, you can specify a separate properties file by using `-P`. If properties are specified on both the command line and in a properties file, the command-line specification takes precedence.

Return Codes

Pig uses return codes, described in Table 2-1, to communicate success or failure.

Table 2-1. Pig return codes

Value	Meaning	Comments
0	Success	
1	Retriable failure	
2	Failure	
3	Partial failure	Used with multiquery; see "Nonlinear Data Flows" on page 72
4	Illegal arguments passed to Pig	
5	`IOException` thrown	Would usually be thrown by a UDF
6	`PigException` thrown	Usually means a Python UDF raised an exception
7	`ParseException` thrown (can happen after parsing if variable substitution is being done)	
8	`Throwable` thrown (an unexpected exception)	

## CHAPTER 3

Grunt

Grunt* is Pig's interactive shell. It enables users to enter Pig Latin interactively and provides a shell for users to interact with HDFS.

To enter Grunt, invoke Pig with no script or command to run. Typing:

```
pig -x local
```

will result in the prompt:

```
grunt>
```

This gives you a Grunt shell to interact with your local filesystem. If you omit the -x local and have a cluster configuration set in PIG_CLASSPATH, this will put you in a Grunt shell that will interact with HDFS on your cluster.

As you would expect with a shell, Grunt provides command-line history and editing, as well as Tab completion. It does not provide filename completion via the Tab key. That is, if you type kil and then press the Tab key, it will complete the command as kill. But if you have a file *foo* in your local directory and type ls fo, and then hit Tab, it will not complete it as ls foo. This is because the response time from HDFS to connect and find whether the file exists is too slow to be useful.

Although Grunt is a useful shell, remember that it is not a full-featured shell. It does not provide a number of commands found in standard Unix shells, such as pipes, redirection, and background execution.

To exit Grunt you can type quit or enter Ctrl-D.

---

* According to Ben Reed, one of the researchers at Yahoo! who helped start Pig, they named the shell "Grunt" because they felt the initial implementation was so limited that it was not worthy even of the name "oink."

Entering Pig Latin Scripts in Grunt

One of the main uses of Grunt is to enter Pig Latin in an interactive session. This can be particularly useful for quickly sampling your data and for prototyping new Pig Latin scripts.

You can enter Pig Latin directly into Grunt. Pig will not start executing the Pig Latin you enter until it sees either a store or dump. However, it will do basic syntax and semantic checking to help you catch errors quickly. If you do make a mistake while entering a line of Pig Latin in Grunt, you can reenter the line using the same alias, and Pig will take the last instance of the line you enter. For example:

```
pig -x local
grunt> dividends = load 'NYSE_dividends' as (exchange, symbol, date, dividend);
grunt> symbols = foreach dividends generate symbl;
...Error during parsing. Invalid alias: symbl ...
grunt> symbols = foreach A generate symbol;
...
```

HDFS Commands in Grunt

Besides entering Pig Latin interactively, Grunt's other major use is to act as a shell for HDFS. In versions 0.5 and later of Pig, all hadoop fs shell commands are available. They are accessed using the keyword fs. The dash (-) used in the hadoop fs is also required:

```
grunt>fs -ls
```

You can see a complete guide to the available commands at *http://hadoop.apache.org/ common/docs/r0.20.2/hdfs_shell.html*. A number of the commands come directly from Unix shells and will operate in ways that are familiar: chgrp, chmod, chown, cp, du, ls, mkdir, mv, rm, and stat. A few of them either look like Unix commands you are used to but behave slightly differently or are unfamiliar, including:

cat *filename*
> Print the contents of a file to stdout. You can apply this command to a directory and it will apply itself in turn to each file in the directory.

copyFromLocal *localfile hdfsfile*
> Copy a file from your local disk to HDFS. This is done serially, not in parallel.

copyToLocal *hdfsfile localfile*
> Copy a file from HDFS to your local disk. This is done serially, not in parallel.

rmr *filename*
> Remove files recursively. This is equivalent to rm -r in Unix. Use this with caution.

In versions of Pig before 0.5, hadoop fs commands were not available. Instead, Grunt had its own implementation of some of these commands: cat, cd, copyFromLocal, copy ToLocal, cp, ls, mkdir, mv, pwd, rm (which acted like Hadoop's rmr, not Hadoop's rm), and rmf. As of Pig 0.8, all of these commands are still available. However, with the

---

exception of cd and pwd, these commands are deprecated in favor of using hadoop fs, and they might be removed at some point in the future.

In version 0.8, a new command was added to Grunt: sh. This command gives you access to the local shell, just as fs gives you access to HDFS. Simple shell commands that do not involve pipes or redirects can be executed. It is better to work with absolute paths, as sh does not always properly track the current working directory.

Controlling Pig from Grunt

Grunt also provides commands for controlling Pig and MapReduce:

kill *jobid*
> Kill the MapReduce job associated with *jobid*. The output of the pig command that spawned the job will list the ID of each job it spawns. You can also find the job's ID by looking at Hadoop's JobTracker GUI, which lists all jobs currently running on the cluster. Note that this command kills a particular MapReduce job. If your Pig job contains other MapReduce jobs that do not depend on the killed MapReduce job, these jobs will still continue. If you want to kill all of the Map-Reduce jobs associated with a particular Pig job, it is best to terminate the process running Pig, and then use this command to kill any MapReduce jobs that are still running. Make sure to terminate the Pig process with a Ctrl-C or a Unix kill, not a Unix kill -9. The latter does not give Pig the chance to clean up temporary files it is using, which can leave garbage in your cluster.

exec [[-param *param_name* = *param_value*]] [[-param_file *filename*]] *script*
> Execute the Pig Latin script *script*. Aliases defined in *script* are not imported into Grunt. This command is useful for testing your Pig Latin scripts while inside a Grunt session. For information on the -param and -param_file options, see "Parameter Substitution" on page 77.

run [[-param *param_name* = *param_value*]] [[-param_file *filename*]] *script*
> Execute the Pig Latin script *script* in the current Grunt shell. Thus all aliases referenced in *script* are available to Grunt, and the commands in *script* are accessible via the shell history. This is another option for testing Pig Latin scripts while inside a Grunt session. For information on the -param and -param_file options, see "Parameter Substitution" on page 77.

CHAPTER 4
Pig's Data Model

Before we take a look at the operators that Pig Latin provides, we first need to understand Pig's data model. This includes Pig's data types, how it handles concepts such as missing data, and how you can describe your data to Pig.

Types

Pig's data types can be divided into two categories: *scalar* types, which contain a single value, and *complex* types, which contain other types.

Scalar Types

Pig's scalar types are simple types that appear in most programming languages. With the exception of bytearray, they are all represented in Pig interfaces by `java.lang` classes, making them easy to work with in UDFs:

int

> An integer. Ints are represented in interfaces by `java.lang.Integer`. They store a four-byte signed integer. Constant integers are expressed as integer numbers, for example, `42`.

long

> A long integer. Longs are represented in interfaces by `java.lang.Long`. They store an eight-byte signed integer. Constant longs are expressed as integer numbers with an L appended, for example, `5000000000L`.

float

> A floating-point number. Floats are represented in interfaces by `java.lang.Float` and use four bytes to store their value. You can find the range of values representable by Java's `Float` type at *http://java.sun.com/docs/books/jls/third_edition/html/typesValues.html#4.2.3*. Note that because this is a floating-point number, in some calculations it will lose precision. For calculations that require no loss of precision, you should use an int or long instead. Constant floats are expressed as a

floating-point number with an f appended. Floating-point numbers can be expressed in simple format, 3.14f, or in exponent format, 6.022e23f.

double

A double-precision floating-point number. Doubles are represented in interfaces by java.lang.Double and use eight bytes to store their value. You can find the range of values representable by Java's Double type at *http://java.sun.com/docs/books/jls/third_edition/html/typesValues.html#4.2.3*. Note that because this is a floating-point number, in some calculations it will lose precision. For calculations that require no loss of precision, you should use an int or long instead. Constant doubles are expressed as a floating-point number in either simple format, 2.71828, or in exponent format, 6.626e-34.

chararray

A string or character array. Chararrays are represented in interfaces by java.lang.String. Constant chararrays are expressed as string literals with single quotes, for example, 'fred'. In addition to standard alphanumeric and symbolic characters, you can express certain characters in chararrays by using backslash codes, such as \t for Tab and \n for Return. Unicode characters can be expressed as \u followed by their four-digit hexadecimal Unicode value. For example, the value for Ctrl-A is expressed as \u0001.

bytearray

A blob or array of bytes. Bytearrays are represented in interfaces by a Java class DataByteArray that wraps a Java byte[]. There is no way to specify a constant bytearray.

Complex Types

Pig has three complex data types: maps, tuples, and bags. All of these types can contain data of any type, including other complex types. So it is possible to have a map where the value field is a bag, which contains a tuple where one of the fields is a map.

Map

A *map* in Pig is a chararray to data element mapping, where that element can be any Pig type, including a complex type. The chararray is called a key and is used as an index to find the element, referred to as the value.

Because Pig does not know the type of the value, it will assume it is a bytearray. However, the actual value might be something different. If you know what the actual type is (or what you want it to be), you can cast it; see "Casts" on page 30. If you do not cast the value, Pig will make a best guess based on how you use the value in your script. If the value is of a type other than bytearray, Pig will figure that out at runtime and handle it. See "Schemas" on page 27 for more information on how Pig handles unknown types.

By default there is no requirement that all values in a map must be of the same type. It is legitimate to have a map with two keys name and age, where the value for name is a chararray and the value for age is an int. Beginning in Pig 0.9, a map can declare its values to all be of the same type. This is useful if you know all values in the map will be of the same type, as it allows you to avoid the casting, and Pig can avoid the runtime type-massaging referenced in the previous paragraph.

Map constants are formed using brackets to delimit the map, a hash between keys and values, and a comma between key-value pairs. For example, ['name'#'bob', 'age'#55] will create a map with two keys, "name" and "age". The first value is a chararray, and the second is an integer.

Tuple

A *tuple* is a fixed-length, ordered collection of Pig data elements. Tuples are divided into *fields*, with each field containing one data element. These elements can be of any type—they do not all need to be the same type. A tuple is analogous to a row in SQL, with the fields being SQL columns. Because tuples are ordered, it is possible to refer to the fields by position; see "Expressions in foreach" on page 37 for details. A tuple can, but is not required to, have a schema associated with it that describes each field's type and provides a name for each field. This allows Pig to check that the data in the tuple is what the user expects, and it allows the user to reference the fields of the tuple by name.

Tuple constants use parentheses to indicate the tuple and commas to delimit fields in the tuple. For example, ('bob', 55) describes a tuple constant with two fields.

Bag

A *bag* is an unordered collection of tuples. Because it has no order, it is not possible to reference tuples in a bag by position. Like tuples, a bag can, but is not required to, have a schema associated with it. In the case of a bag, the schema describes all tuples within the bag.

Bag constants are constructed using braces, with tuples in the bag separated by commas. For example, {('bob', 55), ('sally', 52), ('john', 25)} constructs a bag with three tuples, each with two fields.

Pig users often notice that Pig does not provide a list or set type that can store items of any type. It is possible to mimic a set type using the bag, by wrapping the desired type in a tuple of one field. For instance, if you want to store a set of integers, you can create a bag with a tuple with one field, which is an int. This is a bit cumbersome, but it works.

Bag is the one type in Pig that is not required to fit into memory. As you will see later, because bags are used to store collections when grouping, bags can become quite large. Pig has the ability to spill bags to disk when necessary, keeping only partial sections of the bag in memory. The size of the bag is limited to the amount of local disk available for spilling the bag.

Memory Requirements of Pig Data Types

In the previous sections I often referenced the size of the value stored for each type (four bytes for integer, eight bytes for long, etc.). This tells you how large (or small) a value those types can hold. However, this does not tell you how much memory is actually used by objects of those types. Because Pig uses Java objects to represent these values internally, there is an additional overhead. This overhead depends on your JVM, but it is usually eight bytes per object. It is even worse for chararrays because Java's String uses two bytes per character rather than one.

So, if you are trying to figure out how much memory you need in Pig to hold all of your data (e.g., if you are going to do a join that needs to hold a hash table in memory), do not count the bytes on disk and assume that is how much memory you need. The multiplication factor between disk and memory is dependent on your data, whether your data is compressed on disk, your disk storage format, etc. As a rule of thumb, it takes about four times as much memory as it does disk to represent the uncompressed data.

Nulls

Pig includes the concept of a data element being null. Data of any type can be null. It is important to understand that in Pig the concept of null is the same as in SQL, which is completely different from the concept of null in C, Java, Python, etc. In Pig a null data element means the value is unknown. This might be because the data is missing, an error occurred in processing it, etc. In most procedural languages, a data value is said to be null when it is unset or does not point to a valid address or object. This difference in the concept of null is important and affects the way Pig treats null data, especially when operating on it. See "foreach" on page 37, "Group" on page 41, and "Join" on page 45 for details of how nulls are handled in expressions and relations in Pig.

Unlike SQL, Pig does not have a notion of constraints on the data. In the context of nulls, this means that any data element can always be null. As you write Pig Latin scripts and UDFs, you will need to keep this in mind.

Schemas

Pig has a very lax attitude when it comes to schemas. This is a consequence of Pig's philosophy of eating anything. If a schema for the data is available, Pig will make use of it, both for up-front error checking and for optimization. But if no schema is available, Pig will still process the data, making the best guesses it can based on how the script treats the data. First, we will look at ways that you can communicate the schema to Pig; then, we will examine how Pig handles the case where you do not provide it with the schema.

The easiest way to communicate the schema of your data to Pig is to explicitly tell Pig what it is when you load the data:

```
dividends = load 'NYSE_dividends' as
    (exchange:chararray, symbol:chararray, date:chararray, dividend:float);
```

Pig now expects your data to have four fields. If it has more, it will truncate the extra ones. If it has less, it will pad the end of the record with nulls.

It is also possible to specify the schema without giving explicit data types. In this case, the data type is assumed to be bytearray:

```
dividends = load 'NYSE_dividends' as (exchange, symbol, date, dividend);
```

> You would expect that this also would force your data into a tuple with four fields, regardless of the number of actual input fields, just like when you specify both names and types for the fields. And in Pig 0.9 this is what happens. But in 0.8 and earlier versions it does not; no truncation or null padding is done in the case where you do not provide explicit types for the fields.

Also, when you declare a schema, you do not have to declare the schema of complex types, but you can if you want to. For example, if your data has a tuple in it, you can declare that field to be a tuple without specifying the fields it contains. You can also declare that field to be a tuple that has three columns, all of which are integers. Table 4-1 gives the details of how to specify each data type inside a schema declaration.

Table 4-1. Schema syntax

Data type	Syntax	Example
int	int	as (a:int)
long	long	as (a:long)
float	float	as (a:float)
double	double	as (a:double)
chararray	chararray	as (a:chararray)
bytearray	bytearray	as (a:bytearray)
map	map[] or map[*type*], where *type* is any valid type. This declares all values in the map to be of this type.	as (a:map[], b:map[int])
tuple	tuple() or tuple(*list_of_fields*), where *list_of_fields* is a comma-separated list of field declarations.	as (a:tuple(), b:tuple(x:int, y:int))
bag	bag{} or bag{t:(*list_of_fields*)}, where *list_of_fields* is a comma-separated list of field declarations. Note that, oddly enough, the tuple inside the bag must have a name, here specified as t, even though you will never be able to access that tuple t directly.	(a:bag{}, b:bag{t: (x:int, y:int)})

The runtime declaration of schemas is very nice. It makes it easy for users to operate on data without having to first load it into a metadata system. It also means that if you are interested in only the first few fields, you only have to declare those fields.

But for production systems that run over the same data every hour or every day, it has a couple of significant drawbacks. One, whenever your data changes, you have to change your Pig Latin. Two, although this works fine on data with 5 columns, it is painful when your data has 100 columns. To address these issues, there is another way to load schemas in Pig.

If the load function you are using already knows the schema of the data, the function can communicate that to Pig. (Load functions are how Pig reads data; see "Load" on page 34 for details.) Load functions might already know the schema because it is stored in a metadata repository such as HCatalog, or it might be stored in the data itself (if, for example, the data is stored in JSON format). In this case, you do not have to declare the schema as part of the load statement. And you can still refer to fields by name because Pig will fetch the schema from the load function before doing error checking on your script:

```
mdata = load 'mydata' using HCatLoader();
cleansed = filter mdata by name is not null;
...
```

But what happens when you cross the streams? What if you specify a schema and the loader returns one? If they are identical, all is well. If they are not identical, Pig will determine whether it can adapt the one returned by the loader to match the one you gave. For example, if you specified a field as a long and the loader said it was an int, Pig can and will do that cast. However, if it cannot determine a way to make the loader's schema fit the one you gave, it will give an error. See "Casts" on page 30 for a list of casts Pig can and cannot insert to make the schemas work together.

Now let's look at the case where neither you nor the load function tell Pig what the data's schema is. In addition to being referenced by name, fields can be referenced by position, starting from zero. The syntax is a dollar sign, then the position: $0 refers to the first field. So it is easy to tell Pig which field you want to work with. But how does Pig know the data type? It does not, so it starts by assuming everything is a bytearray. Then it looks at how you use those fields in your script, drawing conclusions about what you think those fields are and how you want to use them. Consider the following:

```
--no_schema.pig
daily = load 'NYSE_daily';
calcs = foreach daily generate $7 / 1000, $3 * 100.0, SUBSTRING($0, 0, 1), $6 - $3;
```

In the expression $7 / 1000, 1000 is an integer, so it is a safe guess that the eighth field of *NYSE_daily* is an integer or something that can be cast to an integer. In the same way, $3 * 100.0 indicates $3 is a double, and the use of $0 in a function that takes a chararray as an argument indicates the type of $0. But what about the last expression, $6 - $3? The - operator is used only with numeric types in Pig, so Pig can safely guess that $3 and $6 are numeric. But should it treat them as integers or floating-point numbers? Here Pig plays it safe and guesses that they are floating points, casting them to doubles. This is the safer bet because if they actually are integers, those can be represented as floating-point numbers, but the reverse is not true. However, because floating-point arithmetic is much slower and subject to loss of precision, if these values really are integers, you should cast them so that Pig uses integer types in this case.

There are also cases where Pig cannot make any intelligent guess:

```
--no_schema_filter
daily = load 'NYSE_daily';
fltrd = filter daily by $6 > $3;
```

> is a valid operator on numeric, chararray, and bytearray types in Pig Latin. So, Pig has no way to make a guess. In this case, it treats these fields as if they were bytearrays, which means it will do a byte-to-byte comparison of the data in these fields.

Pig also has to handle the case where it guesses wrong and must adapt on the fly. Consider the following:

```
--unintended_walks.pig
player    = load 'baseball' as (name:chararray, team:chararray,
               pos:bag{t:(p:chararray)}, bat:map[]);
unintended = foreach player generate bat#'base_on_balls' - bat#'ibbs';
```

Because the values in maps can be of any type, Pig has no idea what type bat#'base_on_balls' and bat#'ibbs' are. By the rules laid out previously, Pig will assume they are doubles. But let's say they actually turn out to be represented internally as integers.* In that case, Pig will need to adapt at runtime and convert what it thought was a cast from bytearray to double into a cast from int to double. Note that it will still produce a double output and not an int output. This might seem nonintuitive; see "How Strongly Typed Is Pig?" on page 32 for details on why this is so. It should be noted that in Pig 0.8 and earlier, much of this runtime adaption code was shaky and often failed. In 0.9, much of this has been fixed. But if you are using an older version of Pig, you might need to cast the data explicitly to get the right results.

Finally, Pig's knowledge of the schema can change at different points in the Pig Latin script. In all of the previous examples where we loaded data without a schema and then passed it to a foreach statement, the data started out without a schema. But after the foreach, the schema is known. Similarly, Pig can start out knowing the schema, but if the data is mingled with other data without a schema, the schema can be lost. That is, lack of schema is contagious:

```
--no_schema_join.pig
divs  = load 'NYSE_dividends' as (exchange, stock_symbol, date, dividends);
daily = load 'NYSE_daily';
jnd   = join divs by stock_symbol, daily by $1;
```

In this example, because Pig does not know the schema of daily, it cannot know the schema of the join of divs and daily.

Casts

The previous sections have referenced casts in Pig without bothering to define how casts work. The syntax for casts in Pig is the same as in Java—the type name in parentheses before the value:

```
--unintended_walks_cast.pig
player     = load 'baseball' as (name:chararray, team:chararray,
                pos:bag{t:(p:chararray)}, bat:map[]);
unintended = foreach player generate (int)bat#'base_on_balls' - (int)bat#'ibbs';
```

The syntax for specifying types in casts is exactly the same as specifying them in schemas, as shown previously in Table 4-1.

Not all conceivable casts are allowed in Pig. Table 4-2 describes which casts are allowed between scalar types. Casts to bytearrays are never allowed because Pig does not know how to represent the various data types in binary format. Casts from bytearrays to any type are allowed. Casts to and from complex types currently are not allowed, except from bytearray, although conceptually in some cases they could be.

---

* That is not the case in the example data. For that to be the case, you would need to use a loader that did load the bat map with these values as integers.

Table 4-2. Supported casts

	To int	To long	To float	To double	To chararray
From int		Yes.	Yes.	Yes.	Yes.
From long	Yes. Any values greater than 2^{31} or less than -2^{31} will be truncated.		Yes.	Yes.	Yes.
From float	Yes. Values will be truncated to int values.	Yes. Values will be truncated to long values.		Yes.	Yes.
From double	Yes. Values will be truncated to int values.	Yes. Values will be truncated to long values.	Yes. Values with precision beyond what float can represent will be truncated.		Yes.
From chararray	Yes. Chararrays with nonnumeric characters result in null.	Yes. Chararrays with nonnumeric characters result in null.	Yes. Chararrays with nonnumeric characters result in null.	Yes. Chararrays with nonnumeric characters result in null.	

One type of casting that requires special treatment is casting from bytearray to other types. Because bytearray indicates a string of bytes, Pig does not know how to convert its contents to any other type. Continuing the previous example, both `bat#'base_on_balls'` and `bat#'ibbs'` were loaded as bytearrays. The casts in the script indicate that you want them treated as ints.

Pig does not know whether integer values in *baseball* are stored as ASCII strings, Java serialized values, binary-coded decimal, or some other format. So it asks the load function, because it is that function's responsibility to cast bytearrays to other types. In general this works nicely, but it does lead to a few corner cases where Pig does not know how to cast a bytearray. In particular, if a UDF returns a bytearray, Pig will not know how to perform casts on it because that bytearray is not generated by a load function.

Before leaving the topic of casts, we need to consider cases where Pig inserts casts for the user. These casts are implicit, compared to explicit casts where the user indicates the cast. Consider the following:

```
--total_trade_estimate.pig
daily = load 'NYSE_daily' as (exchange:chararray, symbol:chararray,
        date:chararray, open:float, high:float, low:float, close:float,
        volume:int, adj_close:float);
rough = foreach daily generate volume * close;
```

In this case, Pig will change the second line to (float)volume * close to do the operation without losing precision. In general, Pig will always widen types to fit when it needs to insert these implicit casts. So, int and long together will result in a long; int or long and float will result in a float; and int, long, or float and double will result in a double. There are no implicit casts between numeric types and chararrays or other types.

How Strongly Typed Is Pig?

In a strongly typed computer language (e.g., Java), the user must declare up front the type for all variables. In weakly typed languages (e.g., Perl), variables can take on values of different type and adapt as the occasion demands. So which is Pig? For the most part it is strongly typed. If you describe the schema of your data, Pig expects your data to be what you said. But when Pig does not know the schema, it will adapt to the actual types at runtime. (Perhaps we should say Pig is "gently typed." It is strong but willing to work with data that does not live up to its expectations.) To see the differences between these two cases, look again at this example:

```
--unintended_walks.pig
player     = load 'baseball' as (name:chararray, team:chararray,
                 pos:bag{t:(p:chararray)}, bat:map[]);
unintended = foreach player generate bat#'base_on_balls' - bat#'ibbs';
```

In this example, remember we are pretending that the values for base_on_balls and ibbs turn out to be represented as integers internally (that is, the load function constructed them as integers). If Pig were weakly typed, the output of unintended would be records with one field typed as an integer. As it is, Pig will output records with one field typed as a double. Pig will make a guess and then do its best to massage the data into the types it guessed.

The downside here is that users coming from weakly typed languages are surprised, and perhaps frustrated, when their data comes out as a type they did not anticipate. However, on the upside, by looking at a Pig Latin script it is possible to know what the output data type will be in these cases without knowing the input data.

## CHAPTER 5

Introduction to Pig Latin

It is time to dig into Pig Latin. This chapter provides you with the basics of Pig Latin, enough to write your first useful scripts. More advanced features of Pig Latin are covered in Chapter 6.

Preliminary Matters

Pig Latin is a dataflow language. Each processing step results in a new data set, or *relation*. In `input = load 'data'`, input is the name of the relation that results from loading the data set *data*. A relation name is referred to as an *alias*. Relation names look like variables, but they are not. Once made, an assignment is permanent. It is possible to reuse relation names; for example, this is legitimate:

```
A = load 'NYSE_dividends' (exchange, symbol, date, dividends);
A = filter A by dividends > 0;
A = foreach A generate UPPER(symbol);
```

However, it is not recommended. It looks here as if you are reassigning A, but really you are creating new relations called A, losing track of the old relations called A. Pig is smart enough to keep up, but it still is not a good practice. It leads to confusion when trying to read your programs (which A am I referring to?) and when reading error messages.

In addition to relation names, Pig Latin also has field names. They name a field (or column) in a relation. In the previous snippet of Pig Latin, dividends and symbol are examples of field names. These are somewhat like variables in that they will contain a different value for each record as it passes through the pipeline, but you cannot assign values to them.

Both relation and field names must start with an alphabetic character, and then they can have zero or more alphabetic, numeric, or _ (underscore) characters. All characters in the name must be ASCII.

Case Sensitivity

Unfortunately, Pig Latin cannot decide whether it is case-sensitive. Keywords in Pig Latin are not case-sensitive; for example, `LOAD` is equivalent to `load`. But relation and field names are. So `A = load 'foo';` is not equivalent to `a = load 'foo';`. UDF names are also case-sensitive, thus `COUNT` is not the same UDF as `count`.

Comments

Pig Latin has two types of comment operators: SQL-style single-line comments (`--`) and Java-style multiline comments (`/* */`). For example:

```
A = load 'foo'; --this is a single-line comment
/*
 * This is a multiline comment.
 */
B = load /* a comment in the middle */'bar';
```

Input and Output

Before you can do anything of interest, you need to be able to add inputs and outputs to your data flows.

Load

The first step to any data flow is to specify your input. In Pig Latin this is done with the `load` statement. By default, `load` looks for your data on HDFS in a tab-delimited file using the default load function `PigStorage`. `divs = load '/data/examples/NYSE_divi dends';` will look for a file called *NYSE_dividends* in the directory */data/examples*. You can also specify relative path names. By default, your Pig jobs will run in your home directory on HDFS, */users/yourlogin*. Unless you change directories, all relative paths will be evaluated from there. You can also specify a full URL for the path, for example, *hdfs://nn.acme.com/data/examples/NYSE_dividends* to read the file from the HDFS instance that has `nn.acme.com` as a NameNode.

In practice, most of your data will not be in tab-separated text files. You also might be loading data from storage systems other than HDFS. Pig allows you to specify the function for loading your data with the `using` clause. For example, if you wanted to load your data from HBase, you would use the loader for HBase:

```
divs = load 'NYSE_dividends' using HBaseStorage();
```

If you do not specify a load function, the built-in function `PigStorage` will be used. You can also pass arguments to your load function via the `using` clause. For example, if you are reading comma-separated text data, `PigStorage` takes an argument to indicate which character to use as a separator:

```
divs = load 'NYSE_dividends' using PigStorage(',');
```

The load statement also can have an **as** clause, which allows you to specify the schema of the data you are loading. (The syntax and semantics of declaring schemas in Pig Latin is discussed in "Schemas" on page 27.)

```
divs = load 'NYSE_dividends' as (exchange, symbol, date, dividends);
```

When specifying a "file" to read from HDFS, you can specify directories. In this case, Pig will find all files under the directory you specify and use them as input for that load statement. So, if you had a directory *input* with two datafiles *today* and *yesterday* under it, and you specified *input* as your file to load, Pig will read both *today* and *yesterday* as input. If the directory you specify has other directories, files in those directories will be included as well.

PigStorage and **TextLoader**, the two built-in Pig load functions that operate on HDFS files, support globs.* With globs, you can read multiple files that are not under the same directory or read some but not all files under a directory. Table 5-1 describes globs that are valid in Hadoop 0.20. Be aware that glob meaning is determined by HDFS underneath Pig, so the globs that will work for you depend on your version of HDFS. Also, if you are issuing Pig Latin commands from a Unix shell command line, you will need to escape many of the glob characters to prevent your shell from expanding them.

Table 5-1. Globs in Hadoop 0.20

Glob	Meaning
?	Matches any single character.
*	Matches zero or more characters.
[abc]	Matches a single character from character set (a,b,c).
[a-z]	Matches a single character from the character range (a..z), inclusive. The first character must be lexicographically less than or equal to the second character.
[^abc]	Matches a single character that is not in the character set (a, b, c). The ^ character must occur immediately to the right of the opening bracket.
[^a-z]	Matches a single character that is not from the character range (a..z), inclusive. The ^ character must occur immediately to the right of the opening bracket.
\c	Removes (escapes) any special meaning of character c.
{ab,cd}	Matches a string from the string set {ab, cd}.

---

* Any loader that uses **FileInputFormat** as its InputFormat will support globs. Most loaders that load data from HDFS use this InputFormat.

Store

After you have finished processing your data, you will want to write it out somewhere. Pig provides the `store` statement for this purpose. In many ways it is the mirror image of the `load` statement. By default, Pig stores your data on HDFS in a tab-delimited file using `PigStorage`:[†]

```
store processed into '/data/examples/processed';
```

Pig will write the results of your processing into a directory *processed* in the directory */data/examples*. You can specify relative path names, as well as a full URL for the path, such as *hdfs://nn.acme.com/data/examples/processed*.

If you do not specify a store function, `PigStorage` will be used. You can specify a different store function with a `using` clause:

```
store processed into 'processed' using
    HBaseStorage();
```

You can also pass arguments to your store function. For example, if you want to store your data as comma-separated text data, `PigStorage` takes an argument to indicate which character to use as a separator:

```
store processed into 'processed' using PigStorage(',');
```

As noted in "Running Pig" on page 13, when writing to a filesystem, *processed* will be a directory with part files rather than a single file. But how many part files will be created? That depends on the parallelism of the last job before the `store`. If it has reduces, it will be determined by the parallel level set for that job. See "Parallel" on page 49 for information on how this is determined. If it is a map-only job, it will be determined by the number of maps, which is controlled by Hadoop and not Pig.

Dump

In most cases you will want to store your data somewhere when you are done processing it. But occasionally you will want to see it on the screen. This is particularly useful during debugging and prototyping sessions. It can also be useful for quick *ad hoc* jobs. `dump` directs the output of your script to your screen:

```
dump processed;
```

Up through version 0.7, the output of `dump` matches the format of constants in Pig Latin. So, longs are followed by an `L`, and floats by an `F`, and maps are surrounded by [] (brackets), tuples by () (parentheses), and bags by {} (braces). Starting with version 0.8, the `L` for longs and `F` for floats have been dropped, though the markers for the complex types have been kept. Nulls are indicated by missing values, and fields are separated by commas. Because each record in the output is a tuple, it is surrounded by ().

[†] A single function can be both a load and store function, as `PigStorage` is.

Relational Operations

Relational operators are the main tools Pig Latin provides to operate on your data. They allow you to transform it by sorting, grouping, joining, projecting, and filtering. This section covers the basic relational operators. More advanced features of these operators, as well as advanced relational operators, are covered in "Advanced Relational Operations" on page 57. What is covered here will be enough to get you started programming in Pig Latin.

foreach

foreach takes a set of expressions and applies them to every record in the data pipeline, hence the name foreach. From these expressions it generates new records to send down the pipeline to the next operator. For those familiar with database terminology, it is Pig's projection operator. For example, the following code loads an entire record, but then removes all but the user and id fields from each record:

```
A = load 'input' as (user:chararray, id:long, address:chararray, phone:chararray,
        preferences:map[]);
B = foreach A generate user, id;
```

Expressions in foreach

foreach supports an array of expressions. The simplest are constants and field references. The syntax for constants has already been discussed in "Types" on page 23. Field references can be by name (as shown in the preceding example) or by position. Positional references are preceded by a $ (dollar sign) and start from 0:

```
prices = load 'NYSE_daily' as (exchange, symbol, date, open, high, low, close,
            volume, adj_close);
gain   = foreach prices generate close - open;
gain2  = foreach prices generate $6 - $3;
```

Relations gain and gain2 will contain the same values. Positional style references are useful in situations where the schema is unknown or undeclared.

In addition to using names and positions, you can refer to all fields using * (asterisk), which produces a tuple that contains all the fields. Beginning in version 0.9, you can also refer to ranges of fields using .. (two periods). This is particularly useful when you have many fields and do not want to repeat them all in your foreach command:

```
prices    = load 'NYSE_daily' as (exchange, symbol, date, open,
                high, low, close, volume, adj_close);
beginning = foreach prices generate ..open; -- produces exchange, symbol, date, open
middle    = foreach prices generate open..close; -- produces open, high, low, close
end       = foreach prices generate volume..; -- produces volume, adj_close
```

Standard arithmetic operators for integers and floating-point numbers are supported: + for addition, - for subtraction, * for multiplication, and / for division. These operators return values of their own type, so 5/2 is 2, whereas 5.0/2.0 is 2.5. In addition, for integers the modulo operator % is supported. The unary negative operator (-) is also supported for both integers and floating-point numbers. Pig Latin obeys the standard mathematical precedence rules. For information on what happens when arithmetic operators are applied across different types (for example, 5/2.0), see "Casts" on page 30.

Null values are viral for all arithmetic operators. That is, x + null = null for all values of x.

Pig also provides a binary condition operator, often referred to as *bincond*. It begins with a Boolean test, followed by a ?, then the value to return if the test is true, then a :, and finally the value to return if the test is false. If the test returns null, bincond returns null. Both value arguments of the bincond must return the same type:

```
2 == 2 ? 1 : 4 --returns 1
2 == 3 ? 1 : 4 --returns 4
null == 2 ? 1 : 4 -- returns null
2 == 2 ? 1 : 'fred' -- type error; both values must be of the same type
```

To extract data from complex types, use the projection operators. For maps this is # (the pound or hash), followed by the name of the key as a string. Keep in mind that the value associated with a key may be of any type. If you reference a key that does not exist in the map, the result is a null:

```
bball = load 'baseball' as (name:chararray, team:chararray,
        position:bag{t:(p:chararray)}, bat:map[]);
avg = foreach bball generate bat#'batting_average';
```

Tuple projection is done with ., the dot operator. As with top-level records, the field can be referenced by name (if you have a schema for the tuple) or by position. Referencing a nonexistent positional field in the tuple will return null. Referencing a field name that does not exist in the tuple will produce an error:

```
A = load 'input' as (t:tuple(x:int, y:int));
B = foreach A generate t.x, t.$1;
```

Bag projection is not as straightforward as map and tuple projection. Bags do not guarantee that their tuples are stored in any order, so allowing a projection of the tuple inside the bag would not be meaningful. Instead, when you project fields in a bag, you are creating a new bag with only those fields:

```
A = load 'input' as (b:bag{t:(x:int, y:int)});
B = foreach A generate b.x;
```

This will produce a new bag whose tuples have only the field x in them. You can project multiple fields in a bag by surrounding the fields with parentheses and separating them by commas:

```
A = load 'input' as (b:bag{t:(x:int, y:int)});
B = foreach A generate b.(x, y);
```

This seemingly pedantic distinction that b.x is a bag and not a scalar value has consequences. Consider the following Pig Latin, which will not work:

```
A = load 'foo' as (x:chararray, y:int, z:int);
B = group A by x; -- produces bag A containing all the records for a given value of x
C = foreach B generate SUM(A.y + A.z);
```

It is clear what the programmer is trying to do here. But because A.y and B.y are bags and the addition operator is not defined on bags, this will produce an error.‡ The correct way to do this calculation in Pig Latin is:

```
A = load 'foo' as (x:chararray, y:int, z:int);
A1 = foreach A generate x, y + z as yz;
B = group A1 by x;
C = foreach B generate SUM(A1.yz);
```

UDFs in foreach

User Defined Functions (UDFs) can be invoked in foreach. These are called evaluation functions, or *eval funcs*. Because they are part of a foreach statement, these UDFs take one record at a time and produce one output. Keep in mind that either the input or the output can be a bag, so this one record can contain a bag of records:

```
-- udf_in_foreach.pig
divs  = load 'NYSE_dividends' as (exchange, symbol, date, dividends);
 --make sure all strings are uppercase
upped = foreach divs generate UPPER(symbol) as symbol, dividends;
grpd  = group upped by symbol;   --output a bag upped for each value of symbol
--take a bag of integers, produce one result for each group
sums  = foreach grpd generate group, SUM(upped.dividends);
```

In addition, eval funcs can take * as an argument, which passes the entire record to the function. They can also be invoked with no arguments at all.

For a complete list of UDFs that are provided with Pig, see Appendix A. For a discussion of how to invoke UDFs not distributed as part of Pig, see "User Defined Functions" on page 51.

Naming fields in foreach

The result of each foreach statement is a new tuple, usually with a different schema than the tuple that was an input to foreach. Pig can infer the data types of the fields in this schema from the foreach statement. But it cannot always infer the names of those fields. For fields that are simple projections with no other operators applied, Pig keeps the same name as before:

```
divs = load 'NYSE_dividends' as (exchange:chararray, symbol:chararray,
           date:chararray, dividends:float);
```

---

‡ You might object and say that Pig could figure out what is intended here and do it, since SUM(A.y + A.z) could be decomposed to "foreach record in A, add y and z and then take the sum." This is true. But when we change the group to a cogroup so that there are two bags A and B involved (see "cogroup" on page 66) and change the sum to SUM(A.y + B.z), because neither A nor B guarantee any ordering, this is not a well-defined operation. In designing the language, we thought it better to be consistent and always say that bags could not be added rather than allow it in some instances and not in others.

```
sym  = foreach divs generate symbol;
describe sym;
```

sym: {symbol: chararray}

Once any expression beyond simple projection is applied, Pig does not assign a name to the field. If you do not explicitly assign a name, the field will be nameless and will be addressable only via a positional parameter, for example, $0. You can assign a name with the as clause:

```
divs     = load 'NYSE_dividends' as (exchange:chararray, symbol:chararray,
             date:chararray, dividends:float);
in_cents = foreach divs generate dividends * 100.0 as dividend, dividends * 100.0;
describe in_cents;
```

in_cents: {dividend: double,double}

Notice that in foreach the as is attached to each expression. This is different than load, where it is attached to the entire statement. The reason for this will become clear when we discuss flatten in "flatten" on page 57.

Filter

The filter statement allows you to select which records will be retained in your data pipeline. A filter contains a predicate. If that predicate evaluates to true for a given record, that record will be passed down the pipeline. Otherwise, it will not.

Predicates can contain the equality operators you expect, including == to test equality, and !=, >, >=, <, and <=. These comparators can be used on any scalar data type. == and != can be applied to maps and tuples. To use these with two tuples, both tuples must have either the same schema or no schema. None of the equality operators can be applied to bags.

Pig Latin follows the operator precedence that is standard in most programming languages, where arithmetic operators have precedence over equality operators. So, x + y == a + b is equivalent to (x + y) == (a + b).

For chararrays, users can test to see whether the chararray matches a regular expression:

```
-- filter_matches.pig
divs       = load 'NYSE_dividends' as (exchange:chararray, symbol:chararray,
             date:chararray, dividends:float);
startswithcm = filter divs by symbol matches 'CM.*';
```

 Pig uses Java's regular expression format (*http://download.oracle.com/ javase/6/docs/api/java/util/regex/Pattern.html*). This format requires the entire chararray to match, not just a portion as in Perl-style regular expressions. For example, if you are looking for all fields that contain the string "fred", you must say '.*fred.*' and not 'fred'. The latter will match only the chararray fred.

You can find chararrays that do not match a regular expression by preceding the test with not:

```
-- filter_not_matches.pig
divs         = load 'NYSE_dividends' as (exchange:chararray, symbol:chararray,
                    date:chararray, dividends:float);
notstartswithcm = filter divs by not symbol matches 'CM.*';
```

You can combine multiple predicates into one by using the Boolean operators and and or, and you can reverse the outcome of any predicate by using the Boolean not operator. As is standard, the precedence of Boolean operators, from highest to lowest, is not, and, or. Thus a and b or not c is equivalent to (a and b) or (not c).

Pig will short-circuit Boolean operations when possible. If the first (left) predicate of an and is false, the second (right) will not be evaluated. So in 1 == 2 and udf(x), the UDF will never be invoked. Similarly, if the first predicate of an or is true, the second predicate will not be evaluted. 1 == 1 or udf(x) will never invoke the UDF.

For Boolean operators, nulls follow the SQL trinary logic. Thus x == null results in a value of null, not true (*even when x is null also*) or false. Filters pass through only those values that are true. So for a field that had three values 2, null, and 4, if you applied a filter x == 2 to it, only the first record where the value is 2 would be passed through the filter. Likewise, x != 2 would return only the last record where the value is 4. The way to look for null values is to use the is null operator, which returns true whenever the value is null. To find values that are not null, use is not null.

Likewise, null neither matches nor fails to match any regular expression value.

Just as there are UDFs to be used in evaluation expressions, there are UDFs specifically for filtering records, called *filter funcs*. These are eval funcs that return a Boolean value and can be invoked in the filter statement. Filter funcs cannot be used in foreach statements.

Group

The group statement collects together records with the same key. It is the first operator we have looked at that shares its syntax with SQL, but it is important to understand that the grouping operator in Pig Latin is fundamentally different than the one in SQL. In SQL the group by clause creates a group that must feed directly into one or more aggregate functions. In Pig Latin there is no direct connection between group and aggregate functions. Instead, group does exactly what it says: collects all records with the same value for the provided key together into a bag. You can then pass this to an aggregate function if you want or do other things with it:

```
-- count.pig
daily = load 'NYSE_daily' as (exchange, stock);
grpd  = group daily by stock;
cnt   = foreach grpd generate group, COUNT(daily);
```

That example groups records by the key stock and then counts them. It is just as legitimate to group them and then store them for processing at a later time:

```
-- group.pig
daily = load 'NYSE_daily' as (exchange, stock);
grpd  = group daily by stock;
store grpd into 'by_group';
```

The records coming out of the group by statement have two fields, the key and the bag of collected records. The key field is named group.§ The bag is named for the alias that was grouped, so in the previous examples it will be named daily and have the same schema as the relation daily. If the relation daily has no schema, the bag daily will have no schema. For each record in the group, the entire record (including the key) is in the bag. Changing the last line of the previous script from store grpd... to describe grpd; will produce:

```
grpd: {group: bytearray,daily: {exchange: bytearray,stock: bytearray}}
```

You can also group on multiple keys, but the keys must be surrounded by parentheses. The resulting records still have two fields. In this case, the group field is a tuple with a field for each key:

```
--twokey.pig
daily = load 'NYSE_daily' as (exchange, stock, date, dividends);
grpd  = group daily by (exchange, stock);
avg   = foreach grpd generate group, AVG(daily.dividends);
describe grpd;
grpd: {group: (exchange: bytearray,stock: bytearray),daily: {exchange: bytearray,
    stock: bytearray,date: bytearray,dividends: bytearray}}
```

You can also use all to group together all of the records in your pipeline:

```
--countall.pig
daily = load 'NYSE_daily' as (exchange, stock);
grpd  = group daily all;
cnt   = foreach grpd generate COUNT(daily);
```

The record coming out of group all has the chararray literal all as a key. Usually this does not matter because you will pass the bag directly to an aggregate function such as COUNT. But if you plan to store the record or use it for another purpose, you might want to project out the artificial key first.

group is the first operator we have looked at that usually will force a reduce phase. Grouping means collecting all records where the key has the same value. If the pipeline is in a map phase, this will force it to shuffle and then reduce. If the pipeline is already in a reduce, this will force it to pass through map, shuffle, and reduce phases.

---

§ Thus the keyword group is overloaded in Pig Latin. This is unfortunate and confusing, but also hard to change now.

Because grouping collects *all* records together with the same value for the key, you often get skewed results. That is, just because you have specified that your job have 100 reducers, there is no reason to expect that the number of values per key will be distributed evenly. They might have a Gaussian or power law distribution.[||] For example, suppose you have an index of web pages and you group by the base URL. Certain values such as yahoo.com are going to have far more entries than most, which means that some reducers get far more data than others. Because your MapReduce job is not finished (and any subsequent ones cannot start) until all your reducers have finished, this skew will significantly slow your processing. In some cases it will also be impossible for one reducer to manage that much data.

Pig has a number of ways that it tries to manage this skew to balance out the load across your reducers. The one that applies to grouping is Hadoop's combiner. For details of how Hadoop's combiner works, see "Combiner Phase" on page 190. This does not remove all skew, but it places a bound on it. And because for most jobs the number of mappers will be at most in the tens of thousands, even if the reducers get a skewed number of records, the absolute number of records per reducer will be small enough that the reducers can handle them quickly.

Unfortunately, not all calculations can be done using the combiner. Calculations that can be decomposed into any number of steps, such as sum, are called *distributive*. These fit nicely into the combiner. Calculations that can be decomposed into an initial step, any number of intermediate steps, and a final step are referred to as *algebraic*. Count is an example of such a function, where the initial step is a count and the intermediate and final steps are sums. Distributive is a special case of algebraic, where the initial, intermediate, and final steps are all the same. Session analysis, where you want to track a user's actions on a website, is an example of a calculation that is not algebraic. You must have all the records sorted by timestamp before you can start analyzing their interaction with the site.

Pig's operators and built-in UDFs use the combiner whenever possible, because of its skew-reducing features and because early aggregation greatly reduces the amount of data shipped over the network and written to disk, thus speeding performance significantly. UDFs can indicate when they can work with the combiner by implementing the Algebraic interface. For information on how to make your UDFs use the combiner, see "Algebraic Interface" on page 135.

For information on how to determine the level of parallelism when executing your group operation, see "Parallel" on page 49. Also, keep in mind that when using group all, you are necessarily serializing your pipeline. That is, this step and any step after it until you split out the single bag now containing all of your records will not be done in parallel.

|| In my experience, the vast majority of data tracking human activity follows a power law distribution.

Finally, group handles nulls in the same way that SQL handles them: by collecting all records with a null key into the same group. Note that this is in direct contradiction to the way expressions handle nulls (remember that neither null == null nor null != null are true) and to the way join (see "Join" on page 45) handles nulls.

Order by

The order statement sorts your data for you, producing a total order of your output data. Total order means that not only is the data sorted in each partition of your data, it is also guaranteed that all records in partition n are less than all records in partition n - 1 for all n. When your data is stored on HDFS, where each partition is a part file, this means that cat will output your data in order.

The syntax of order is similar to group. You indicate a key or set of keys by which you wish to order your data. One glaring difference is that there are no parentheses around the keys when multiple keys are indicated in order:

```
--order.pig
daily   = load 'NYSE_daily' as (exchange:chararray, symbol:chararray,
            date:chararray, open:float, high:float, low:float, close:float,
            volume:int, adj_close:float);
bydate = order daily by date;

--order2key.pig
daily        = load 'NYSE_daily' as (exchange:chararray, symbol:chararray,
                  date:chararray, open:float, high:float, low:float,
                  close:float, volume:int, adj_close:float);
bydatensymbol  = order daily by date, symbol;
```

It is also possible to reverse the order of the sort by appending desc to a key in the sort. In order statements with multiple keys, desc applies only to the key it immediately follows. Other keys will still be sorted in ascending order:

```
--orderdesc.pig
daily   = load 'NYSE_daily' as (exchange:chararray, symbol:chararray,
            date:chararray, open:float, high:float, low:float, close:float,
            volume:int, adj_close:float);
byclose = order daily by close desc, open;
dump byclose; -- open still sorted in ascending order
```

Data is sorted based on the types of the indicated fields: numeric values are sorted numerically, chararray fields are sorted lexically, and bytearray fields are sorted lexically, using byte values rather than character values. Sorting by maps, tuples, or bags produces errors. For all data types, nulls are taken to be smaller than all possible values for that type, and thus will always appear first (or last when desc is used).

As discussed earlier in "Group" on page 41, skew of the values in data is very common. This affects order just as it does group, causing some reducers to take significantly longer than others. To address this, Pig balances the output across reducers. It does this by first sampling the input of the order statement to get an estimate of the key distribution. Based on this sample, it then builds a partitioner that produces a balanced total order (for details on what a partitioner is, see "Shuffle Phase" on page 191). For example, suppose you are ordering on a chararray field with the values a, b, e, e, e, e, e, e, m, q, r, z, and you have three reducers. The partitioner in this case would decide to partition your data such that values a-e go to reducer 1, e goes to reducer 2, and m-z go to reducer 3. Notice that the value e can be sent to either reducer 1 or 2. Some records with key e will be sent to reducer 1 and some to 2. This allows the partitioner to distribute the data evenly. In practice, we rarely see variance in reducer time exceed 10% when using this algorithm.

An important side effect of the way Pig distributes records to minimize skew is that it breaks the MapReduce convention that all instances of a given key are sent to the same partition. If you have other processing that depends on this convention, do not use Pig's order statement to sort data for it.

order always causes your data pipeline to go through a reduce phase. This is necessary to collect all equal records together. Also, Pig adds an additional MapReduce job to your pipeline to do the sampling. Because this sampling is very lightweight (it reads only the first record of every block), it generally takes less than 5% of the total job time.

Distinct

The distinct statement is very simple. It removes duplicate records. It works only on entire records, not on individual fields:

```
--distinct.pig
-- find a distinct list of ticker symbols for each exchange
-- This load will truncate the records, picking up just the first two fields.
daily   = load 'NYSE_daily' as (exchange:chararray, symbol:chararray);
uniq    = distinct daily;
```

Because it needs to collect like records together in order to determine whether they are duplicates, distinct forces a reduce phase. It does make use of the combiner to remove any duplicate records it can delete in the map phase.

The use of distinct shown here is equivalent to select distinct x in SQL. To learn how to do the equivalent of select count(distinct x), see "Nested foreach" on page 59.

Join

join is one of the workhorses of data processing, and it is likely to be in many of your Pig Latin scripts. join selects records from one input to put together with records from another input. This is done by indicating keys for each input. When those keys are equal,# the two rows are joined. Records for which no match is found are dropped:

```
--join.pig
daily = load 'NYSE_daily' as (exchange, symbol, date, open, high, low, close,
            volume, adj_close);
divs  = load 'NYSE_dividends' as (exchange, symbol, date, dividends);
jnd   = join daily by symbol, divs by symbol;
```

You can also join on multiple keys. In all cases you must have the same number of keys, and they must be of the same or compatible types (where compatible means that an implicit cast can be inserted; see "Casts" on page 30):

```
-- join2key.pig
daily = load 'NYSE_daily' as (exchange, symbol, date, open, high, low, close,
            volume, adj_close);
divs  = load 'NYSE_dividends' as (exchange, symbol, date, dividends);
jnd   = join daily by (symbol, date), divs by (symbol, date);
```

Like foreach, join preserves the names of the fields of the inputs passed to it. It also prepends the name of the relation the field came from, followed by a ::. Adding describe jnd; to the end of the previous example produces:

```
jnd: {daily::exchange: bytearray,daily::symbol: bytearray,daily::date: bytearray,
daily::open: bytearray,daily::high: bytearray,daily::low: bytearray,
daily::close: bytearray,daily::volume: bytearray,daily::adj_close: bytearray,
divs::exchange: bytearray,divs::symbol: bytearray,divs::date: bytearray,
divs::dividends: bytearray}
```

The daily:: prefix needs to be used only when the field name is no longer unique in the record. In this example, you will need to use daily::date or divs::date if you wish to refer to one of the date fields after the join. But fields such as open and divs do not need a prefix because there is no ambiguity.

Pig also supports *outer joins*. In outer joins, records that do not have a match on the other side are included, with null values being filled in for the missing fields. Outer joins can be left, right, or full. A left outer join means records from the left side will be included even when they do not have a match on the right side. Likewise, a right outer joins means records from the right side will be included even when they do not have a match on the left side. A full outer join means records from both sides are taken even when they do not have matches:

```
--leftjoin.pig
daily = load 'NYSE_daily' as (exchange, symbol, date, open, high, low, close,
            volume, adj_close);
divs  = load 'NYSE_dividends' as (exchange, symbol, date, dividends);
jnd   = join daily by (symbol, date) left outer, divs by (symbol, date);
```

#Actually, joins can be on any condition, not just equality, but Pig only supports joins on equality (called equi-joins). See "cross" on page 68 for information on how to do non-equi-joins in Pig.

outer is a noise word and can be omitted. Unlike some SQL implementations, full is not a noise word. C = join A by x outer, B by u; will generate a syntax error, not a full outer join.

Outer joins are supported only when Pig knows the schema of the data on the side(s) for which it might need to fill in nulls. Thus for left outer joins, it must know the schema of the right side; for right outer joins, it must know the schema of the left side; and for full outer joins, it must know both. This is because, without the schema, Pig will not know how many null values to fill in.[*]

As in SQL, null values for keys do not match anything, *even null values from the other input*. So, for inner joins, all records with null key values are dropped. For outer joins, they will be retained but will not match any records from the other input.

Pig can also do multiple joins in a single operation, as long as they are all being joined on the same key(s). This can be done only for inner joins:

```
A = load 'input1' as (x, y);
B = load 'input2' as (u, v);
C = load 'input3' as (e, f);
alpha = join A by x, B by u, C by e;
```

Self joins are supported, though the data must be loaded twice:

```
--selfjoin.pig
-- For each stock, find all dividends that increased between two dates
divs1     = load 'NYSE_dividends' as (exchange:chararray, symbol:chararray,
                date:chararray, dividends);
divs2     = load 'NYSE_dividends' as (exchange:chararray, symbol:chararray,
                date:chararray, dividends);
jnd       = join divs1 by symbol, divs2 by symbol;
increased = filter jnd by divs1::date < divs2::date and
                divs1::dividends < divs2::dividends;
```

If the preceding code were changed to the following, it would fail:

```
--selfjoin.pig
-- For each stock, find all dividends that increased between two dates
divs1     = load 'NYSE_dividends' as (exchange:chararray, symbol:chararray,
                date:chararray, dividends);
jnd       = join divs1 by symbol, divs1 by symbol;
increased = filter jnd by divs1::date < divs2::date and
                divs1::dividends < divs2::dividends;
```

It seems like this ought to work, since Pig could split the divs1 data set and send it to join twice. But the problem is that field names would be ambiguous after the join, so the load statement must be written twice. The next best thing would be for Pig to figure

---

[*] You may object that Pig could determine this by looking at other records in the join and inferring the correct number of fields. However, this does not work for two reasons. First, when no schema is present, Pig does not enforce a semantic that every record has the same schema. So, assuming Pig can infer one record from another is not valid. Second, there might be no records in the join that match, and thus Pig might have no record to infer from.

out that these two load statements are loading the same input and then run the load only once, but it does not do that currently.

Pig does these joins in MapReduce by using the map phase to annotate each record with which input it came from. It then uses the join key as the shuffle key. Thus join forces a new reduce phase. Once all of the records with the same value for the key are collected together, Pig does a cross product between the records from both inputs. To minimize memory usage, it has MapReduce order the records coming into the reducer using the input annotation it added in the map phase. Thus all of the records for the left input arrive first. Pig caches these in memory. All of the records for the right input arrive second. As each of these records arrives, it is crossed with each record from the left side to produce an output record. In a multiway join, the left n - 1 inputs are held in memory, and the nth is streamed through. It is important to keep this in mind when writing joins in your Pig queries if you know that one of your inputs has more records per value of the chosen key. Placing that input on the right side of your join will lower memory usage and possibly increase your script's performance.

Limit

Sometimes you want to see only a limited number of results. limit allows you do this:

```
--limit.pig
divs    = load 'NYSE_dividends';
first10 = limit divs 10;
```

The example here will return at most 10 lines (if your input has less than 10 lines total, it will return them all). Note that for all operators except order, Pig does not guarantee the order in which records are produced. Thus, because *NYSE_dividends* has more than 10 records, the example script could return different results every time. Putting an order *immediately* before the limit will guarantee that the same results are returned every time.

limit causes an additional reduce phase, since it needs to collect the records together to count how many it is returning. It does optimize this phase by limiting the output of each map and then applying the limit again in the reducer. In the case where limit is combined with order, the two are done together on the map and reduce. That is, on the map side, the records are sorted by MapReduce and the limit applied in the combiner. They are sorted again by MapReduce as part of the shuffle, and Pig applies the limit again in the reducer.

One possible optimization that Pig does not do is terminate reading of the input early once it has reached the number of records specified by limit. So, in the example, if you hoped to use this to read just a tiny slice of your input, you will be disappointed. Pig will still read it all.

Sample

sample offers a simple way to get a sample of your data. It reads through all of your data but returns only a percentage of rows. What percentage it returns is expressed as a double value, between 0 and 1. So, in the following example, 0.1 indicates 10%:

```
--sample.pig
divs = load 'NYSE_dividends';
some = sample divs 0.1;
```

Currently the sampling algorithm is very simple. The sample A by 0.1 is rewritten to filter A by random() <= 0.1. Obviously this is nondeterministic, so results of a script with sample will vary with every run. Also, the percentage will not be an exact match, but close. There has been discussion about adding more sophisticated sampling techniques, but it has not been done yet.

Parallel

One of Pig's core claims is that it provides a language for parallel data processing. One of the tenets of Pig's philosophy is that Pigs are domestic animals (see "Pig Philosophy" on page 9), so Pig prefers that you tell it how parallel to be. To do this, it provides the parallel clause.

The parallel clause can be attached to any relational operator in Pig Latin. However, it controls only reduce-side parallelism, so it makes sense only for operators that force a reduce phase. These are: group*, order, distinct, join*, limit, cogroup*, and cross. Operators marked with an asterisk have multiple implementations, some of which force a reduce and some which do not. For details on this and on operators not covered in this chapter, see Chapter 6. parallel is ignored in local mode because all operations happen serially in local mode:

```
--parallel.pig
daily   = load 'NYSE_daily' as (exchange, symbol, date, open, high, low, close,
             volume, adj_close);
bysymbl = group daily by symbol parallel 10;
```

In this example, parallel will cause the MapReduce job spawned by Pig to have 10 reducers. parallel clauses apply only to the statement to which they are attached; they do not carry through the script. So if this group were followed by an order, parallel would need to be set for that order separately. Most likely the group will reduce your data size significantly and you will want to change the parallelism:

```
--parallel.pig
daily   = load 'NYSE_daily' as (exchange, symbol, date, open, high, low, close,
             volume, adj_close);
bysymbl = group daily by symbol parallel 10;
average = foreach bysymbl generate group, AVG(daily.close) as avg;
sorted  = order average by avg desc parallel 2;
```

If, however, you do not want to set `parallel` separately for every reduce-invoking operator in your script, you can set a script-wide value using the `set` command:

```
--defaultparallel.pig
set default_parallel 10;
daily   = load 'NYSE_daily' as (exchange, symbol, date, open, high, low, close,
                volume, adj_close);
bysymbl = group daily by symbol;
average = foreach bysymbl generate group, AVG(daily.close) as avg;
sorted  = order average by avg desc;
```

In this script, all MapReduce jobs will be done with 10 reduces. When you set a default parallel level, you can still add a `parallel` clause to any statement to override the default value. Thus it can be helpful to set a default value as a base to use in most cases, and specifically add a `parallel` clause only when you have an operator that needs a different value.

All of this is rather static, however. What happens if you run the same script across different inputs that have different characteristics? Or what if your input data varies significantly sometimes? You do not want to have to edit your script each time. Using parameter substitution, you can write your parallel clauses with variables, providing values for those variables at runtime. See "Parameter Substitution" on page 77 for details.

So far we have assumed that you know what your parallel value should be. See "Select the Right Level of Parallelism" on page 105 for information on how to determine that.

Finally, what happens if you do not specify a parallel level? Before version 0.8, Pig lets MapReduce set the parallelism in that case. The MapReduce default parallelism is controlled by your cluster configuration. The installation default value is one, and most people do not change that. This most likely means that you will be running with only one reducer. This is rarely what you want.

To avoid this situation, Pig added a heuristic in 0.8 to do a gross estimate of what the parallelism should be set to if it is not set. It looks at the initial input size, assumes there will be no data size changes, and then allocates a reducer for every 1G of data. It must be emphasized that this is not a good algorithm. It is provided only to prevent mistakes that result in scripts running very slowly, and, in some extreme cases, mistakes that cause MapReduce itself to have problems. This is a safety net, not an optimizer.

Map Parallelism

`parallel` only lets you set reduce parallelism. What about map parallelism? MapReduce only allows users to set reduce parallelism: it controls map parallelism itself. Because Pig cannot control map parallelism, it cannot expose that to its users either.

In MapReduce, data is read using a class called `InputFormat`. Part of `InputFormat`'s purpose is to tell MapReduce how many map tasks to run. It also suggests where they should be run.

Although Pig cannot give you direct control over how many map tasks to run, it does let you build and run your own `InputFormat` as part of building your own load function. See Chapter 11 for details on how to do this.

User Defined Functions

Much of the power of Pig lies in its ability to let users combine irs operators with their own or others' code via UDFs. Up through version 0.7, all UDFs must be written in Java and are implemented as Java classes.[†] This makes it very easy to add new UDFs to Pig by writing a Java class and telling Pig about your JAR file.

As of version 0.8, UDFs can also be written in Python. Pig uses Jython to execute Python UDFs, so they must be compatible with Python 2.5 and cannot use Python 3 features.

Pig itself comes packaged with some UDFs. Prior to version 0.8, this was a very limited set, including only the standard SQL aggregate functions and a few others. In 0.8, a large number of standard string-processing, math, and complex-type UDFs were added. For a complete list and description of built-in UDFs, see "Built-in UDFs" on page 171.

Piggybank is a collection of user-contributed UDFs that is packaged and released along with Pig. Piggybank UDFs are not included in the Pig JAR, and thus you have to register them manually in your script. See "Piggybank" on page 187 for more information.

Of course you can also write your own UDFs or use those written by other users. For details of how to write your own, see Chapter 10. Finally, you can use some static Java functions as UDFs as well.

Registering UDFs

When you use a UDF that is not already built into Pig, you have to tell Pig where to look for that UDF. This is done via the `register` command. For example, let's say you want to use the `Reverse` UDF provided in Piggybank (for information on where to find the Piggybank JAR, see "Piggybank" on page 187):

```
--register.pig
register 'your_path_to_piggybank/piggybank.jar';
divs     = load 'NYSE_dividends' as (exchange:chararray, symbol:chararray,
               date:chararray, dividends:float);
backwards = foreach divs generate
               org.apache.pig.piggybank.evaluation.string.Reverse(symbol);
```

[†] This is why UDF names are case-sensitive in Pig.

This example tells Pig that it needs to include code from *your_path_to_piggybank/piggybank.jar* when it produces a JAR to send to Hadoop. Pig opens all of the registered JARs, takes out the files, and places them in the JAR that it sends to Hadoop to run your jobs.

In this example, we have to give Pig the full package and class name of the UDF. This verbosity can be alleviated in two ways. The first option is to use the `define` command (see "define and UDFs" on page 53). The second option is to include a set of paths on the command line for Pig to search when looking for UDFs. So if instead of invoking Pig as `pig register.pig` we change our invocation to `pig -Dudf.import.list=org.apache.pig.piggybank.evaluation.string register.pig`, we can change our script to:

```
register 'your_path_to_piggybank/piggybank.jar';
divs     = load 'NYSE_dividends' as (exchange:chararray, symbol:chararray,
               date:chararray, dividends:float);
backwards = foreach divs generate Reverse(symbol);
```

Using yet another property, we can get rid of the register command as well. If we add `-Dpig.additional.jars=/usr/local/pig/piggybank/piggybank.jar` to our command line, the register command is no longer necessary.

In many cases it is better to deal with registration and definition issues explicitly in the script via the `register` and `define` commands than use these properties. Otherwise, everyone who runs your script has to know how to configure the command line. However, in some situations your scripts will always use the same set of JARs and always look in the same places for them. For instance, you might have a set of JARs used by everyone in your company. In this case, placing these properties in a shared properties file and using that with your Pig scripts will make sharing those UDFs easier and assure that everyone is using the correct versions of them.

In 0.8 and later versions, the `register` command can also take HDFS paths. If your JARs are stored in HDFS, you could then say `register 'hdfs://user/jar/acme.jar';`. Starting in 0.9, `register` accepts globs. So if all of the JARs you need are stored in one directory, you could include them all with `register '/usr/local/share/pig/udfs/*.jar'`.

Registering Python UDFs

`register` is also used to locate resources for Python UDFs that you use in your Pig Latin scripts. In this case you do not register a JAR, but rather a Python script that contains your UDF. The Python script must be in your current directory. Using the examples provided in the example code, copying *udfs/python/production.py* to the *data* directory looks like this:

```
--batting_production.pig
register 'production.py' using jython as bballudfs;
players  = load 'baseball' as (name:chararray, team:chararray,
                pos:bag{t:(p:chararray)}, bat:map[]);
nonnull  = filter players by bat#'slugging_percentage' is not null and
             bat#'on_base_percentage' is not null;
calcprod = foreach nonnull generate name, bballudfs.production(
               (float)bat#'slugging_percentage',
               (float)bat#'on_base_percentage');
```

The important differences here are the using jython and as bballudfs portions of the register statement. using jython tells Pig that this UDF is written in Python, not Java, and it should use Jython to compile that UDF. Pig does not know where on your system the Jython interpreter is, so you must include *jython.jar* in your classpath when invoking Pig. This can be done by setting the PIG_CLASSPATH environment variable.

as bballudfs defines a namespace that UDFs from this file are placed in. All UDFs from this file must now be invoked as bballudfs.*udfname*. Each Python file you load should be given a separate namespace. This avoids naming collisions when you register two Python scripts with duplicate function names.

One caveat: Pig does not trace dependencies inside your Python scripts and send the needed Python modules to your Hadoop cluster. You are required to make sure the modules you need reside on the task nodes in your cluster and that the PYTHONPATH environment variable is set on those nodes such that your UDFs will be able to find them for import. This issue has been fixed after 0.9, but as of this writing is not yet released.

define and UDFs

As was alluded to earlier, define can be used to provide an alias so that you do not have to use full package names for your Java UDFs. It can also be used to provide constructor arguments to your UDFs. define also is used in defining streaming commands, but this section covers only its UDF-related features. For information on using define with streaming, see "stream" on page 69. The following provides an example of using define to provide an alias for org.apache.pig.piggybank.evaluation.string.Reverse:

```
--define.pig
register 'your_path_to_piggybank/piggybank.jar';
define reverse org.apache.pig.piggybank.evaluation.string.Reverse();
divs     = load 'NYSE_dividends' as (exchange:chararray, symbol:chararray,
                date:chararray, dividends:float);
backwards = foreach divs generate reverse(symbol);
```

Eval and filter functions can also take one or more strings as constructor arguments. If you are using a UDF that takes constructor arguments, define is the place to provide those arguments. For example, consider a method CurrencyConverter that takes two constructor arguments, the first indicating which currency you are converting from and the second which currency you are converting to:

```
--define_constructor_args.pig
register 'acme.jar';
define convert com.acme.financial.CurrencyConverter('dollar', 'euro');
divs      = load 'NYSE_dividends' as (exchange:chararray, symbol:chararray,
                  date:chararray, dividends:float);
backwards = foreach divs generate convert(dividends);
```

Calling Static Java Functions

Java has a rich collection of utilities and libraries. Because Pig is implemented in Java, some of these functions can be exposed to Pig users. Starting in version 0.8, Pig offers *invoker* methods that allow you to treat certain static Java functions as if they were Pig UDFs.

Any public static Java function that takes no arguments or some combination of int, long, float, double, String, or arrays thereof,[‡] and returns int, long, float, double, or String can be invoked in this way.

Because Pig Latin does not support overloading on return types, there is an invoker for each return type: InvokeForInt, InvokeForLong, InvokeForFloat, InvokeForDouble, and InvokeForString. You must pick the appropriate invoker for the type you wish to return. This method takes two constructor arguments. The first is the full package, classname, and method name. The second is a space-separated list of parameters the Java function expects. Only the types of the parameters are given. If the parameter is an array, [] (square brackets) are appended to the type name. If the method takes no parameters, the second constructor argument is omitted.

For example, if you wanted to use Java's Integer class to translate decimal values to hexadecimal values, you could do:

```
--invoker.pig
define hex InvokeForString('java.lang.Integer.toHexString', 'int');
divs = load 'NYSE_daily' as (exchange, symbol, date, open, high, low,
          close, volume, adj_close);
nonnull = filter divs by volume is not null;
inhex = foreach nonnull generate symbol, hex((int)volume);
```

If your method takes an array of types, Pig will expect to pass it a bag where each tuple has a single field of that type. So if you had a Java method com.yourcompany.Stats.stdev that took an array of doubles, you could use it like this:

```
define stdev InvokeForDouble('com.acme.Stats.stdev', 'double[]');
A = load 'input' as (id: int, dp:double);
B = group A by id;
C = foreach B generate group, stdev(A.dp);
```

‡ For int, long, float, and double, invoker methods can call Java functions that take the scalar types but not the associated Java classes (so int but not Integer, etc.).

Invokers do not use the `Accumulator` or `Algebraic` interfaces, and are thus likely to be much slower and to use much more memory than UDFs written specifically for Pig. This means that before you pass an array argument to an invoked method, you should think carefully about whether those inefficiencies are acceptable. For more information on these interfaces, see "Accumulator Interface" on page 139 and "Algebraic Interface" on page 135.

Invoking Java functions in this way does have a small cost because reflection is used to find and invoke the methods.

Invoker functions throw Java an `IllegalArgumentException` when they are passed null input. You should place a filter before the invocation to prevent this.

## CHAPTER 6

Advanced Pig Latin

In the previous chapter we worked through the basics of Pig Latin. In this chapter we will plumb its depths, and we will also discuss how Pig handles more complex data flows. Finally, we will look at how to use macros and modules to modularize your scripts.

Advanced Relational Operations

We will now discuss the more advanced Pig Latin operators, as well as additional options for operators that were introduced in the previous chapter.

Advanced Features of foreach

In our introduction to foreach (see "foreach" on page 37), we discussed how it could take a list of expressions to output for every record in your data pipeline. Now we will look at ways it can explode the number of records in your pipeline, and also how it can be used to apply a set of operations to each record.

flatten

Sometimes you have data in a bag or a tuple and you want to remove that level of nesting. The *baseball* data available on GitHub (see "Code Examples in This Book" on page xi) can be used as an example. Because a player can play more than one position, position is stored in a bag. This allows us to still have one entry per player in the *baseball* file.[*] But when you want to switch around your data on the fly and group

---

[*] Those with database experience will notice that this is a violation of the first normal form as defined by E. F. Codd. This intentional denormalization of data is very common in OLAP systems in general, and in large data-processing systems such as Hadoop in particular. RDBMS systems tend to make joins common and then work to optimize them. In systems such as Hadoop, where storage is cheap and joins are expensive, it is generally better to use nested data structures to avoid the joins.

by a particular position, you need a way to pull those entries out of the bag. To do this, Pig provides the `flatten` modifier in `foreach`:

```
--flatten.pig
players = load 'baseball' as (name:chararray, team:chararray,
            position:bag{t:(p:chararray)}, bat:map[]);
pos     = foreach players generate name, flatten(position) as position;
bypos   = group pos by position;
```

A `foreach` with a `flatten` produces a cross product of every record in the bag with all of the other expressions in the `generate` statement. Looking at the first record in *baseball*, we see it is the following (replacing tabs with commas for clarity):

```
Jorge Posada,New York Yankees,{(Catcher),(Designated_hitter)},...
```

Once this has passed through the `flatten` statement, it will be two records:

```
Jorge Posada,Catcher
Jorge Posada,Designated_hitter
```

If there is more than one bag and both are flattened, this cross product will be done with members of each bag as well as other expressions in the `generate` statement. So rather than getting n rows (where n is the number of records in one bag), you will get n * m rows.

One side effect that surprises many users is that if the bag is empty, no records are produced. So if there had been an entry in *baseball* with no position, either because the bag is null or empty, that record would not be contained in the output of *flatten.pig*. The record with the empty bag would be swallowed by `foreach`. There are a couple of reasons for this behavior. One, since Pig may or may not have the schema of the data in the bag, it might have no idea how to fill in nulls for the missing fields. Two, from a mathematical perspective, this is what you would expect. Crossing a set S with the empty set results in the empty set. If you wish to avoid this, use a bincond to replace empty bags with a constant bag:

```
--flatten_noempty.pig
players = load 'baseball' as (name:chararray, team:chararray,
            position:bag{t:(p:chararray)}, bat:map[]);
noempty = foreach players generate name,
            ((position is null or IsEmpty(position)) ? {('unknown')} : position)
            as position;
pos     = foreach noempty generate name, flatten(position) as position;
bypos   = group pos by position;
```

`flatten` can also be applied to a tuple. In this case, it does not produce a cross product; instead, it elevates each field in the tuple to a top-level field. Again, empty tuples will remove the entire record.

If the fields in a bag or tuple that is being flattened have names, Pig will carry those names along. As with `join`, to avoid ambiguity, the field name will have the bag's name and `::` prepended to it. As long as the field name is not ambiguous, you are not required to use the *bagname*`::` prefix.

If you wish to change the names of the fields, or if the fields initially did not have names, you can attach an **as** clause to your **flatten**, as in the preceding example. If there is more than one field in the bag or tuple that you are assigning names to, you must surround the set of field names with parentheses.

Finally, if you flatten a bag or tuple without a schema and do not provide an **as** clause, the resulting records coming out of your **foreach** will have a null schema. This is because Pig will not know how many fields the **flatten** will result in.[†]

Nested foreach

So far, all of the examples of **foreach** that we have seen immediately generate one or more lines of output. But **foreach** is more powerful than this. It can also apply a set of relational operations to each record in your pipeline. This is referred to as a *nested foreach*, or inner foreach. One example of how this can be used is to find the number of unique entries in a group. For example, to find the number of unique stock symbols for each exchange in the *NYSE_daily* data:

```
--distinct_symbols.pig
daily    = load 'NYSE_daily' as (exchange, symbol); -- not interested in other fields
grpd     = group daily by exchange;
uniqcnt  = foreach grpd {
            sym      = daily.symbol;
            uniq_sym = distinct sym;
            generate group, COUNT(uniq_sym);
};
```

There are several new things here to unpack; we will walk through each. In this example, rather than **generate** immediately following **foreach**, a { (open brace) signals that we will be nesting operators inside this **foreach**. In this nested code, each record passed to **foreach** is handled one at a time.

In the first line we see a syntax that we have not seen outside of **foreach**. In fact, **sym = daily.symbol** would not be legal outside of **foreach**. It is roughly equivalent to the top-level statement **sym = foreach grpd generate daily.symbol**, but it is not stated that way inside the **foreach** because it is not really another **foreach**. There is no relation for it to be associated with (that is, grpd is not defined here). This line takes the bag **daily** and produces a new relation **sym**, which is a bag with tuples that have only the field **symbol**.

The second line applies the **distinct** operator to the relation **sym**. Note that even inside **foreach**, relational operators can be applied only to relations; they cannot be applied to expressions. For example, the statement **uniq_sym = distinct daily.symbol** will produce a syntax error because **daily.symbol** is an expression, not a relation. **sym** is a relation. This distinction may seem arbitrary, but it results in Pig Latin having a

---

[†] In versions 0.8 and earlier, there is a bug where this **flatten** is assigned a schema of one field, which is a **bytearray**, instead of causing the schema to be null. This bug has been fixed in 0.9.

coherent definition as a language. Without this, strange statements such as C = dis tinct 1 + 2 would be legal. One way to think about this is that the assignment operator inside foreach can be used to take an expression and create a relation, as happens in this example.

The last line in a nested foreach must always be generate. This tells Pig how to take the results of the nested operations and produce a record to be put in the outer relation (in this case, uniqcnt). So, generate is the operator that takes the inner relations and turns them back into expressions for inclusion in the outer relation. That is, if the script read generate group, uniq_sym, uniq_sym would be treated as a bag for the purpose of the generate statement.

Theoretically, any Pig Latin relational operator should be legal inside foreach. However, at the moment, only distinct, filter, limit, and order are supported.

Let's look at a few more examples of how this feature can be useful, such as to sort the contents of a bag before the bag is passed to a UDF. This is convenient for UDFs that require all of their input to come in a certain order. Consider a stock-analysis UDF that wants to track information about a particular stock over time. The UDF will want input sorted by timestamp:

```
--analyze_stock.pig
register 'acme.jar';
define analyze com.acme.financial.AnalyzeStock();
daily    = load 'NYSE_daily' as (exchange:chararray, symbol:chararray,
               date:chararray, open:float, high:float, low:float,
               close:float, volume:int, adj_close:float);
grpd     = group daily by symbol;
analyzed = foreach grpd {
               sorted = order daily by date;
               generate group, analyze(sorted);
};
```

Doing the sorting in Pig Latin, rather than in your UDF, is important for a couple of reasons. One, it means Pig can offload the sorting to MapReduce. MapReduce has the ability to sort data by a secondary key while grouping it. So, the order statement in this case does not require a separate sorting operation. Two, it means that your UDF does not need to wait for all data to be available before it starts processing. Instead, it can use the Accumulator interface (see "Accumulator Interface" on page 139), which is much more memory efficient.

This feature can be used to find the top *k* elements in a group. The following example will find the top three dividends payed for each stock:

```
--hightest_dividend.pig
divs = load 'NYSE_dividends' as (exchange:chararray, symbol:chararray,
            date:chararray, dividends:float);
grpd = group divs by symbol;
top3 = foreach grpd {
            sorted = order divs by dividends desc;
            top    = limit sorted 3;
```

```
            generate group, flatten(top);
    };
```

Currently, these nested portions of code are always run serially for each record handed to them. Of course the `foreach` itself will be running in multiple map or reduce tasks, but each instance of the `foreach` will not spawn subtasks to do the nested operations in parallel. So if we added a `parallel 10` clause to the `grpd = group divs by symbol` statement in the previous example, this ordering and limiting would take place in 10 reducers. But each group of stocks would be sorted and the top three records taken serially within one of those 10 reducers.

There is, of course, no requirement that the pipeline inside the `foreach` be a simple linear pipeline. For example, if you wanted to calculate two distinct counts together, you could do the following:

```
--double_distinct.pig
divs = load 'NYSE_dividends' as (exchange:chararray, symbol:chararray);
grpd = group divs all;
uniq = foreach grpd {
            exchanges      = divs.exchange;
            uniq_exchanges = distinct exchanges;
            symbols        = divs.symbol;
            uniq_symbols   = distinct symbols;
            generate COUNT(uniq_exchanges), COUNT(uniq_symbols);
    };
```

For simplicity, Pig actually runs this pipeline once for each expression in `generate`. Here this has no side effects because the two data flows are completely disjointed. However, if you constructed a pipeline where there was a split in the flow, and you put a UDF in the shared portion, you would find that it was invoked more often than you expected.

Using Different Join Implementations

When we covered `join` in the previous chapter (see "Join" on page 45), we discussed only the default join behavior. However, Pig offers multiple join implementations, which we will discuss here.

In RDBMS systems, traditionally the SQL optimizer chooses a join implementation for the user. This is nice as long as the optimizer chooses well, which it does in most cases. But Pig has taken a different approach. In the Pig team we like to say that our optimizer is located between the user's chair and keyboard. We empower the user to make these choices rather than having Pig make them. So for operators such as `join` where there are multiple implementations, Pig lets the user indicate his choice via a `using` clause.

This approach fits well with our philosophy that Pigs are domestic animals (i.e., Pig does what you tell it; see "Pig Philosophy" on page 9). Also, as a relatively new product, Pig has a lot of functionality to add. It makes more sense to focus on adding implementation choices and letting the user choose which ones to use, rather than focusing on building an optimizer capable of choosing well.

Joining small to large data

A common type of join is doing a lookup in a smaller input. For example, suppose you were processing data where you needed to translate a US ZIP code (postal code) to the state and city it referred to. As there are at most 100,000 zip codes in the US, this translation table should easily fit in memory. Rather than forcing a reduce phase that will sort your big file plus this tiny zip code translation file, it makes sense instead to send the zip code file to every machine, load it into memory, and then do the join by streaming through the large file and looking up each record in the zip code file. This is called a *fragment-replicate join* (because you fragment one file and replicate the other):

```
--repljoin.pig
daily = load 'NYSE_daily' as (exchange:chararray, symbol:chararray,
            date:chararray, open:float, high:float, low:float,
            close:float, volume:int, adj_close:float);
divs  = load 'NYSE_dividends' as (exchange:chararray, symbol:chararray,
            date:chararray, dividends:float);
jnd   = join daily by (exchange, symbol), divs by (exchange, symbol)
            using 'replicated';
```

The using 'replicated' tells Pig to use the fragment-replicate algorithm to execute this join. Because no reduce phase is necessary, all of this can be done in the map task.

The second input listed in the join (in this case, divs) is always the input that is loaded into memory. Pig does not check beforehand that the specified input will fit into memory. If Pig cannot fit the replicated input into memory, it will issue an error and fail.

 Due to the way Java stores objects in memory, the size of the data on disk will not be the size of the data in memory. See "Memory Requirements of Pig Data Types" on page 26 for a discussion of how data expands in memory in Pig. You will need more memory for a replicated join than you need space on disk to store the replicated input.

Fragment-replicate join supports only inner and left outer joins. It cannot do a right outer join, because when a given map task sees a record in the replicated input that does not match any record in the fragmented input, it has no idea whether it would match a record in a different fragment. So, it does not know whether to emit a record. If you want a right or full outer join, you will need to use the default join operation.

Fragment-replicate join can be used with more than two tables. In this case, all but the first (left-most) table are read into memory.

Pig implements the fragment-replicate join by loading the replicated input into Hadoop's *distributed cache*. The distributed cache is a tool provided by Hadoop that preloads a file onto the local disk of nodes that will be executing the maps or reduces for that job. This has two important benefits. First, if you have a fragment-replicate join that is going to run on 1,000 maps, opening one file in HDFS from 1,000 different machines all at once puts a serious strain on the NameNode and the three data nodes that contain the block for that file. The distributed cache is built specifically to manage these kinds of issues without straining HDFS. Second, if multiple map tasks are located on the same physical machine, the files in the distributed cache are shared between those instances, thus reducing the number of times the file has to be copied.

Pig runs a map-only MapReduce job to preprocess the file and get it ready for loading into the distributed cache. If there is a `filter` or `foreach` between the `load` and `join`, these will be done as part of this initial job so that the file to be stored in the distributed cache is as small as possible. The join itself will be done in a second map-only job.

Joining skewed data

As we have seen elsewhere, much of the data you will be processing with Pig has significant skew in the number of records per key. For example, if you were building a map of the Web and joining by the domain of the URL (your key), you would expect to see significant skew for values such as yahoo.com. Pig's default join algorithm is very sensitive to skew, because it collects all of the records for a given key together on a single reducer. In many data sets, there are a few keys that have three or more orders of magnitude more records than other keys. This results in one or two reducers that will take much longer than the rest. To deal with this, Pig provides *skew join*.

Skew join works by first sampling one input for the join. In that input it identifies any keys that have so many records that skew join estimates it will not be able to fit them all into memory. Then, in a second MapReduce job, it does the join. For all records except those identified in the sample, it does a standard join, collecting records with the same key onto the same reducer. Those keys identified as too large are treated differently. Based on how many records were seen for a given key, those records are split across the appropriate number of reducers. The number of reducers is chosen based on Pig's estimate of how wide the data must be split such that each reducer can fit its split into memory. For the input to the join that is not split, those keys that were split are then replicated to each reducer that contains that key.[‡]

For example, let's look at how the following Pig Latin script would work:

```
users = load 'users' as (name:chararray, city:chararray);
cinfo = load 'cityinfo' as (city:chararray, population:int);
jnd   = join cinfo by city, users by city using 'skewed';
```

Assume that the cities in *users* are distributed such that 20 users live in Barcelona, 100,000 in New York, and 350 in Portland. Let's further assume that Pig determined that it could fit 75,000 records into memory on each reducer. When this data was joined, New York would be identified as a key that needed to be split across reducers. During the join phase, all records with keys other than New York would be treated as in a default join. Records from *users* with New York as the key would be split between

---

[‡] This algorithm was proposed in the paper "Practical Skew Handling in Parallel Joins," presented by David J. DeWitt, Jeffrey F. Naughton, Donovan A. Schneider, and S. Seshadri at the 18th International Conference on Very Large Databases.

two separate reducers. Records from *cityinfo* with New York as a key would be duplicated and sent to both of those reducers.

The second input in the join, in this case users, is the one that will be sampled and have its keys with a large number of values split across reducers. The first input will have records with those values replicated across reducers.

This algorithm addresses skew in only one input. If both inputs have skew, this algorithm will still work, but it will be slow. Much of the motivation behind this approach was that it guarantees the join will still finish, given time. Before Pig introduced skew join in version 0.4, data that was skewed on both sides could not be joined in Pig because it was not possible to fit all the records for the high-cardinality key values in memory for either side.

Skew join can be done on inner or outer joins. However, it can take only two join inputs. Multiway joins must be broken into a series of joins if they need to use skew join.

Since data often has skew, why not use skew join all of the time? There is a small performance penalty for using skew join, because one of the inputs must be sampled first to find any key values with a large number of records. This usually adds about 5% to the time it takes to calculate the join. If your data frequently has skew, it might be worth it to always use skew join and pay the 5% tax in order to avoid failing or running very slowly with the default join and then needing to rerun using skewed join.

As stated earlier, Pig estimates how much data it can fit into memory when deciding which key values to split and how wide to split them. For the purposes of this calculation, Pig looks at the record sizes in the sample and assumes it can use 30% of the JVM's heap to materialize records that will be joined. In your particular case you might find you need to increase or decrease this size. You should decrease the value if your join is still failing with out-of-memory errors even when using skew join. This indicates that Pig is estimating memory usage improperly, so you should tell it to use less. If profiling indicates that Pig is not utilizing all of your heap, you might want to increase the value in order to do the join more efficiently; the less ways the key values are split, the more efficient the join will be. You can do that by setting the property pig.skewed join.reduce.memusage to a value between 0 and 1. For example, if you wanted it to use 25% instead of 30%, you could add -Dpig.skewedjoin.reduce.memusage=0.25 to your Pig command line or define the value in your properties file.

 Like order, skew join breaks the MapReduce convention that all records with the same key will be processed by the same reducer. This means records with the same key might be placed in separate part files. If you plan to process the data in a way that depends on all records with the same key being in the same part file, you cannot use skew join.

Joining sorted data

A common database join strategy is to first sort both inputs on the join key and then walk through both inputs together, doing the join. This is referred to as a sort-merge join. In MapReduce, because a sort requires a full MapReduce job, as does Pig's default join, this technique is not more efficient than the default. However, if your inputs are already sorted on the join key, this approach makes sense. The join can be done in the map phase by opening both files and walking through them. Pig refers to this as a *merge join* because it is a sort-merge join, but the sort has already been done:

```
--mergejoin.pig
-- use sort_for_mergejoin.pig to build NYSE_daily_sorted and NYSE_dividends_sorted
daily = load 'NYSE_daily_sorted' as (exchange:chararray, symbol:chararray,
            date:chararray, open:float, high:float, low:float,
            close:float, volume:int, adj_close:float);
divs  = load 'NYSE_dividends_sorted' as (exchange:chararray, symbol:chararray,
            date:chararray, dividends:float);
jnd   = join daily by symbol, divs by symbol using 'merge';
```

To execute this join, Pig will first run a MapReduce job that samples the second input, *NYSE_dividends_sorted*. This sample builds an index that tells Pig the value of the join keys, symbol in the first record in every input split (usually each HDFS block). Because this sample reads only one record per split, it runs very quickly. Pig will then run a second MapReduce job that takes the first input, *NYSE_daily_sorted*, as its input. When each map reads the first record in its split of *NYSE_daily_sorted*, it takes the value of symbol and looks it up in the index built by the previous job. It looks for the last entry that is less than its value of symbol. It then opens *NYSE_dividends_sorted* at the corresponding block for that entry. For example, if the index contained entries (CA, 1), (CHY, 2), (CP, 3), and the first symbol in a given map's input split of *NYSE_daily_sorted* was CJA, that map would open block 2 of *NYSE_dividends_sorted*. (Even if CP was the first user ID in *NYSE_daily_sorted*'s split, block 2 of *NYSE_dividends_sorted* would be opened, as there could be records with a key of CP in that block.) Once *NYSE_dividends_sorted* is opened, Pig throws away records until it reaches a record with symbol of CJA. Once it finds a match, it collects all the records with that value into memory and then does the join. It then advances the first input, *NYSE_daily_sorted*. If the key is the same, it again does the join. If not, it advances the second input, *NYSE_dividends_sorted*, again until it finds a value greater than or equal to the next value in the first input, *NYSE_daily_sorted*. If the value is greater, it advances the first input and continues. Because both inputs are sorted, it never needs to look in the index after the initial lookup.

All of this can be done without a reduce phase, and so it is more efficient than a default join. This algorithm, which was introduced in version 0.4, currently supports only two-way inner joins.

cogroup

cogroup is a generalization of group. Instead of collecting records of one input based on a key, it collects records of *n* inputs based on a key. The result is a record with a key and one bag for each input. Each bag contains all records from that input that have the given value for the key:

```
A = load 'input1' as (id:int, val:float);
B = load 'input2' as (id:int, val2:int);
C = cogroup A by id, B by id;
describe C;

C: {group: int,A: {id: int,val: float},B: {id: int,val2: int}}
```

Another way to think of cogroup is as the first half of a join. The keys are collected together, but the cross product is not done. In fact, cogroup plus foreach, where each bag is flattened, is equivalent to a join—as long as there are no null values in the keys.

cogroup handles null values in the keys similarly to group and unlike join. That is, all records with a null value in the key will be collected together.

cogroup is useful when you want to do join-like things but not a full join. For example, Pig Latin does not have a semi-join operator, but you can do a semi-join:

```
--semijoin.pig
daily = load 'NYSE_daily' as (exchange:chararray, symbol:chararray,
            date:chararray, open:float, high:float, low:float,
            close:float, volume:int, adj_close:float);
divs  = load 'NYSE_dividends' as (exchange:chararray, symbol:chararray,
            date:chararray, dividends:float);
grpd  = cogroup daily by (exchange, symbol), divs by (exchange, symbol);
sjnd  = filter grpd by not IsEmpty(divs);
final = foreach sjnd generate flatten(daily);
```

Because cogroup needs to collect records with like keys together, it requires a reduce phase.

union

Sometimes you want to put two data sets together by concatenating them instead of joining them. Pig Latin provides union for this purpose. If you had two files you wanted to use for input and there was no glob that could describe them, you could do the following:

```
A = load '/user/me/data/files/input1';
B = load '/user/someoneelse/info/input2';
C = union A, B;
```

Unlike union in SQL, Pig does not require that both inputs share the
same schema. If both do share the same schema, the output of the union
will have that schema. If one schema can be produced from another by
a set of implicit casts, the union will have that resulting schema. If neither of these conditions hold, the output will have no schema (that is,
different records will have different fields). This schema comparison
includes names, so even different field names will result in the output
having no schema. You can get around this by placing a foreach before
the union that renames fields.

```
A = load 'input1' as (x:int, y:float);
B = load 'input2' as (x:int, y:float);
C = union A, B;
describe C;
```

```
C: {x: int,y: float}
```

```
A = load 'input1' as (x:int, y:float);
B = load 'input2' as (x:int, y:double);
C = union A, B;
describe C;
```

```
C: {x: int,y: double}
```

```
A = load 'input1' as (x:int, y:float);
B = load 'input2' as (x:int, y:chararray);
C = union A, B;
describe C;
```

```
Schema for C unknown.
```

union does not perform a mathematical set union. That is, duplicate records are not
eliminated. In this manner it is like SQL's union all. Also, union does not require a
separate reduce phase.

Sometimes your data changes over time. If you have data you collect every month, you
might add a new column this month. Now you are prevented from using union because
your schemas do not match. If you want to union this data and force your data into a
common schema, you can add the keyword onschema to your union statement:

```
A = load 'input1' as (w:chararray, x:int, y:float);
B = load 'input2' as (x:int, y:double, z:chararray);
C = union onschema A, B;
describe C;
```

```
C: {w: chararray,x: int,y: double,z: chararray}
```

union onschema requires that all inputs have schemas. It also requires that a shared
schema for all inputs can be produced by adding fields and implicit casts. Matching of
fields is done by name, not position. So, in the preceding example, w:chararray is added
from *input1* and z:chararray is added from *input2*. Also, a cast from float to double is

added for *input1* so that field y is a double. If a shared schema cannot be produced by this method, an error is returned. When the data is read, nulls are inserted for fields not present in a given input.

cross

cross matches the mathematical set operation of the same name. In the following Pig Latin, cross takes every record in *NYSE_daily* and combines it with every record in *NYSE_dividends*:

```
--cross.pig
-- you may want to run this in a cluster, it produces about 3G of data
daily     = load 'NYSE_daily' as (exchange:chararray, symbol:chararray,
                date:chararray, open:float, high:float, low:float,
                close:float, volume:int, adj_close:float);
divs      = load 'NYSE_dividends' as (exchange:chararray, symbol:chararray,
                date:chararray, dividends:float);
tonsodata = cross daily, divs parallel 10;
```

cross tends to produce a lot of data. Given inputs with n and m records respectively, cross will produce output with n x m records.

Pig does implement cross in a parallel fashion. It does this by generating a synthetic join key, replicating rows, and then doing the cross as a join. The previous script is rewritten to:

```
daily     = load 'NYSE_daily' as (exchange:chararray, symbol:chararray,
                date:chararray, open:float, high:float, low:float,
                close:float, volume:int, adj_close:float);
divs      = load 'NYSE_dividends' as (exchange:chararray, symbol:chararray,
                date:chararray, dividends:float);
A         = foreach daily generate flatten(GFCross(0, 2)), flatten(*);
B         = foreach divs generate flatten(GFCross(1, 2)), flatten(*);
C         = cogroup A by ($0, $1), B by ($0, $1) parallel 10;
tonsodata = foreach C generate flatten(A), flatten(B);
```

GFCross is an internal UDF. The first argument is the input number, and the second argument is the total number of inputs. In this example, the output is a bag that contains four records.[§] These records have a schema of (int, int). The field that is the same number as the first argument to GFCross contains a random number between zero and three. The other field counts from zero to three. So, if we assume for a given two records, one in each input, that the random number for the first input is 3 and for the second is 2, then the outputs of GFCross would look like:

```
A {(3, 0), (3, 1), (3, 2), (3, 3)}
B {(0, 2), (1, 2), (2, 2), (3, 2)}
```

[§] In 0.8 and earlier, the number of records is always 10. In 0.9, this is changed to be the square root of the parallel factor, rounded up.

When these records are flattened, four copies of each input record will be created in the map. They then are joined on the artificial keys. For every record in each input, it is guaranteed that there is one and only one instance of the artificial keys that will match and produce a record. Because the random numbers are chosen differently for each record, the resulting joins are done on an even distribution of the reducers.

This algorithm does enable crossing of data in parallel. However, it creates a burden on the shuffle phase by increasing the number of records in each input being shuffled. Also, no matter what you do, `cross` outputs a lot of data. Writing all of this data to disk is expensive, even when done in parallel.

This is not to say you should not use `cross`. There are instances when it is indispensable. Pig's `join` operator supports only equi-joins, that is, joins on an equality condition. Because general join implementations (ones that do not depend on the data being sorted or small enough to fit in memory) in MapReduce depend on collecting records with the same join key values onto the same reducer, non-equi-joins (also called *theta joins*) are difficult to do. They can be done in Pig using `cross` followed by `filter`:

```
--thetajoin.pig
--I recommend running this one on a cluster too
daily    = load 'NYSE_daily' as (exchange:chararray, symbol:chararray,
               date:chararray, open:float, high:float, low:float,
               close:float, volume:int, adj_close:float);
divs     = load 'NYSE_dividends' as (exchange:chararray, symbol:chararray,
               date:chararray, dividends:float);
crossed = cross daily, divs;
tjnd     = filter crossed by daily::date < divs::date;
```

Fuzzy joins could also be done in this manner, where the fuzzy comparison is done after the cross. However, whenever possible, it is better to use a UDF to conform fuzzy values to a standard value and then do a regular join. For example, if you wanted to join two inputs on `city` but wanted to join any time two cities were in the same metropolitan area (e.g., you wanted "Los Angeles" and "Pasadena" to be viewed as equal), you could first run your records through a UDF that generated a single join key for all cities in a metropolitan area and then do the join.

Integrating Pig with Legacy Code and MapReduce

One tenet of Pig's philosophy is that Pig allows users to integrate their own code with Pig wherever possible (see "Pig Philosophy" on page 9). The most obvious way Pig does that is through its UDFs. But it also allows you to directly integrate other executables and MapReduce jobs.

stream

To specify an executable that you want to insert into your data flow, use `stream`. You may want to do this when you have a legacy program that you do not want to modify or are unable to change. You can also use stream when you have a program you use frequently, or one you have tested on small data sets and now want to apply to a large data set. Let's look at an example where you have a Perl program *highdiv.pl* that filters out all stocks with a dividend below $1.00:

```
-- streamsimple.pig
divs = load 'NYSE_dividends' as (exchange, symbol, date, dividends);
highdivs = stream divs through `highdiv.pl` as (exchange, symbol, date, dividends);
```

Notice the as clause in the stream command. This is not required. But Pig has no idea what the executable will return, so if you do not provide the as clause, the relation highdivs will have no schema.

The executable *highdiv.pl* is invoked once on every map or reduce task. It is not invoked once per record. Pig instantiates the executable and keeps feeding data to it via *stdin*. It also keeps checking *stdout*, passing any results to the next operator in your data flow. The executable can choose whether to produce an output for every input, only every so many inputs, or only after all inputs have been received.

The preceding example assumes that you already have *highdiv.pl* installed on your grid, and that it is runnable from the working directory on the task machines. If that is not the case, which it usually will not be, you can ship the executable to the grid. To do this, use a define statement:

```
--streamship.pig
define hd `highdiv.pl` ship('highdiv.pl');
divs = load 'NYSE_dividends' as (exchange, symbol, date, dividends);
highdivs = stream divs through hd as (exchange, symbol, date, dividends);
```

This define does two things. First, it defines the executable that will be used. Now in stream we refer to *highdiv.pl* by the alias we gave it, hp, rather than referring to it directly. Second, it tells Pig to pick up the file *./highdiv.pl* and ship it to Hadoop as part of this job. This file will be picked up from the specified location on the machine where you launch the job. It will be placed in the working directory of the task on the task machines. So, the command you pass to stream must refer to it relative to the current working directory, not via an absolute path. If your executable depends on other modules or files, they can be specified as part of the ship clause as well. For example, if *highdiv.pl* depends on a Perl module called *Financial.pm*, you can send them both to the task machines:

```
define hd `highdiv.pl` ship('highdiv.pl', 'Financial.pm');
divs = load 'NYSE_dividends' as (exchange, symbol, date, dividends);
highdivs = stream divs through hd as (exchange, symbol, date, dividends);
```

Many scripting languages assume certain paths for modules based on their hierarchy. For example, Perl expects to find a module Acme::Financial in *Acme/Financial.pm*. However, the ship clause always puts files in your current working directory, and it does not take directories, so you could not ship *Acme*. The workaround for this is to create a TAR file and ship that, and then have a step in your executable that unbundles the TAR file. You then need to set your module include path (for Perl, `-I` or the `PERL LIB` environment variables) to contain . (dot).

`ship` moves files into the grid from the machine where you are launching your job. But sometimes the file you want is already in the grid. If you have a grid file that will be accessed by every map or reduce task in your job, the proper way to access it is via the *distributed cache*. The distributed cache is a mechanism Hadoop provides to share files. It reduces the load on HDFS by preloading the file to the local disk on the machine that will be executing the task. You can use the distributed cache for your executable by using the cache clause in `define`:

```
crawl      = load 'webcrawl' as (url, pageid);
normalized = foreach crawl generate normalize(url);
define blc `blacklistchecker.py` cache('/data/shared/badurls#badurls');
goodurls   = stream normalized through blc as (url, pageid);
```

The string before the # is the path on HDFS, in this case, */data/shared/badurls*. The string after the # is the name of the file as viewed by the executable. So, Hadoop will put a copy of */data/shared/badurls* into the task's working directory and call it *badurls*.

So far we have assumed that your executable takes data on *stdin* and writes it to *stdout*. This might not work, depending on your executable. If your executable needs a file to read from, write to, or both, you can specify that with the `input` and `output` clauses in the `define` command. Continuing with our previous example, let's say that *blacklistchecker.py* expects to read its input from a file specified by `-i` on its command line and write to a file specified by `-o`:

```
crawl      = load 'webcrawl' as (url, pageid);
normalized = foreach crawl generate normalize(url);
define blc `blacklistchecker.py -i urls -o good` input('urls') output('good');
goodurls   = stream normalized through blc as (url, pageid);
```

Again, file locations are specified from the working directory on the task machines. In this example, Pig will write out all the input for a given task for *blacklistchecker.py* to *urls*, then invoke the executable, and then read *good* to get the results. Again, the executable will be invoked only once per map or reduce task, so Pig will first write out all the input to the file.

mapreduce

Beginning in Pig 0.8, you can also include MapReduce jobs directly in your data flow with the `mapreduce` command. This is convenient if you have processing that is better done in MapReduce than Pig but must be integrated with the rest of your Pig data flow. It can also make it easier to incorporate legacy processing written in MapReduce with newer processing you want to write in Pig Latin.

MapReduce jobs expect to read their input from and write their output to a storage device (usually HDFS). So to integrate them with your data flow, Pig first has to store the data, then invoke the MapReduce job, and then read the data back. This is done via `store` and `load` clauses in the `mapreduce` statement that invoke regular load and store functions. You also provide Pig with the name of the JAR that contains the code for your MapReduce job.

As an example, let's continue with the blacklisting of URLs that we considered in the previous section. Only now let's assume that this is done by a MapReduce job instead of a Python script:

```
crawl      = load 'webcrawl' as (url, pageid);
normalized = foreach crawl generate normalize(url);
goodurls   = mapreduce 'blacklistchecker.jar'
                 store normalized into 'input'
                 load 'output' as (url, pageid);
```

`mapreduce` takes as its first argument the JAR containing the code to run a MapReduce job. It uses `load` and `store` phrases to specify how data will be moved from Pig's data pipeline to the MapReduce job. Notice that the input alias is contained in the `store` clause. As with `stream`, the output of `mapreduce` is opaque to Pig, so if we want the resulting relation `goodurls` to have a schema, we have to tell Pig what it is. This example also assumes that the Java code in *blacklistchecker.jar* knows which input and output files to look for and has a default class to run specified in its manifest. Often this will not be the case. Any arguments you wish to pass to the invocation of the Java command that will run the MapReduce task can be put in backquotes after the `load` clause:

```
crawl      = load 'webcrawl' as (url, pageid);
normalized = foreach crawl generate normalize(url);
goodurls   = mapreduce 'blacklistchecker.jar'
                 store normalized into 'input'
                 load 'output' as (url, pageid)
                 `com.acmeweb.security.BlackListChecker -i input -o output`;
```

The string in the backquotes will be passed directly to your MapReduce job as is. So if you wanted to pass Java options, etc., you can do that as well.

The `load` and `store` clauses of the `mapreduce` command have the same syntax as the `load` and `store` statements, so you can use different load and store functions, pass constructor arguments, and so on. See "Load" on page 34 and "Store" on page 36 for full details.

Nonlinear Data Flows

So far our examples have been linear data flows or trees. In a linear data flow, one input is loaded, processed, and stored. We have looked at operators that combine multiple data flows: `join`, `cogroup`, `union`, and `cross`. With these you can build tree structures where multiple inputs all flow to a single output. But in complex data-processing situations, you often also want to split your data flow. That is, one input will result in more than one output. You might also have diamonds, places where the data flow is split and eventually joined back together. Pig supports these directed acyclic graph (DAG) data flows.

Splits in your data flow can be either implicit or explicit. In an implicit split, no specific operator or syntax is required in your script. You simply refer to a given relation multiple times. Let's consider data from our *baseball* example data. You might, for example, want to analyze players by position and by team at the same time:

```
--multiquery.pig
players    = load 'baseball' as (name:chararray, team:chararray,
                 position:bag{t:(p:chararray)}, bat:map[]);
pwithba    = foreach players generate name, team, position,
                 bat#'batting_average' as batavg;
byteam     = group pwithba by team;
avgbyteam  = foreach byteam generate group, AVG(pwithba.batavg);
store avgbyteam into 'by_team';
flattenpos = foreach pwithba generate name, team,
                 flatten(position) as position, batavg;
bypos      = group flattenpos by position;
avgbypos   = foreach bypos generate group, AVG(flattenpos.batavg);
store avgbypos into 'by_position';
```

The `pwithba` relation is referred to by the `group` operators for both the `byteam` and `bypos` relations. Pig builds a data flow that takes every record from `pwithba` and ships it to both `group` operators.

Splitting data flows can also be done explicitly via the `split` operator, which allows you to split your data flow as many ways as you like. Let's take an example where you want to split data into different files depending on the date the record was created:

```
wlogs = load 'weblogs' as (pageid, url, timestamp);
split wlogs into apr03 if timestamp < '20110404',
          apr02 if timestamp < '20110403' and timestamp > '20110401',
          apr01 if timestamp < '20110402' and timestamp > '20110331';
store apr03 into '20110403';
store apr02 into '20110402';
store apr01 into '20110401';
```

At first glance, `split` looks like a `switch` or `case` statement, *but it is not*. A single record can go to multiple legs of the split since you use different filters for each `if` clause. And a record can go to no leg. In the preceding example, if a record were found with a date of `20110331`, it would be dropped. And there is no default clause—no way to send any leftover records to a particular alias.

`split` is semantically identical to an implicit split that users filters. The previous example could be rewritten as:

```
wlogs = load 'weblogs' as (pageid, url, timestamp);
apr03 = filter wlogs by timestamp < '20110404';
apr02 = filter wlogs by timestamp < '20110403' and timestamp > '20110401';
apr01 = filter wlogs by timestamp < '20110402' and timestamp > '20110331';
store apr03 into '20110403';
store apr02 into '20110402';
store apr01 into '20110401';
```

In fact, Pig will internally rewrite the original script that has `split` in exactly this way.

Let's take a look at how Pig executes these nonlinear data flows. Whenever possible, it combines them into single MapReduce jobs. This is referred to as a *multiquery*. In cases where all operators will fit into a single map task, this is easy. Pig creates separate pipelines inside the map and sends the appropriate records to each pipeline. The example using `split` to store data by date will be executed in this way.

Pig can also combine multiple `group` operators together in many cases. In the example given at the beginning of this section, where the baseball data is grouped by both team and position, this entire Pig Latin script will be executed inside one MapReduce job. Pig accomplishes this by duplicating records on the map side and annotating each record with its pipeline number. When the data is partitioned during the shuffle, the appropriate key is used for each record. That is, records from the pipeline grouping by `team` will use `team` as their shuffle key, and records from the pipeline grouping by `position` will use `position` as their shuffle key. This is done by declaring the key type to be `tuple` and placing the correct values in the key tuple for each record. Once the data has been collected to reducers, the pipeline number is used as part of the sort key so that records from each pipeline and group are collected together. In the reduce task, Pig instantiates multiple pipelines, one for each group operator. It sends each record down the appropriate pipeline based on its annotated pipeline number. In this way, input data can be scanned once but grouped many different ways. An example of how one record flows through this pipeline is shown in Figure 6-1. Although this does not provide linear speedup, we find it often approaches it.

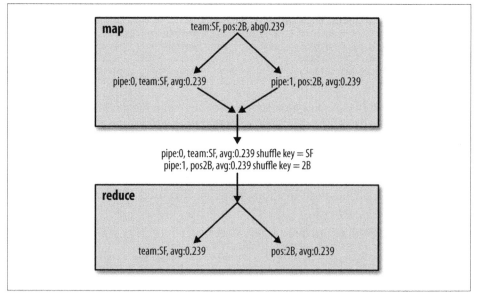

Figure 6-1. Multiquery illustration

There are cases where Pig will not combine multiple operators into a single MapReduce job. Pig does not use multiquery for any of the multiple-input operators: `join`, `union`, cross, or cogroup. It does not use multiquery for order statements either. Also, if it has multiple group statements and some would use Hadoop's combiner and some would not, it combines only those statements that use Hadoop's combiner into a multiquery. This is because we have found that combining the Hadoop combiner and non-Hadoop combiner jobs together does not perform well.

Multiquery scripts tend to perform better than loading the same input multiple times, but this approach does have limits. Because it requires replicating records in the map, it does slow down the shuffle phase. Eventually the increased cost of the shuffle phase outweighs the reduced cost of rescanning the input data. Pig has no way to estimate when this will occur. Currently, the optimizer is optimistic and always combines jobs with multiquery whenever it can. If it combines too many jobs and becomes slower than splitting some of the jobs, you can turn off multiquery or you can rewrite your Pig Latin into separate scripts so Pig does not attempt to combine them all. To turn off multiquery, you can pass either -M or -no_multiquery on the command line or set the property opt.multiquery to false.

We must also consider what happens when one job in a multiquery fails but others succeed. If all jobs succeed, Pig will return 0, meaning success. If all of the jobs fail, Pig will return 2. If some jobs fail and some succeed, Pig will return 3. By default, if one of the jobs fails, Pig will continue processing the other jobs. However, if you want Pig to stop as soon as one of the jobs fails, you can pass -F or -stop_on_failure. In this case, any jobs that have not yet been finished will be terminated, and any that have not started will not be started. Any jobs that are already finished will not be cleaned up.

Controlling Execution

In addition to providing many relational and dataflow operators, Pig Latin provides ways for you to control how your jobs execute on MapReduce. It allows you to set values that control your environment and details of MapReduce, such as how your data is partitioned.

set

The set command is used to set the environment in which Pig runs the MapReduce jobs. Table 6-1 shows Pig-specific parameters that can be controlled via set.

Table 6-1. Pig-specific set parameters

Parameter	Value type	Description
debug	string	Sets the logging level to DEBUG. Equivalent to passing -debug DEBUG on the command line.
default_parallel	integer	Sets a default parallel level for all reduce operations in the script. See "Parallel" on page 49 for details.

Parameter	Value type	Description
job.name	string	Assigns a name to the Hadoop job. By default the name is the filename of the script being run, or a randomly generated name for interactive sessions.
job.priority	string	If your Hadoop cluster is using the Capacity Scheduler with priorities enabled for queues, this allows you to set the priority of your Pig job. Allowed values are very_low, low, normal, high, and very_high.

For example, to set the default parallelism of your Pig Latin script and set the job name to my_job:

```
set default_parallel 10;
set job.name my_job;
users = load 'users';
```

In addition to these predefined values, set can be used to pass Java property settings to Pig and Hadoop. Both Pig and Hadoop use a number of Java properties to control their behavior. Consider an example where you want to turn multiquery off for a given script, and you want to tell Hadoop to use a higher value than usual for its map-side sort buffer:

```
set opt.multiquery false;
set io.sort.mb 2048; --give it 2G
```

You can also use this mechanism to pass properties to UDFs. All of the properties are passed to the tasks on the Hadoop nodes when they are executed. They are not set as Java properties in that environment; rather, they are placed in a Hadoop object called JobConf. UDFs have access to the JobConf. Thus, anything you set in the script can be seen by your UDFs. This can be a convenient way to control UDF behavior. For information on how to retrieve this information in your UDFs, see "Constructors and Passing Data from Frontend to Backend" on page 128.

Values that are set in your script are global for the whole script. If they are reset later in the script, that second value will overwrite the first and be used *throughout the whole script*.

Setting the Partitioner

Hadoop uses a class called Partitioner to partition records to reducers during the shuffle phase. For details on partitioners, see "Shuffle Phase" on page 191. Pig does not override the default partitioner, except for order and skew join. The balancing operations in these require special Partitioners.

Beginning in version 0.8, Pig allows you to set the partitioner, except in the cases where it is already overriding it. To do this, you need to tell Pig which Java class to use to partition your data. This class must extend Hadoop's org.apache.hadoop.mapre duce.Partitioner<KEY,VALUE>. Note that this is the newer (version 0.20 and later) map reduce API and not the older mapred:

```
register acme.jar; --jar containing the partitioner
users = load 'users' as (id, age, zip);
grp   = group users by id partition by com.acme.userpartitioner parallel 100;
```

Operators that reduce data can take the `partition` clause. These operators are `cogroup`, `cross`, `distinct`, `group`, and `join` (again, not in conjunction with skew join).

Pig Latin Preprocessor

Pig Latin has a preprocessor that runs before your Pig Latin script is parsed. In 0.8 and earlier, this provided parameter substitution, roughly similar to a very simple version of `#define` in C. Starting with 0.9, it also provides inclusion of other Pig Latin scripts and function-like macro definitions, so that you can write Pig Latin in a modular way.

Parameter Substitution

Pig Latin scripts that are used frequently often have elements that need to change based on when or where they are run. A script that is run every day is likely to have a date component in its input files or filters. Rather than edit and change the script every day, you want to pass in the date as a parameter. *Parameter substitution* provides this capability with a basic string-replacement functionality. Parameters must start with a letter or an underscore and can then have any amount of letters, numbers, or underscores. Values for the parameters can be passed in on the command line or from a parameter file:

```
--daily.pig
daily     = load 'NYSE_daily' as (exchange:chararray, symbol:chararray,
               date:chararray, open:float, high:float, low:float, close:float,
               volume:int, adj_close:float);
yesterday = filter daily by date == '$DATE';
grpd      = group yesterday all;
minmax    = foreach grpd generate MAX(yesterday.high), MIN(yesterday.low);
```

When you run *daily.pig*, you must provide a definition for the parameter DATE; otherwise, you will get an error telling you that you have undefined parameters:

```
pig -p DATE=2009-12-17 daily.pig
```

You can repeat the -p command-line switch as many times as needed. Parameters can also be placed in a file, which is convenient if you have more than a few of them. The format of the file is *parameter=value*, one per line. Comments in the file should be preceded by a #. You then indicate the file to be used with -m or -param_file:

```
pig -param_file daily.params daily.pig
```

Parameters passed on the command line take precedence over parameters provided in files. This way, you can provide all your standard parameters in a file and override a few as needed on the command line.

Parameters can contain other parameters. So, for example, you could have the following parameter file:

```
#Param file
YEAR=2009-
MONTH=12-
DAY=17
DATE=$YEAR$MONTH$DAY
```

A parameter must be defined before it is referenced. The parameter file here would produce an error if the DAY line came after the DATE line. The other caveat is that there is no special character to delimit the end of a parameter. Any alphanumeric or underscore character will be interpreted as part of the parameter, and any other character will be interpreted as itself. So, if you had a script that ran at the first of every month, you could not do the following:

```
wlogs = load 'clicks/$YEAR$MONTH01' as (url, pageid, timestamp);
```

This would try to resolve a parameter MONTH01 when you meant MONTH.

When using parameter substitution, all parameters in your script must be resolved after the preprocessor is finished. If not, Pig will issue an error message and not continue. You can see the results of your parameter substitution by using the -dryrun flag on the Pig command line. Pig will write out a version of your Pig Latin script with the parameter substitution done, but it will not execute the script.

You can also define parameters inside your Pig Latin script using %declare and %default. %declare allows you to define a parameter in the script itself. %default is useful to provide a common default value that can be overridden when needed. Consider a case where most of the time your script is run on one Hadoop cluster, but occasionally it is run on a different cluster with different hardware:

```
%default parallel_factor 10;
wlogs = load 'clicks' as (url, pageid, timestamp);
grp   = group wlogs by pageid parallel $parallel_factor;
cntd  = foreach grp generate group, COUNT(wlogs);
```

When running your script in the usual configuration, there is no need to set the parameter parallel_factor. On the occasions it is run in a different setup, the parallel factor can be changed by passing a value on the command line.

Macros

Starting in 0.9, Pig added the ability to define macros. This makes it possible to make your Pig Latin scripts modular. It also makes it possible to share segments of Pig Latin code among users. This can be particularly useful for defining standard practices and making sure all data producers and consumers use them.

Macros are declared with the define statement. A macro takes a set of input parameters, which are string values that will be substituted for the parameters when the macro is expanded. By convention, input relation names are placed first before other parameters.

The output relation name is given in a `returns` statement. The operators of the macro are enclosed in {} (braces). Anywhere the parameters—including the output relation name—are referenced inside the macro, they must be preceded by a $ (dollar sign). The macro is then invoked in your Pig Latin by assigning it to a relation:

```
--macro.pig
-- Given daily input and a particular year, analyze how
-- stock prices changed on days dividends were paid out.
define dividend_analysis (daily, year, daily_symbol, daily_open, daily_close)
returns analyzed {
    divs         = load 'NYSE_dividends' as (exchange:chararray,
                        symbol:chararray, date:chararray, dividends:float);
    divsthisyear  = filter divs by date matches '$year-.*';
    dailythisyear = filter $daily by date matches '$year-.*';
    jnd           = join divsthisyear by symbol, dailythisyear by $daily_symbol;
    $analyzed     = foreach jnd generate dailythisyear::$daily_symbol,
                        $daily_close - $daily_open;
};

daily   = load 'NYSE_daily' as (exchange:chararray, symbol:chararray,
            date:chararray, open:float, high:float, low:float, close:float,
            volume:int, adj_close:float);
results = dividend_analysis(daily, '2009', 'symbol', 'open', 'close');
```

It is also possible to have a macro that does not return a relation. In this case, the `returns` clause of the `define` statement is changed to `returns void`. This can be useful when you want to define a macro that controls how data is partitioned and sorted before being stored to a particular output, such as HBase or a database.

These macros are expanded inline. This is where an important difference between macros and functions becomes apparent. Macros cannot be invoked recursively. Macros can invoke other macros, so a macro A can invoke a macro B, but A cannot invoke itself. And once A has invoked B, B cannot invoke A. Pig will detect these loops and throw an error.

Parameter substitution (see "Parameter Substitution" on page 77) cannot be used inside of macros. Parameters should be passed explicitly to macros, and parameter substitution should be used only at the top level.

You can use the `-dryrun` command-line argument to see how the macros are expanded inline. When the macros are expanded, the alias names are changed to avoid collisions with alias names in the place the macro is being expanded. If we take the previous example and use `-dryrun` to show us the resulting Pig Latin, we will see the following (reformatted slightly to fit on the page):

```
daily = load 'NYSE_daily' as (exchange:chararray, symbol:chararray,
            date:chararray, open:float, high:float, low:float, close:float,
            volume:int, adj_close:float);
macro_dividend_analysis_divs_0 = load 'NYSE_dividends' as (exchange:chararray,
            symbol:chararray, date:chararray, dividends:float);
macro_dividend_analysis_divsthisyear_0 =
            filter macro_dividend_analysis_divs_0 BY (date matches '2009-.*');
```

```
macro_dividend_analysis_dailythisyear_0 = filter daily BY (date matches '2009-.*');
macro_dividend_analysis_jnd_0 =
            join macro_dividend_analysis_divsthisyear_0 by (symbol),
            macro_dividend_analysis_dailythisyear_0 by (symbol);
results = foreach macro_dividend_analysis_jnd_0 generate
            macro_dividend_analysis_dailythisyear_0::symbol, close - open;
```

As you can see, the aliases in the macro are expanded with a combination of the macro name and the invocation number. This provides a unique key so that if other macros use the same aliases, or the same macro is used multiple times, there is still no duplication.

Including Other Pig Latin Scripts

For a long time in Pig Latin, the entire script needed to be in one file. This produced some rather unpleasant multithousand-line Pig Latin scripts. Starting in 0.9, the preprocessor can be used to include one Pig Latin script in another. Taken together with the macros (also added in 0.9; see "Macros" on page 78), it is now possible to write modular Pig Latin that is easier to debug and reuse.

import is used to include one Pig Latin script in another:

```
--main.pig
import '../examples/ch6/dividend_analysis.pig';

daily   = load 'NYSE_daily' as (exchange:chararray, symbol:chararray,
            date:chararray, open:float, high:float, low:float, close:float,
            volume:int, adj_close:float);
results = dividend_analysis(daily, '2009', 'symbol', 'open', 'close');
```

import writes the imported file directly into your Pig Latin script in place of the import statement. In the preceding example, the contents of *dividend_analysis.pig* will be placed immediately before the load statement. Note that a file cannot be imported twice. If you wish to use the same functionality multiple times, you should write it as a macro and import the file with that macro.

In the example just shown, we used a relative path for the file to be included. Fully qualified paths also can be used. By default, relative paths are taken from the current working directory of Pig when you launch the script. You can set a search path by setting the pig.import.search.path property. This is a comma-separated list of paths that will be searched for your files. The current working directory, . (dot), is always in the search path:

```
set pig.import.search.path '/usr/local/pig,/grid/pig';
import 'acme/macros.pig';
```

Imported files are not in separate namespaces. This means that all macros are in the same namespace, even when they have been imported from separate files. Thus, care should be taken to choose unique names for your macros.

## CHAPTER 7

Developing and Testing Pig Latin Scripts

The last few chapters focused on Pig Latin the language. Now we will turn to the practical matters of developing and testing your scripts. This chapter covers helpful debugging tools such as `describe` and `explain`. It also covers ways to test your scripts. Information on how to make your scripts perform better will be covered in the next chapter.

Development Tools

Pig provides several tools and diagnostic operators to help you develop your applications. In this section we will explore these and also look at some tools others have written to make it easier to develop Pig with standard editors and integrated development environments (IDEs).

Syntax Highlighting and Checking

Syntax highlighting often helps users write code correctly, at least syntactically, the first time around. Syntax highlighting packages exist for several popular editors. The packages listed in Table 7-1 were created and added at various times, so how their highlighting conforms with current Pig Latin syntax varies.

Table 7-1. Pig Latin syntax highlighting packages

Tool	URL
Eclipse	http://code.google.com/p/pig-eclipse
Emacs	http://github.com/cloudera/piglatin-mode, http://sf.net/projects/pig-mode
TextMate	http://www.github.com/kevinweil/pig.tmbundle
Vim	http://www.vim.org/scripts/script.php?script_id=2186

In addition to these syntax highlighting packages, Pig will also let you check the syntax of your script without running it. If you add -c or -check to the command line, Pig will just parse and run semantic checks on your script. The -dryrun command-line option will also check your syntax, expand any macros and imports, and perform parameter substitution.

describe

describe shows you the schema of a relation in your script. This can be very helpful as you are developing your scripts. It is especially useful as you are learning Pig Latin and understanding how various operators change the data. describe can be applied to any relation in your script, and you can have multiple describes in a script:

```
--describe.pig
divs    = load 'NYSE_dividends' as (exchange:chararray, symbol:chararray,
            date:chararray, dividends:float);
trimmed = foreach divs generate symbol, dividends;
grpd    = group trimmed by symbol;
avgdiv  = foreach grpd generate group, AVG(trimmed.dividends);

describe trimmed;
describe grpd;
describe avgdiv;

trimmed: {symbol: chararray,dividends: float}
grpd: {group: chararray,trimmed: {(symbol: chararray,dividends: float)}}
avgdiv: {group: chararray,double}
```

describe uses Pig's standard schema syntax. For information on this syntax, see "Schemas" on page 27. So, in this example, the relation trimmed has two fields: symbol, which is a chararray, and dividends, which is a float. grpd also has two fields, group (the name Pig always assigns to the group by key) and a bag trimmed, which matches the name of the relation that Pig grouped to produce the bag. Tuples in trimmed have two fields: symbol and dividends. Finally, in avgdiv there are two fields, group and a double, which is the result of the AVG function and is unnamed.

explain

One of Pig's goals is to allow you to think in terms of data flow instead of MapReduce. But sometimes you need to peek into the barn and see how Pig is compiling your script into MapReduce jobs. Pig provides explain for this. explain is particularly helpful when you are trying to optimize your scripts or debug errors. It was written so that Pig developers could examine how Pig handled various scripts, thus its output is not the most user-friendly. But with some effort, explain can help you write better Pig Latin.

There are two ways to use explain. You can explain any alias in your Pig Latin script, which will show the execution plan Pig would use if you stored that relation. You can also take an existing Pig Latin script and apply explain to the whole script in Grunt.

This has a couple of advantages. One, you do not have to edit your script to add the `explain` line. Two, it will work with scripts that do not have a single store, showing how Pig will execute the entire script:

```
--explain.pig
divs  = load 'NYSE_dividends' as (exchange, symbol, date, dividends);
grpd  = group divs by symbol;
avgdiv = foreach grpd generate group, AVG(divs.dividends);
store avgdiv into 'average_dividend';

bin/pig -x local -e 'explain -script explain.pig'
```

This will produce a printout of several graphs in text format; we will examine this output momentarily. When using `explain` on a script in Grunt, you can also have it print out the plan in graphical format. To do this, add `-dot -out` *filename* to the preceding command line. This prints out a file in DOT language containing diagrams explaining how your script will be executed. Tools that can read this language and produce graphs can then be used to view the graphs. For some tools, you might need to split the three graphs in the file into separate files.

Pig goes through several steps to transform a Pig Latin script to a set of MapReduce jobs. After doing basic parsing and semantic checking, it produces a *logical plan*. This plan describes the logical operators that Pig will use to execute the script. Some optimizations are done on this plan. For example, filters are pushed as far up[*] as possible in the logical plan. The logical plan for the preceding example is shown in Figure 7-1. I have trimmed a few extraneous pieces to make the output more readable (scary that this is more readable, huh?). If you are using Pig 0.9, the output will look slightly different, but close enough that it will be recognizable.

The flow of this chart is bottom to top so that the `Load` operator is at the very bottom. The lines between operators show the flow. Each of the four operators created by the script (`Load`, `CoGroup`, `ForEach`, and `Store`) can be seen. Each of these operators also has a schema, described in standard schema syntax. The `CoGroup` and `ForEach` operators also have expressions attached to them (the lines dropping down from those operators). In the `CoGroup` operator, the projection indicates which field is the grouping key (in this case, field 1). The `ForEach` operator has a projection expression that projects field 0 (the group field) and a UDF expression, which indicates that the UDF being used is `org.apache.pig.builtin.AVG`. Notice how each of the `Project` operators has an `Input` field, indicating from which operator they are drawing their input. Figure 7-2 shows how this plan looks when the `-dot` option is used instead.

---

[*] Or down, whichever you prefer. Database textbooks usually talk of pushing filters down, closer to the scan. Because Pig Latin scripts start with a `load` at the top and go down, we tend to refer to it as pushing filters up toward the `load`.

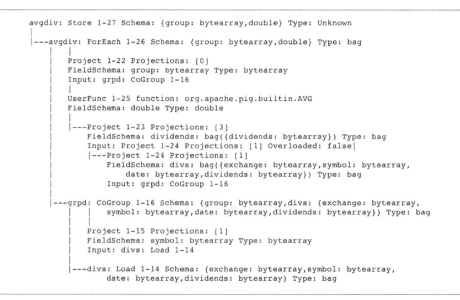

```
avgdiv: Store 1-27 Schema: {group: bytearray,double} Type: Unknown
|
|---avgdiv: ForEach 1-26 Schema: {group: bytearray,double} Type: bag
|       |
|       Project 1-22 Projections: [0]
|       FieldSchema: group: bytearray Type: bytearray
|       Input: grpd: CoGroup 1-16
|       |
|       UserFunc 1-25 function: org.apache.pig.builtin.AVG
|       FieldSchema: double Type: double
|       |
|       |---Project 1-23 Projections: [3]
|           FieldSchema: dividends: bag({dividends: bytearray}) Type: bag
|           Input: Project 1-24 Projections: [1] Overloaded: false|
|           |---Project 1-24 Projections: [1]
|               FieldSchema: divs: bag({exchange: bytearray,symbol: bytearray,
|                   date: bytearray,dividends: bytearray}) Type: bag
|               Input: grpd: CoGroup 1-16
|
|---grpd: CoGroup 1-16 Schema: {group: bytearray,divs: {exchange: bytearray,
|       |       symbol: bytearray,date: bytearray,dividends: bytearray}} Type: bag
|       |
|       Project 1-15 Projections: [1]
|       FieldSchema: symbol: bytearray Type: bytearray
|       Input: divs: Load 1-14
|       |
|       |---divs: Load 1-14 Schema: {exchange: bytearray,symbol: bytearray,
|               date: bytearray,dividends: bytearray} Type: bag
```

Figure 7-1. Logical plan

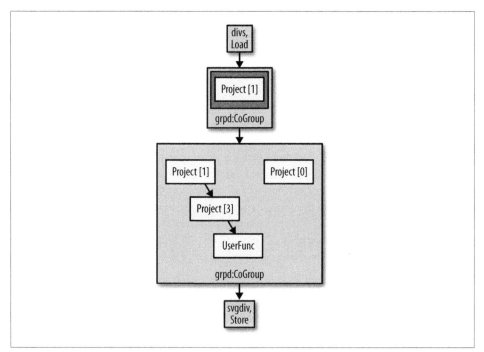

Figure 7-2. Logical plan diagram

After optimizing the logical plan, Pig produces a physical plan. This plan describes the physical operators Pig will use to execute the script, without reference to how they will be executed in MapReduce. The physical plan for our plan in Figure 7-1 is shown in Figure 7-3.

```
avgdiv: Store(file:///home/gates/git/programmingpig/data/average_dividend:
|       org.apache.pig.builtin.PigStorage)
|
|---avgdiv: New For Each(false,false)[bag]
    |    |
    |    Project[bytearray][0]
    |    |
    |    POUserFunc(org.apache.pig.builtin.AVG)[double]
    |    |
    |    |---Project[bag][3]
    |        |
    |        |---Project[bag][1]
    |
    |---grpd: Package[tuple]{bytearray}
        |
        |---grpd: Global Rearrange[tuple]
            |
            |---grpd: Local Rearrange[tuple]{bytearray}(false)
                |    |
                |    Project[bytearray][1]
                |
                |---divs: Load(file:///home/gates/git/programmingpig/data/
                    NYSE_dividends:org.apache.pig.builtin.PigStorage)
```

Figure 7-3. Physical plan

This looks like the logical plan, but with a few differences. The load and store functions that will be used have been resolved (in this case to org.apache.pig.builtin.PigStor age, the default load and store function), and the actual paths that will be used have been resolved. This example was run in local mode, so the paths are local files. If it had been run on a cluster, it would have showed a path like *hdfs://nn.machine.domain/ filepath*.

The other noticeable difference is that the CoGroup operator was replaced by three operators, Local Rearrange, Global Rearrange, and Package. Local Rearrange is the operator Pig uses to prepare data for the shuffle by setting up the key. Global Rearrange is a stand-in for the shuffle. Package sits in the reduce phase and directs records to the proper bag. Figure 7-4 shows a graphical representation of this plan.

Finally, Pig takes the physical plan and decides how it will place its operators into one or more MapReduce jobs. First, it walks the physical plan looking for all operators that require a new reduce. This occurs anywhere there is a Local Rearrange, Global Rear range, and Package. After it has done this, it sees whether there are places that it can do physical optimizations. For example, it looks for places the combiner can be used, and whether sorts can be avoided by including them as part of the sorting Hadoop does in the shuffle. After all of this is done, Pig has a MapReduce plan. This plan describes the

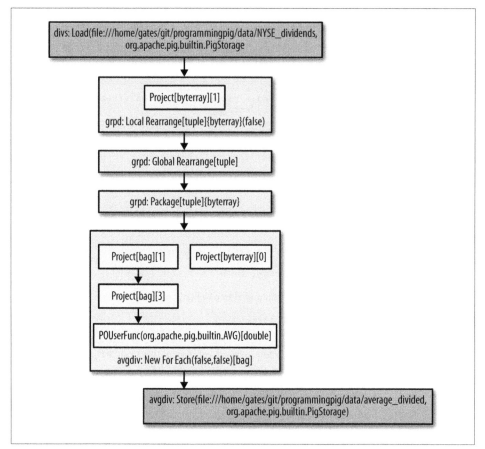

Figure 7-4. Physical plan diagram

maps, combines, and reduces, along with the physical operations Pig will perform in each stage. Completing our example, the MapReduce plan is shown in Figure 7-5.

This looks much the same as the physical plan. The pipeline is now broken into three stages: map, combine, and reduce. The `Global Rearrange` operator is gone because it was a stand-in for the shuffle. The `AVG` UDF has been broken up into three stages: `Initial` in the map, `Intermediate` in the combiner, and `Final` in the reduce. If there were multiple MapReduce jobs in this example, they would all be shown in this output. The graphical version is shown in Figure 7-6.

```
MapReduce node
Map Plan
grpd: Local Rearrange[tuple]{bytearray}(false)
|    |
|    Project[bytearray][0]
|
|---avgdiv: New For Each(false,false)[bag]
|       |    |
|       |    Project[bytearray][0]
|       |    |
|       |    POUserFunc(org.apache.pig.builtin.AVG$Initial)[tuple]
|       |    |
|       |    |---Project[bag][3]
|       |         |
|       |         |---Project[bag][1]
|       |
|       |---Pre Combiner Local Rearrange[tuple]{Unknown}
|            |
|            |---divs: Load(file:///home/gates/git/programmingpig/data/
|                          NYSE_dividends:org.apache.pig.builtin.PigStorage)


Combine Plan
grpd: Local Rearrange[tuple]{bytearray}(false)
|    |
|    Project[bytearray][0]
|
|---avgdiv: New For Each(false,false)[bag]
|       |    |
|       |    Project[bytearray][0]
|       |    |
|       |    POUserFunc(org.apache.pig.builtin.AVG$Intermediate)[tuple]
|       |    |
|       |    |---Project[bag][1]
|       |
|       |---POCombinerPackage[tuple]{bytearray}


Reduce Plan
avgdiv: Store(file:///home/gates/git/programmingpig/data/average_dividend:
|          org.apache.pig.builtin.PigStorage)
|
|---avgdiv: New For Each(false,false)[bag]
|       |    |
|       |    Project[bytearray][0]
|       |    |
|       |    POUserFunc(org.apache.pig.builtin.AVG$Final)[double]
|       |    |
|       |    |---Project[bag][1]
|       |
|       |---POCombinerPackage[tuple]{bytearray}
Global sort: false
```

Figure 7-5. MapReduce plan

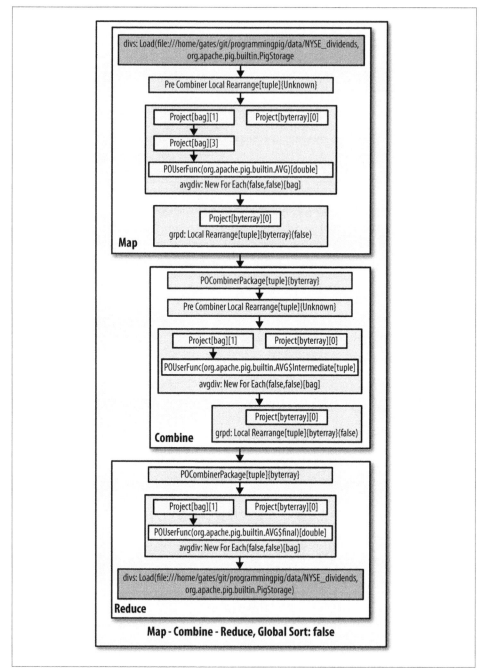

Figure 7-6. MapReduce plan diagram

illustrate

Often one of the best ways to debug your Pig Latin script is to run your data through it. But if you are using Pig, the odds are that you have a large data set. If it takes several hours to process your data, this makes for a very long debugging cycle. One obvious solution is to run your script on a sample of your data. For simple scripts this works fine. But sampling has another problem: it is not always trivial to pick a sample that will exercise your script properly. For example, if you have a join, you have to be careful to sample records from each input such that at least some have the same key. Otherwise, your join will return no results.

To address this issue, the scientists in Yahoo! Research built `illustrate` into Pig. `illustrate` takes a sample of your data and runs it through your script, but as it encounters operators that remove data (such as `filter`, `join`, etc.), it makes sure that some records pass through the operator and some do not. When necessary, it will manufacture records that look like yours (i.e., that have the same schema) but are not in the sample it took. For example, if your script had `B = filter A by x > 100;` and every record that `illustrate` sampled had a value of less than 100 for x, `illustrate` would keep at least one of these records (to show the filter removing a record), and it would manufacture a record with x greater than 100.

To use `illustrate`, apply it to an alias in your script, just as you would `describe`. Figure 7-7 shows the results of illustrating the following script:

```
--illustrate.pig
divs   = load 'NYSE_dividends' as (e:chararray, s:chararray, d:chararray, div:float);
recent = filter divs by d > '2009-01-01';
trimmd = foreach recent generate s, div;
grpd   = group trimmd by s;
avgdiv = foreach grpd generate group, AVG(trimmd.div);
illustrate avgdiv;
```

For each relation here, `illustrate` shows us records as they look coming out of the relation. For the line `recent = filter divs by d > '2009-01-01';`, I intentionally chose a filter that would remove no records in the input to show how `illustrate` manufactures a record that will be removed—in this case, the last record shown in the `divs` output.

Like `explain`, `illustrate` can be given as a command-line option rather than modifying your script; for example, `bin/pig -e 'illustrate -script illustrate.pig'`.

`illustrate` was added to Pig in version 0.2, but it was not well maintained for a time. In version 0.9, it has been revived. In versions 0.7 and 0.8, it works for some Pig operators but not for others.

```
------------------------------------------------------------------------
| divs    | e:chararray   | s:chararray   | d:chararray    | div:float  |
------------------------------------------------------------------------
|         | NYSE          | CUB           | 2009-03-06     | 0.09       |
|         | NYSE          | CUB           | 2009-08-19     | 0.09       |
|         | NYSE          | CUB           | 2009-01-0      | 0.09       |
------------------------------------------------------------------------

------------------------------------------------------------------------
| recent  | e:chararray   | s:chararray   | d:chararray    | div:float  |
------------------------------------------------------------------------
|         | NYSE          | CUB           | 2009-03-06     | 0.09       |
|         | NYSE          | CUB           | 2009-08-19     | 0.09       |
------------------------------------------------------------------------

----------------------------------------------------
| trimmd  | s:chararray    | div:float    |
----------------------------------------------------
|         | CUB            | 0.09         |
|         | CUB            | 0.09         |
----------------------------------------------------

------------------------------------------------------------------------------
| grpd    | group:chararray    | trimmd:bag{:tuple(s:chararray,div:float)}  |
------------------------------------------------------------------------------
|         | CUB                | {(CUB, 0.09), (CUB, 0.09)}                  |
------------------------------------------------------------------------------

-----------------------------------------------------------------
| avgdiv  | group:chararray    | :double              |
-----------------------------------------------------------------
|         | CUB                | 0.09000000357627869  |
-----------------------------------------------------------------
```

Figure 7-7. illustrate output

Pig Statistics

Beginning in version 0.8, Pig produces a summary set of statistics at the end of every run:

```
--stats.pig
a = load '/user/pig/tests/data/singlefile/studenttab20m' as (name, age, gpa);
b = load '/user/pig/tests/data/singlefile/votertab10k'
      as (name, age, registration, contributions);
c = filter a by age < '50';
d = filter b by age < '50';
e = cogroup c by (name, age), d by (name, age) parallel 20;
f = foreach e generate flatten(c), flatten(d);
g = group f by registration parallel 20;
h = foreach g generate group, SUM(f.d::contributions);
i = order h by $1, $0 parallel 20;
store i into 'student_voter_info';
```

Running *stats.pig* produces the statistics shown in Figure 7-8, reformatted slightly so it will fit on the page.

The first couple of lines give a brief summary of the job. StartedAt is the time Pig submits the job, not the time the first job starts running the Hadoop cluster. Depending on how busy your cluster is, these may vary significantly. Similarly, FinishedAt is the time Pig finishes processing the job, which will be slightly after the time the last MapReduce job finishes.

```
HadoopVersion PigVersion UserId  StartedAt            FinishedAt            Features
0.20.2        0.8.1      gates   2011-05-04 18:20:34  2011-05-04 18:23:22   COGROUP,
                                                                            GROUP_BY,
                                                                            ORDER_BY,
                                                                            FILTER


Success!

Job Stats (time in seconds):
JobId Maps Reduces Max  Min  Avg  Max    Min    Avg    Alias      Feature   Outputs
                   Map  Map  Map  Reduce Reduce Reduce
                   Time Time Time Time   Time   Time
3451  8    20      27   3    22   42     33     35     a,b,c,d,e  COGROUP
3452  4    20      15   12   14   12     12     12     g,h        GROUP_BY,
                                                                  COMBINER
3453  1    1       3    3    3    12     12     12     i          SAMPLER
3454  1    20      3    3    3    12     12     12     i          ORDER_BY  bla

Input(s):
Successfully read 20000000 records from: "studenttab20m"
Successfully read 10000 records from: "votertab10k"

Output(s):
Successfully stored 6 records (186 bytes) in: "hdfs://nn.acme.com/user/gates/bla"

Counters:
Total records written : 6
Total bytes written : 186
Spillable Memory Manager spill count : 0
Total bags proactively spilled: 0
Total records proactively spilled: 0

Job DAG:
3451   ->    3452,
3452   ->    3453,
3453   ->    3454,
3454
```

Figure 7-8. Statistics output of stats.pig

The section labeled `Job Stats` gives a breakdown of each MapReduce job that was run. This includes how many map and reduce tasks each job had, statistics on how long these tasks took, and a mapping of aliases in your Pig Latin script to the jobs. This last feature is especially useful when trying to understand which operators in your script are running in which MapReduce job, which can be helpful when determining why a particular job is failing or producing unexpected results.

The `Input`, `Output`, and `Counters` sections are self-explanatory. The statistics on spills record how many times Pig spilled records to local disk to avoid running out of memory. In local mode the `Counters` section will be missing because Hadoop does not report counters in local mode.

The `Job DAG` section at the end describes how data flowed between MapReduce jobs. In this case, the flow was linear.

MapReduce Job Status

When you are running your Pig Latin scripts on your Hadoop cluster, finding the status and logs of your job can be challenging. Logs generated by Pig while it plans and manages your query are stored in the current working directory. You can select a different directory by passing -l *logdir* on the command line. However, Hadoop does not provide a way to fetch back the logs from its tasks. So, the logfile created by Pig contains only log entries generated on your machine. Log entries generated during the execution, including those generated by your UDFs, stay on the task nodes in your Hadoop cluster. All data written to stdout and stderr by map and reduce tasks is also kept in the logs on the task nodes.

The first step to locating your logs is to connect to the JobTracker's web page. This page gives you the status of all jobs currently running on your Hadoop cluster, plus the list of the last hundred or so finished jobs. Generally, it is located at http:// *jt.acme.com:50030*/jobtracker.jsp, where *jt.acme.com* is the address of your Job-Tracker. Figure 7-9 shows a sample page taken from a cluster running in pseudodistributed mode on a Linux desktop.

In this screenshot there, is only one job that has been run on the cluster recently. The user who ran the job, the job ID, and the job name are all listed. Jobs started by Pig are assigned the name of the Pig Latin script that you ran, unless you use the command-line option to change the job name. All jobs started by a single script will share the same name. In most cases you will have more than one MapReduce job resulting from your Pig job. As discussed earlier in "Pig Statistics" on page 90, Pig prints a summary at the end of its execution telling you which aliases and operators were placed in which jobs. When you have multiple jobs with the same name, this will help you determine which MapReduce job you are interested in. For the job in the screenshot shown in Figure 7-9, the relevant portions of the summary look like this:

```
Job Stats (time in seconds):
JobId                   ... Alias                 Feature
job_201104081526_0019       daily,grpd,uniqcnt    GROUP_BY,COMBINER
```

Given this job ID, you now know which job to look at on the JobTracker page.

Note that jobs are shown on the JobTracker page only once they start to execute on your Hadoop cluster. It takes Pig a few seconds to parse your script and plan the Map-Reduce jobs it will run. It then takes a few seconds after Pig submits the first job before Hadoop begins running it. Also, the necessary resources might not be available, in which case your job will not appear until it has been assigned resources.

Clicking on the job ID will take you to a screen that summarizes the execution of the job, including when the job started and stopped, how many maps and reduces it ran, and the results of all of the counters, as shown in Figure 7-10.

Let's say you want to look at the logs for the single map task in this job. In the table toward the top of the page that summarizes the results of the map and reduce tasks,

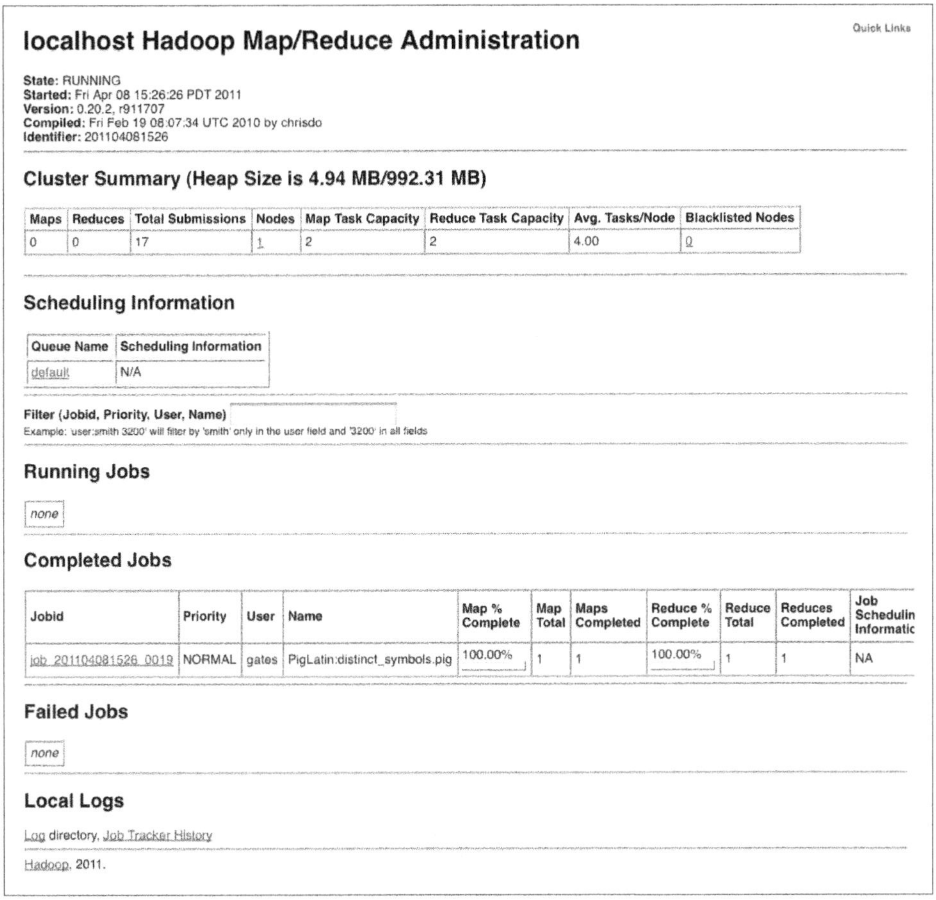

localhost Hadoop Map/Reduce Administration

State: RUNNING
Started: Fri Apr 08 15:26:26 PDT 2011
Version: 0.20.2, r911707
Compiled: Fri Feb 19 08:07:34 UTC 2010 by chrisdo
Identifier: 201104081526

Cluster Summary (Heap Size is 4.94 MB/992.31 MB)

Maps	Reduces	Total Submissions	Nodes	Map Task Capacity	Reduce Task Capacity	Avg. Tasks/Node	Blacklisted Nodes
0	0	17	1	2	2	4.00	0

Scheduling Information

Queue Name	Scheduling Information
default	N/A

Filter (Jobid, Priority, User, Name)
Example: 'user:smith 3200' will filter by 'smith' only in the user field and '3200' in all fields

Running Jobs

none

Completed Jobs

Jobid	Priority	User	Name	Map % Complete	Map Total	Maps Completed	Reduce % Complete	Reduce Total	Reduces Completed	Job Schedulin Informatic
job_201104081526_0019	NORMAL	gates	PigLatin:distinct_symbols.pig	100.00%	1	1	100.00%	1	1	NA

Failed Jobs

none

Local Logs

Log directory, Job Tracker History

Hadoop, 2011.

Figure 7-9. JobTracker web page

clicking on "map" in the far-left column produces a list of all map tasks that were run as part of this job. Selecting any particular task will show you the machine the task ran on, its status, its start and end times, and will then provide a link to its logfile. Clicking on that link will (finally) allow you to see the log for that individual task.

Of course, in this example, finding the map task we wanted was easy because there was only one. But what happens when your job has 10,000 map tasks? How do you know which one to look at? This is a good question that does not always have a concise answer. If your tasks are failing only periodically, you can examine the logs of the failing tasks. If they are all failing, you should be able to pick any of them, since they are all running the same code. If your job is running slower than it seems like it should, you can look for tasks that took much longer than others. It is also often useful to look to see if all maps or all reduces take about the same amount of time. If not, you have a skew problem.

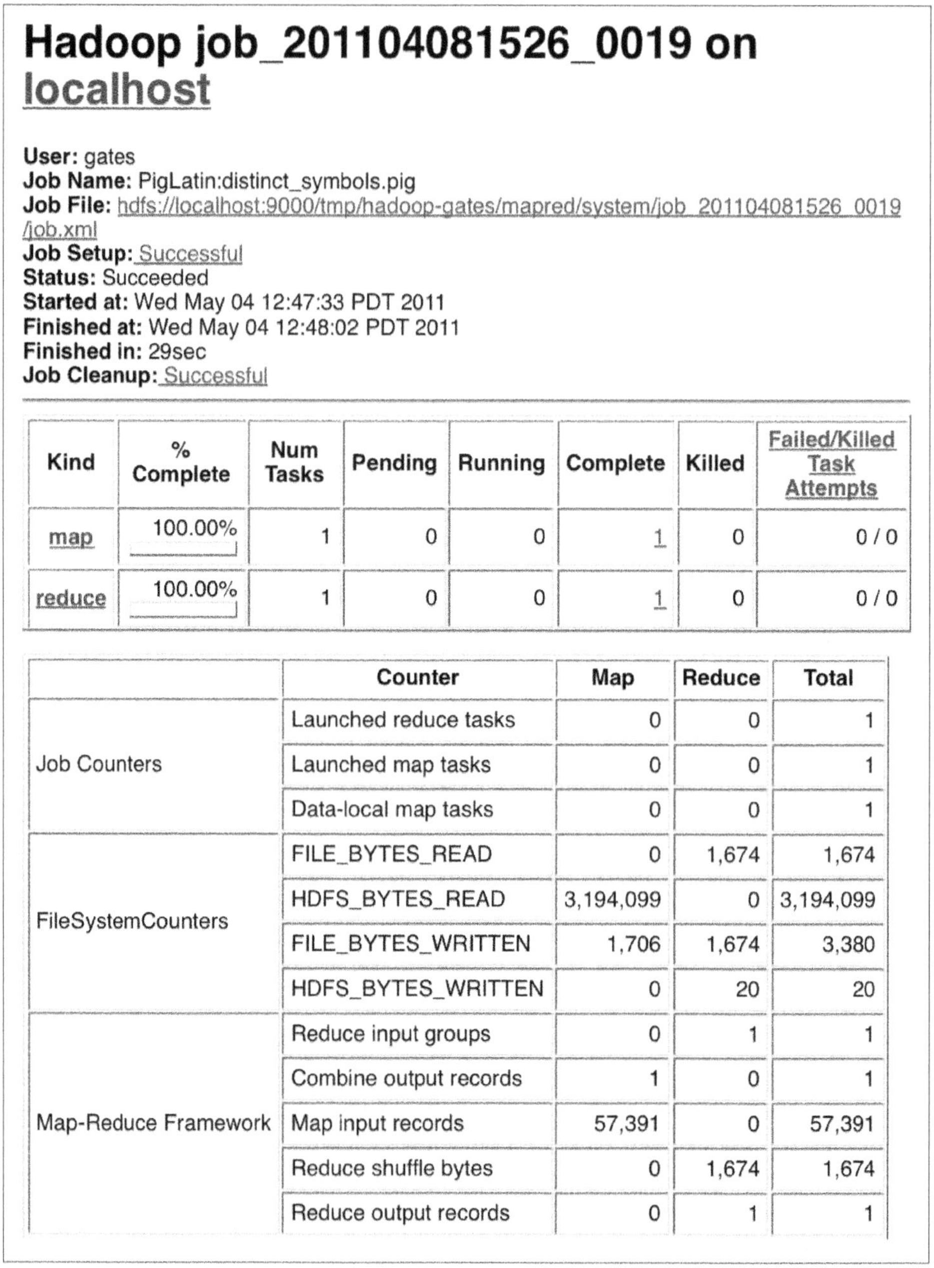

Hadoop job_201104081526_0019 on localhost

User: gates
Job Name: PigLatin:distinct_symbols.pig
Job File: hdfs://localhost:9000/tmp/hadoop-gates/mapred/system/job_201104081526_0019/job.xml
Job Setup: Successful
Status: Succeeded
Started at: Wed May 04 12:47:33 PDT 2011
Finished at: Wed May 04 12:48:02 PDT 2011
Finished in: 29sec
Job Cleanup: Successful

Kind	% Complete	Num Tasks	Pending	Running	Complete	Killed	Failed/Killed Task Attempts
map	100.00%	1	0	0	1	0	0 / 0
reduce	100.00%	1	0	0	1	0	0 / 0

	Counter	Map	Reduce	Total
Job Counters	Launched reduce tasks	0	0	1
	Launched map tasks	0	0	1
	Data-local map tasks	0	0	1
FileSystemCounters	FILE_BYTES_READ	0	1,674	1,674
	HDFS_BYTES_READ	3,194,099	0	3,194,099
	FILE_BYTES_WRITTEN	1,706	1,674	3,380
	HDFS_BYTES_WRITTEN	0	20	20
Map-Reduce Framework	Reduce input groups	0	1	1
	Combine output records	1	0	1
	Map input records	57,391	0	57,391
	Reduce shuffle bytes	0	1,674	1,674
	Reduce output records	0	1	1

Figure 7-10. Job web page

Debugging Tips

Beyond the tools covered previously, there are a few things I have found useful in debugging Pig Latin scripts. First, if `illustrate` does not do what you need, use local mode to test your script before running it on your Hadoop cluster. In most cases, this requires you to work with a sample of your data, which could be difficult, as explained earlier in "illustrate" on page 89. But local mode has several advantages. One, despite its slowness, it is a faster turnaround than using a Hadoop grid, where you may have to wait to get slots, and the minimum job setup time is 30 seconds (versus about 10 seconds in local mode). Two, the logs for your operations appear on your screen, instead of being left on a task node somewhere. Three, local mode runs all in your local process. This means that you can attach a debugger to the process. This is particularly useful when you need to debug your UDFs.

A second tip I have found useful is that sometimes you need to turn off particular features to see whether they are the source of your problem. These can include particular optimizations that Pig attempts or new features that have not had all the bugs worked out yet.[†] Table 7-2 lists features that can be turned off. All of these are options that can be passed to Pig on the command line.

Table 7-2. Turning off features

Command-line option	What it does	When you might want to turn it off
`-t SplitFilter`	Prevents Pig from splitting filter predicates so portions of them can be pushed higher in the data flow.	Your filter is not removing the rows you expect.
`-t MergeFilter`	Prevents Pig from merging adjacent filter operators to evaluate them more efficiently.	Your filter is not removing the rows you expect.
`-t PushUpFilter`	Prevents Pig from pushing filter operators in front of adjacent operators in the data flow.	Your filter is not removing the rows you expect.
`-t PushDownForEachFlatten`	Prevents Pig from pushing `foreach` operators with a `flatten` behind adjacent operators in the data flow.	Your `foreach` is not producing the rows or fields you expect.
`-t ColumnMapKeyPrune`	Prevents Pig from determining all fields your script uses and telling the loader to load only those fields.	Your load function is not returning the fields you expect.
`-t LimitOptimizer`	Prevents Pig from pushing `limit` operators in front of adjacent operators in the data flow.	Your `limit` is not returning the number of rows you expect.

---

† If you find you are turning off a feature to avoid a bug, please file a JIRA ticket (*https://issues.apache.org/jira/browse/PIG*) so that the problem can be fixed.

Command-line option	What it does	When you might want to turn it off
`-t AddForEach`	Prevents Pig from placing `foreach` operators in your script to trim out unneeded fields.	Your results do not contain the fields you expect.
`-t MergeForEach`	Prevents Pig from merging adjacent `foreach` operators to evaluate them more efficiently.	Your `foreach` is not producing the rows or fields you expect.
`-t LogicalExpressionsSimplifier`	Prevents Pig from doing some expression simplifications.	Your `foreach` is not producing the values you expect.
`-t All`	Turns off all logical optimizations. Physical optimizations (such as use of combiner, multiquery, etc.) will still be done.	Your script is not producing the rows you expect and you want to understand whether the logical optimizer is part of the problem.
`-D pig.usenewlogicalplan=false`	Prevents Pig from using the new logical plan introduced in 0.8. This works only in 0.8 and 0.8.1.	Scripts that worked in previous versions of Pig stop working in 0.8.
`-D pig.exec.nocombiner=true`	Prevents Pig from using Hadoop's combiner.	Helps you check if your UDF has a problem in its `Algebraic` implementation, as this is called only when the combiner is used.
`-D opt.multiquery=true`	Prevents Pig from combining multiple data pipelines into a single MapReduce job.	Your multiquery scripts are running out of memory, underperforming, or otherwise failing.
`-D pig.noSplitCombination=true`	Prevents Pig from combining input splits to reduce the number of map tasks.	Some input formats, such as HBase, cannot have their splits combined.

In Pig 0.8.0, the logical optimizer and logical plan were completely rewritten. The new optimizer and plan are used by default in 0.8.0, but old ones are available as a backup. After releasing 0.8.0, a number of issues were found with the new optimizer and plan. If you are using 0.8.0, I strongly encourage you to upgrade to Pig 0.8.1. As of the time of this writing, all known logical plan and optimizer issues in 0.8.0 were fixed in 0.8.1. If upgrading is not an option, the workaround is to turn off the new logical plan as described in Table 7-2. In Pig 0.9, the old logical plan has been removed.

Testing Your Scripts with PigUnit

As part of your development, you will want to test your Pig Latin scripts. Even once they are finished, regular testing helps assure that changes to your UDFs, to your scripts, or in the versions of Pig and Hadoop that you are using do not break your code. *PigUnit* provides a unit-testing framework that plugs into JUnit to help you write unit tests that can be run on a regular basis. PigUnit was added in Pig 0.8.

Let's walk through an example of how to test a script with PigUnit. First, you need a script to test:

```
--pigunit.pig
divs   = load 'NYSE_dividends' as (exchange, symbol, date, dividends);
grpd   = group divs all;
avgdiv = foreach grpd generate AVG(divs.dividends);
store avgdiv into 'average_dividend';
```

Second, you will need the *pigunit.jar* JAR file. This is not distributed as part of the standard Pig distribution, but you can build it from the source code included in your distribution. To do this, go to the directory your distribution is in and type `ant jar pigunit-jar`. Once this is finished, there should be two files in the directory: *pig.jar* and *pigunit.jar*. You will need to place these in your classpath when running PigUnit tests.

Third, you need data to run through your script. You can use an existing input file, or you can manufacture some input in your test and run that through your script. We will look at how to do both.

Finally, you need to write a Java class that JUnit can use to run your test. Let's start with a simple example that runs the preceding script:

```java
// java/example/PigUnitExample.java
public class PigUnitExample {
    private PigTest test;
    private static Cluster cluster;

    @Test
    public void testDataInFile() throws ParseException, IOException {
        // Construct an instance of PigTest that will use the script
        // pigunit.pig.
        test = new PigTest("../pigunit.pig");

        // Specify our expected output.  The format is a string for each line.
        // In this particular case we expect only one line of output.
        String[] output = { "(0.27305267014925455)" };

        // Run the test and check that the output matches our expectation.
        // The "avgdiv" tells PigUnit what alias to check the output value
        // against.  It inserts a store for that alias and then checks the
        // contents of the stored file against output.
        test.assertOutput("avgdiv", output);
    }
}
```

You can also specify the input inline in your test rather than relying on an existing datafile:

```
// java/example/PigUnitExample.java
    @Test
    public void testTextInput() throws ParseException, IOException  {
        test = new PigTest("../pigunit.pig");

        // Rather than read from a file, generate synthetic input.
        // Format is one record per line, tab-separated.
        String[] input = {
            "NYSE\tCPO\t2009-12-30\t0.14",
            "NYSE\tCPO\t2009-01-06\t0.14",
            "NYSE\tCCS\t2009-10-28\t0.414",
            "NYSE\tCCS\t2009-01-28\t0.414",
            "NYSE\tCIF\t2009-12-09\t0.029",
        };

        String[] output = { "(0.22739999999999996)" };

        // Run the example script using the input we constructed
        // rather than loading whatever the load statement says.
        // "divs" is the alias to override with the input data.
        // As with the previous example, "avgdiv" is the alias
        // to test against the value(s) in output.
        test.assertOutput("divs", input, "avgdiv", output);
    }
```

It is also possible to specify the Pig Latin script in your test and to test the output against an existing file that contains the expected results:

```
// java/example/PigUnitExample.java
    @Test
    public void testFileOutput() throws ParseException, IOException {
        // The script as an array of strings, one line per string.
        String[] script = {
            "divs   = load '../../../data/NYSE_dividends' as (exchange, symbol,
            "grpd   = group divs all;",
            "avgdiv = foreach grpd generate AVG(divs.dividends);",
            "store avgdiv into 'average_dividend';",
        };
        test = new PigTest(script);

        // Test output against an existing file that contains the
        // expected output.
        test.assertOutput(new File("../expected.out"));
    }
```

Finally, let's look at how to integrate PigUnit with parameter substitution, and how to specify expected output that will be compared against the stored result (rather than specifying an alias to check):

```
// java/example/PigUnitExample.java
    @Test
    public void testWithParams() throws ParseException, IOException {
        // Parameters to be substituted in Pig Latin script before the
```

```
        // test is run.  Format is one string for each parameter,
        // parameter=value
        String[] params = {
            "input=../../../data/NYSE_dividends",
            "output=average_dividend2"
        };
        test = new PigTest("../pigunitwithparams.pig", params);

        String[] output = { "(0.27305267014925455)" };

        // Test output in stored file against specified result
        test.assertOutput(output);
    }
```

These examples can be run by using the *build.xml* file included in the examples from this chapter. These examples are not exhaustive; see the code itself for a complete listing. For more in-depth examples, you can check out the tests for PigUnit located in *test/org/apache/pig/test/pigunit/TestPigTest.java* in your Pig distribution. This file exercises most of the features of PigUnit.

## CHAPTER 8

Making Pig Fly

Who says Pigs can't fly? Knowing how to optimize your Pig Latin scripts can make a significant difference in how they perform. Pig is still a young project and does not have a sophisticated optimizer that can make the right choices. Instead, consistent with Pig's philosophy of user choice, it relies on you to make these choices. Beyond just optimizing your scripts, Pig and MapReduce can be tuned to perform better based on your workload. And there are ways to optimize your data layout as well. This chapter covers a number of features you can use to help Pig fly.

Before diving into the details of how to optimize your Pig Latin, it is worth understanding what items tend to create bottlenecks in Pig jobs:

Input size

It does not seem that a massively parallel system should be I/O bound. Hadoop's parallelism reduces I/O bound but does not entirely remove it. You can always add more map tasks. However, the law of diminishing returns comes into effect. Additional maps take more time to start up, and MapReduce has to find more slots in which to run them. If you have twice as many maps as you have slots to run them, it will take twice your average map time to run all of your maps. Adding one more map in that case will actually make it worse because the map time will increase to three times the average. Also, every record that is read might need to be decompressed and will need to be deserialized.

Shuffle size

By shuffle size I mean the data that is moved from your map tasks to your reduce tasks. All of this data has to be serialized, sorted, moved over the network, merged, and deserialized. Also, the number of maps and reduces matters. Every reducer has to go to every mapper, find the portion of the map's output that belongs to it, and copy that. So if there are m maps and r reduces, the shuffle will have m x r network connections. And if reducers have too many map inputs to merge in one pass, they will have to do a multipass merge, reading the data from and writing it to disk multiple times (see "Combiner Phase" on page 190 for details).

Output size

> Every record written out by a MapReduce job has to be serialized, possibly compressed, and written to the store. When the store is HDFS, it must be written to three separate machines before it is considered written.

Intermediate results size

> Pig moves data between MapReduce jobs by storing it in HDFS. Thus the size of these intermediate results is affected by the input size and output size factors mentioned previously.

Memory

> Some calculations require your job to hold a lot of information in memory, for example, joins. If Pig cannot hold all of the values in memory simultaneously, it will need to spill some to disk. This causes a significant slowdown, as records must be written to and read from disk, possibly multiple times.

Writing Your Scripts to Perform Well

There are a number of things you can do when writing Pig Latin scripts to help reduce the bottlenecks discussed earlier. It may be helpful to review which operators force new MapReduce jobs in Chapters 5 and 6.

Filter Early and Often

Getting rid of data as quickly as possible will help your script perform better. Pushing `filters` higher in your script can reduce the amount of data you are shuffling or storing in HDFS between MapReduce jobs. Pig's logical optimizer will push your `filters` up whenever it can. In cases where a `filter` has multiple predicates joined by and, and one or more of the predicates can be applied before the operator preceding the `filter`, Pig will split the `filter` at the and and push the eligible predicate(s). This allows Pig to push parts of the `filter` when it might not be able to push the `filter` as a whole. Table 8-1 describes when these `filter` predicates will and will not be pushed once they have been split.

Table 8-1. When Pig pushes filters

Preceding operator	Filter will be pushed before?	Comments
cogroup	Sometimes	The `filter` will be pushed if it applies to only one input of the `cogroup` and does not contain a UDF.
cross	Sometimes	The `filter` will be pushed if it applies to only one input of the `cross`.
distinct	Yes	
filter	No	Will seek to merge them with and to avoid passing data through a second operator. This is done only after all `filter` pushing is complete.

Preceding operator	Filter will be pushed before?	Comments
foreach	Sometimes	The filter will be pushed if it references only fields that exist before and after the foreach, and foreach does not transform those fields.
group	Sometimes	The filter will be pushed if it does not contain a UDF.
join	Sometimes	The filter will be pushed if it applies to only one input of the join, and if the join is not outer for that input.
load	No	
mapreduce	No	mapreduce is opaque to Pig, so it cannot know whether pushing will be safe.
sort	Yes	
split	No	
store	No	
stream	No	stream is opaque to Pig, so it cannot know whether pushing will be safe.
union	Yes	

Also, consider adding filters that are implicit in your script. For example, all of the records with null values in the key will be thrown out by an inner join. If you know that more than a few hundred of your records have null key values, put a filter input by key is not null before the join. This will enhance the performance of your join.

Project Early and Often

For earlier versions of Pig, we told users to employ foreach to remove fields they were not using as soon as possible. As of version 0.8, Pig's logical optimizer does a fair job of removing fields aggressively when it can tell that they will no longer be used:

```
-- itemid does not need to be loaded, since it is not used in the script
txns        = load 'purchases' as (date, storeid, amount, itemid);
todays      = filter txns by date == '20110513'; -- date not needed after this
bystore     = group todays by storeid;
avgperstore = foreach bystore generate group, AVG(todays.amount);
```

However, you are still smarter than Pig's optimizer, so there are situations where you can tell that a field is no longer needed but Pig cannot. If AVG(todays.amount) were changed to COUNT(todays) in the preceding example, Pig would not be able to determine that, after the filter, only storeid and amount were required. It cannot see that COUNT does not need all of the fields in the bag it is being passed. Whenever you pass a UDF the entire record (udf(*)) or an entire complex field, Pig cannot determine which fields are required. In this case, you will need to put in the foreach yourself to remove unneeded data as early as possible.

Set Up Your Joins Properly

Joins are one of the most common data operations, and also one of the costliest. Choosing the correct join implementation can improve your performance significantly. The flowchart in Figure 8-1 will help you make the correct selection.

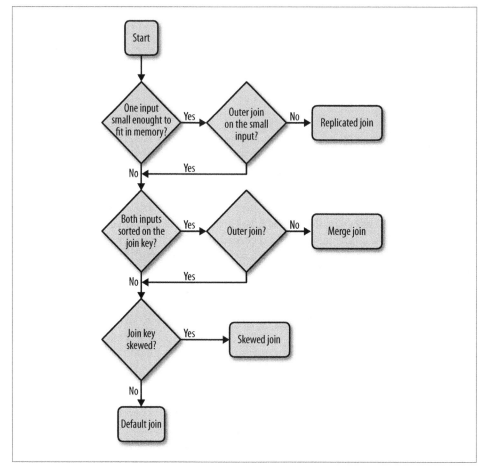

Figure 8-1. Choosing a join implementation

Once you have selected your join implementation, make sure to arrange your inputs in the correct order as well. For replicated joins, the small table must be given as the last input. For skewed joins, the second input is the one that is sampled for large keys. For the default join, the rightmost input has its records streamed through, whereas the other input(s) have their records for a given key value materialized in memory. Thus if you have one join input that you know has more records per key value, you should place it in the rightmost position in the join. For merge join, the left input is taken as the input for the MapReduce job, and thus the number of maps started are based on this input. If one input is much larger than the other, you should place it on the left in order to get more map tasks dedicated to your jobs. This will also reduce the size of the sampling step that builds the index for the right side. For complete details on each of these join implementations, see the sections "Join" on page 45 and "Using Different Join Implementations" on page 61.

Use Multiquery When Possible

Whenever you are doing operations that can be combined by multiquery, such as grouping and filtering, these should be written together in one Pig Latin script so that Pig can combine them. Although adding extra operations does increase the total processing time, it is still much faster than running jobs separately.

Choose the Right Data Type

As discussed elsewhere, Pig can run with or without data type information. In cases where the load function you are using creates data that is already typed, there is little you need to do to optimize the performance. However, if you are using the default PigStorage load function that reads tab-delimited files, then whether you use types will affect your performance.

On the one hand, converting fields from bytearray to the appropriate type has a cost. So, if you do not need type information, you should not declare it. For example, if you are just counting records, you can omit the type declaration without affecting the outcome of your script.

On the other hand, if you are doing integer calculations, types can help your script perform better. When Pig is asked to do a numeric calculation on a bytearray, it treats that bytearray as a double because this is the safest assumption. But floating-point arithmetic is much slower than integer arithmetic on most machines. For example, if you are doing a SUM over integer values, you will get better performance by declaring them to be of type integer.

Select the Right Level of Parallelism

Setting your parallelism properly can be difficult, as there are a number of factors. Before we discuss the factors, a little background will be helpful. It would be natural to think more parallelism is always better; however, that is not the case. Like any other resource, parallelism has a network cost, as discussed under the shuffle size performance bottleneck.

Second, increasing parallelism adds latency to your script because there is a limited number of reduce slots in your cluster, or a limited number that your scheduler will assign to you. If 100 reduce slots are available to you and you specify parallel 200, you still will be able to run only 100 reduces at a time. Your reducers will run in two separate waves. Because there is overhead in starting and stopping reduce tasks, and the shuffle gets less efficient as parallelism increases, it is often not efficient to select more reducers than you have slots to run them. In fact, it is best to specify slightly fewer reducers than the number of slots that you can access. This leaves room for MapReduce to restart a few failed reducers and use speculative execution without doubling your reduce time. See "Handling Failure" on page 192 for information on speculative execution.

Also, it is important to keep in mind the effects of skew on parallelism. MapReduce generally does a good job partitioning *keys* equally to the reducers, but the number of records per key often varies radically. Thus a few reducers that get keys with a large number of records will significantly lag the other reducers. Pig cannot start the next MapReduce job until all of the reducers have finished in the previous job. So the slowest reducer defines the length of the job. If you have 10G of input to your reducers and you set `parallel` to 10, but one key accounts for 50% of the data (not an uncommon case), nine of your reducers will finish quite quickly while the last lags. Increasing your parallelism will not help; it will just waste more cluster resources. Instead, you need to use Pig's mechanisms to handle skew.

Writing Your UDF to Perform

Pig has a couple of features intended to enable aggregate functions to run significantly faster. The `Algebraic` interface allows UDFs to use Hadoop's combiner (see "Combiner Phase" on page 190). The `Accumulator` interface allows Pig to break a collection of records into several sets and give each set to the UDF separately. This avoids the need to materialize all of the records simultaneously, and thus spill to disk when there are too many records. For details on how to use these interfaces, see "Algebraic Interface" on page 135 and "Accumulator Interface" on page 139. Whenever possible, you should write your aggregate UDFs to make use of these features.

Pig also has optimizations to help loaders minimize the amount of data they load. Pig can tell a loader which fields it needs and which keys in a map it needs. It can also push down certain types of filters. For information on this, see "Pushing down projections" on page 156 and "Loading metadata" on page 153.

Tune Pig and Hadoop for Your Job

On your way out of a commercial jet airliner, have you ever peeked around the flight attendant to gaze at all the dials, switches, and levers in the cockpit? This is sort of what tuning Hadoop is like: many, many options, some of which make an important difference. But without the proper skills, it can be hard to know which is the right knob to turn. Table 8-2 looks at a few of the important features.

This table is taken from Tables 6-1 and 6-2 in *Hadoop: The Definitive Guide*, Second Edition, by Tom White (O'Reilly), used with permission. See those tables for a more complete list of parameters.

Table 8-2. MapReduce performance-tuning properties

Property name	Type	Default value	Description
io.sort.mb	int	100	The size, in megabytes, of the memory buffer to use while sorting map output. Increasing this will decrease the number of spills from the map and make the combiner more efficient, but will leave less memory for your map tasks.
io.sort.factor	int	10	The maximum number of streams to merge at once when sorting files. It is fairly common to increase this to 100.
min.num.spills.for.combine	int	3	The minimum number of spill files (from the map) needed for the combiner to run.
mapred.job.shuffle.input.buffer.percent	float	0.7	The proportion of total heap size to be allocated to the map outputs buffer (reducer buffer for storing map outputs) during the copy phase of the shuffle.
mapred.job.shuffle.merge.percent	float	0.66	The threshold usage proportion for the map outputs buffer (defined by mapred.job.shuffle.input.buffer.percent) for starting the process of merging the outputs and spilling to disk.

Compared to Hadoop, tuning Pig is much simpler. There are a couple of memory-related parameters that will help ensure Pig uses its memory in the best way possible. These parameters are covered in Table 8-3.

Table 8-3. Pig performance-tuning properties

Property name	Type	Default value	Description
pig.cached bag.memusage	float	0.1	Percentage of the heap that Pig will allocate for all of the bags in a map or reduce task. Once the bags fill up this amount, the data is spilled to disk. Setting this to a higher value will reduce spills to disk during execution but increase the likelihood of a task running out of heap.
pig.skewed join.reduce.mem usage	float	0.3	Percentage of the heap Pig will use during a skew join when trying to materialize one side in memory. Setting this to a higher value will reduce the number of ways that large keys are split and thus how many times their records must be replicated, but it will increase the likelihood of a reducer running out of memory.

All of these values for Pig and MapReduce can be set using the set option in your Pig Latin script (see "set" on page 75) or by passing them with -D on the command line.

Using Compression in Intermediate Results

As is probably clear by now, some of the biggest costs in Pig are moving data between map and reduce phases and between MapReduce jobs. Compression can be used to reduce the amount of data to be stored to disk and written over the network. By default, compression is turned off, both between map and reduce tasks and between MapReduce jobs.

To enable compression between map and reduce tasks, two Hadoop parameters are used: `mapred.compress.map.output` and `mapred.map.output.compression.codec`. To turn on compression, set `mapred.compress.map.output` to `true`. You will also need to select a compression type to use. The most commonly used types are gzip and LZO. gzip is more CPU-intensive but compresses better. To use gzip, set `mapred.map.output.com pression.codec` to `org.apache.hadoop.io.compress.GzipCodec`. In most cases, LZO provides a better performance boost. See the sidebar "Setting Up LZO on Your Cluster" on page 108 for details. To use LZO as your codec, set `mapred.map.output.com pression.codec` to `com.hadoop.compression.lzo.LzopCodec`.

Compressing data between MapReduce jobs can also have a significant impact on Pig performance. This is particularly true of Pig scripts that include joins or other operators that expand your data size. To turn on compression, set `pig.tmpfilecompression` to `true`. Again, you can choose between gzip and LZO by setting `pig.tmpfilecompres sion.codec` to `gzip` or `lzo`, respectively. In the testing we did while developing this feature, we saw performance improvements of up to four times when using LZO, and slight performance degradation when using gzip.

Setting Up LZO on Your Cluster

LZO is licensed under the GNU Public License (GPL) and thus cannot be distributed as part of Apache Hadoop or Apache Pig. To use it, you first need to build and install the LZO plug-in for Hadoop and configure your cluster to use it.

To download LZO, go to *http://code.google.com/a/apache-extras.org/p/hadoop-gpl-com pression* and click on the Downloads tab. Download the *hadoop-gpl-compression* tarball onto your machine and untar it. Then you will need to build the native LZO library on your system. Be sure to do this build on a system that matches your grid machines, as this is C code and not portable. Once you have built the native library, you need to install it on your cluster. Details for both of these tasks are given at *http://code.google .com/a/apache-extras.org/p/hadoop-gpl-compression/wiki/FAQ*. A number of fixes for bugs found in this tarball have been committed to GitHub (*https://github.com/kevin weil/hadoop-lzo*). You might want to clone and build this version if you have issues with the official tarball.

Data Layout Optimization

How you lay out your data can have a significant impact on how your Pig jobs perform. On the one hand, you want to organize your files such that Pig can scan the minimal set of records. For example, if you have regularly collected data that you usually read on an hourly basis, it likely makes sense to place each hour's data in a separate file. On the other hand, the more files you create, the more pressure you put on your Name-Node. And MapReduce operates more efficiently on larger files than it does on files that are less than one HDFS block (64 MB by default). You will need to find a balance between these two competing forces.

Beginning in 0.8, when your inputs are files and they are smaller than half an HDFS block, Pig will automatically combine the smaller sections when using the file as input. This allows MapReduce to be more efficient and start fewer map tasks. This is almost always better for your cluster utilization. It is not always better for the performance of your individual query, however, because you will be losing locality of data reads for many of the combined blocks, and your map tasks may run longer. If you need to turn this feature off, pass `-Dpig.noSplitCombination=true` on your command line or set the property in your *pig.properties* file.

Bad Record Handling

When processing gigabytes or terabytes of data, the odds are overwhelming that at least one row is corrupt or will cause an unexpected result. An example is division by zero, even though no records were supposed to have a zero in the denominator. Causing an entire job to fail over one bad record is not good. To avoid these failures, Pig inserts a null, issues a warning, and continues processing. This way, the job still finishes. Warnings are aggregated and reported as a count at the end. You should check the warnings to be sure that the failure of a few records is acceptable in your job. If you need to know more details about the warnings, you can turn off the aggregation by passing `-w` on the command line.

## CHAPTER 9

Embedding Pig Latin in Python

Pig Latin is a dataflow language. Unlike general-purpose programming languages, it does not include control flow constructs such as if and for. For many data-processing applications, the operators Pig provides are sufficient. But there are classes of problems that either require the data flow to be repeated an indefinite number of times or need to branch based on the results of an operator. Iterative processing, where a calculation needs to be repeated until the margin of error is within an acceptable limit, is one example. It is not possible to know beforehand how many times the data flow will need to be run before processing begins.

Blending data flow and control flow in one language is difficult to do in a way that is useful and intuitive. Building a general-purpose language and all the associated tools, such as IDEs and debuggers, is a considerable undertaking; also, there is no lack of such languages already. If we turned Pig Latin into a general-purpose language, it would require users to learn a much bigger language to process their data. For these reasons, we decided to embed Pig in existing scripting languages. This avoids the need to invent a new language while still providing users with the features they need to process their data.[*]

As with UDFs, we chose to use Python for the initial release of embedded Pig in version 0.9. The embedding interface is a Java class, so a Jython interpreter is used to run these Python scripts that embed Pig. This means Python 2.5 features can be used but Python 3 features cannot. In the future we hope to extend the system to other scripting languages that can access Java objects, such as JavaScript[†] and JRuby. Of course, since the Pig infrastructure is all in Java, it is possible to use this same interface to embed Pig into Java scripts.

---

[*] In some of the documentation, wiki pages, and issues on JIRA, embedded Pig is referred to as Turing Complete Pig. This was what the project was called when it first started, even though we did not make Pig itself Turing complete.

[†] There is already an experimental version of JavaScript in 0.9.

This embedding is done in a JDBC-like style, where your Python script first compiles a Pig Latin script, then binds variables from Python to it, and finally runs it. It is also possible to do filesystem operations, register JARs, and perform other utility operations through the interface. The top-level class for this interface is `org.apache.pig.script ing.Pig`.

Throughout this chapter we will use an example of calculating page rank from a web crawl. You can find this example under *examples/ch9* in the example code. This code iterates over a set of URLs and links to produce a page rank for each URL.[‡] The input to this example is the *webcrawl* data set found in the examples. Each record in this input contains a URL, a starting rank of 1, and a bag with a tuple for each link found at that URL:

```
http://pig.apache.org/privacypolicy.html 1 {(http://www.google.com/privacy.html)}
http://www.google.com/privacypolicy.html 1 {(http://www.google.com/faq.html)}
http://desktop.google.com/copyrights.html 1 {}
```

Even though control flow is done via a Python script, it can still be run using Pig's *bin/ pig* script. *bin/pig* looks for the #! line and calls the appropriate interpreter. This allows you to use these scripts with systems that expect to invoke a Pig Latin script. It also allows Pig to include UDFs from this file automatically and to give correct line numbers for error messages.

In order to use the `Pig` class and related objects, the code must first import them into the Python script:

```
from org.apache.pig.scripting import *
```

Compile

Calling the static method `Pig.compile` causes Pig to do an initial compilation of the code. Because we have not bound the variables yet, this check cannot completely verify the script. Type checking and other semantic checking is not done at this phase—only the syntax is checked. `compile` returns a `Pig` object that can be bound to a set of variables:

```
# pagerank.py
P = Pig.compile("""
previous_pagerank = load '$docs_in' as (url:chararray, pagerank:float,
                        links:{link:(url:chararray)});
outbound_pagerank = foreach previous_pagerank generate
                        pagerank / COUNT(links) as pagerank,
                        flatten(links) as to_url;
cogrpd            = cogroup outbound_pagerank by to_url,
                        previous_pagerank by url;
new_pagerank      = foreach cogrpd generate group as url,
                        (1 - $d) + $d * SUM (outbound_pagerank.pagerank)
                        as pagerank,
                        flatten(previous_pagerank.links) as links,
```

‡ The example code was graciously provided by Julien Le Dem.

```
                    flatten(previous_pagerank.pagerank) AS previous_pagerank;
store new_pagerank into '$docs_out';
nonulls           = filter new_pagerank by previous_pagerank is not null and
                    pagerank is not null;
pagerank_diff     = foreach nonulls generate ABS (previous_pagerank - pagerank);
grpall            = group pagerank_diff all;
max_diff          = foreach grpall generate MAX (pagerank_diff);
store max_diff into '$max_diff';
""")
```

The only pieces of this Pig Latin script that we have not seen before are the four parameters, marked in the script as $d, $docs_in, $docs_out, and $max_diff. The syntax for these parameters is the same as for parameter substitution. However, Pig expects these to be supplied by the control flow script when bind is called.

There are three other compilation methods in addition to the one shown in this example. compile(*String name, String script*) takes a name in addition to the Pig Latin to be compiled. This name can be used in other Pig Latin code blocks to import this block:

```
P1 = Pig.compile("initial", """
A = load 'input';
...
""")
    P2 = Pig.compile("""
import initial;
B = load 'more_input';
...
""")
```

There are two compilation methods called compileFromFile. These take the same arguments as compile, but they expect the script argument to refer to a file containing the script, rather than the script itself.

Bind

Once your script has been compiled successfully, the next step is to bind variables in the control flow to variables in Pig Latin. In our example script this is done by providing a map to the bind call. The keys are the name of the variables in Pig Latin. The values in the following example are literal string values that are updated as the script progresses. They also could be references to Python variables:

```
# pagerank.py
params = { 'd': '0.5', 'docs_in': 'data/webcrawl' }

for i in range(10):
    out = "out/pagerank_data_" + str(i + 1)
    max_diff = "out/max_diff_" + str(i + 1)
    params["docs_out"] = out
    params["max_diff"] = max_diff
    Pig.fs("rmr " + out)
    Pig.fs("rmr " + max_diff)
    bound = P.bind(params)
```

```
stats = bound.runSingle()
if not stats.isSuccessful():
    raise 'failed'
mdv = float(str(stats.result("max_diff").iterator().next().get(0)))
print "max_diff_value = " + str(mdv)
if mdv < 0.01:
    print "done at iteration " + str(i)
    break
params["docs_in"] = out
```

For the initial run, the Pig Latin $d will take on the value of 0.5, $docs_in the filename *webcrawl*, $docs_out *out/pagerank_data_1*, and $max_diff *out/max_diff_1*.

bind returns a BoundScript object. This object can be run, explained, described, or illustrated. As is shown in this script, a single Pig object can be bound multiple times. A compile is necessary only on the first pass, with different values being bound to it each time.

In our example, bind is given a mapping of the variables to bind. If all of your Python variables and Pig Latin variables have the same name, you can call bind with no arguments. This will cause bind to look in the Python context for variables of the same name as the parameters in Pig and use them. If it cannot find appropriate variables, it will throw an error. We could change our example script to look like this:

```
# pagerankbindnoarg.py
d = 0.5
docs_in = 'data/webcrawl'

for i in range(10):
    docs_out = "out/pagerank_data_" + str(i + 1)
    max_diff = "out/max_diff_" + str(i + 1)
    Pig.fs("rmr " + docs_out)
    Pig.fs("rmr " + max_diff)
    bound = P.bind()
    stats = bound.runSingle()
    if not stats.isSuccessful():
        raise 'failed'
    mdv = float(str(stats.result("max_diff").iterator().next().get(0)))
    print "max_diff_value = " + str(mdv)
    if mdv < 0.01:
        print "done at iteration " + str(i)
        break
    docs_in = docs_out
```

Binding Multiple Sets of Variables

Our example page rank script binds its compiled Pig Latin to different variables multiple times in order to iterate over the data. Each of these jobs is run separately, as is required by the iterative nature of calculating page rank. However, sometimes you want to run a set of jobs together; for example, consider calculating census data from countries all over the world. You want to run the same Pig Latin for each country, but you do not want to run them separately. There is no point in having a massively parallel system such as Hadoop if you are going to run jobs one at a time. You want to tell Pig to take your script and run it against input from all the countries at the same time.

There is a form of bind that provides this capability. Instead of taking a map of parameters, it takes a list of maps of parameters. It still returns a single BoundScript object, but when run is called on this object, all of the separate instantiations of the script will be run together:

```python
#!/usr/bin/python
from org.apache.pig.scripting import *
pig = Pig.compile("""
    input = load '$country' using CensusLoader();
    ...
    store output into '$country_out';
""")

params = [{'country': 'Afghanistan', 'country_out': 'af.out'},
    ...
          {'country': 'Zimbabwe', 'country_out': 'zw.out'}]

bound = pig.bind(params)
stats = bound.run()
```

Run

Once we have our BoundScript object, we can call runSingle to run it. This tells Pig to run a single Pig Latin script. This is appropriate when you have bound your script to just one set of variables. runSingle returns a PigStats object. This object allows you to get your results and examine what happened in your script, including status, error codes and messages if there was an error, and statistics about the run itself. Table 9-1 summarizes the more important methods available for PigStats.

Table 9-1. PigStats methods

Method	Returns
result(*String alias*)	Given an alias, returns an OutputStats object that describes the output stored from that alias. You can get a results iterator from OutputStats.
isSuccessful()	Returns true if all went well, and false otherwise.
getReturnCode()	Gets the return code from running Pig. See Table 2-1 for return code details.
getErrorMessage()	Returns the error message if the run failed. This will try to pick the most relevant error message that was returned, most likely the last.
getAllErrorMessages()	Returns a list of all of the error messages if the run failed.
getOutputLocations()	Returns a list of location strings that were stored in the script. For example, if you wrote output to a file on HDFS, this will return the filename.
getOutputNames()	Returns a list of aliases that were stored in the script.
getRecordWritten()	Returns the total number of records written by the script.
getBytesWritten()	Returns the total number of bytes written by the script.

Method	Returns
getNumberRecords(String location)	Given an output location, returns the number of records written to that location.
getNumberBytes(String location)	Given an output location, returns the number of bytes written to that location.
getDuration()	Wall clock time it took the script to run.
getNumberJobs()	Number of MapReduce jobs run by this script.

As seen in the example, the OutputStats object returned by result() can be used to get an iterator on the result set. With this you can iterate through the tuples of your data, processing them in your Python script. Standard Tuple methods such as get() can be used to inspect the contents of each record. See "Interacting with Pig values" on page 122 for a discussion of working with Tuples. Based on the results read in the iterator, your Python script can decide whether to cease iteration and declare success, raise an error, or continue with another iteration.

For this iterator to work, the store function you use to store results from the alias *must* also be a load function. Pig attempts to use the same class to load the results as was used to store it. The default PigStorage works well for this.

Running Multiple Bindings

If you bound your Pig object to a list of maps of parameters, rather than call runSin gle, you should call run. This will cause Pig to start a thread for each binding and run it. All these jobs will be submitted to Hadoop at the same time, making use of Hadoop's parallelism. run returns a list of PigStats objects. The PigStats objects are guaranteed to be in the same order in the list as in the maps of bound variables passed to bind. Thus the results of the first binding map are in the first position of the PigStats list, etc.

Utility Methods

In addition to the compile, bind, and run methods presented so far, there are also utility methods provided by Pig and BoundScript.

Filesystem operations can be done by calling the static method Pig.fs. The string passed to it should be a valid string for use in the Grunt shell (see Chapter 3). The return code from running the shell command will be returned.

You can use register, define, and set in your compiled Pig Latin statements as you do in nonembedded Pig Latin. However, you might wish to register a JAR, define a function alias, or set a value that you want to be effective through all your Pig Latin code blocks. In these cases you can use the static methods of Pig described in Table 9-2. The registers, defines, and sets done by these methods will affect all Pig Latin code compiled after they are called:

```
# register etc. will not affect this block.
p1 = Pig.compile("...")

Pig.registerJar("acme.jar")
Pig.registerUDF("acme_python.py", "acme")
Pig.define("d_to_e", "com.acme.financial.CurrencyConverter('dollar', 'euro'"))
Pig.set("default_parallel", "100")

# register etc. will affect p2 and p3
p2 = Pig.compile("...")
p3 = Pig.compile("...")
```

Table 9-2. Pig utility methods

Method	Arguments	Pig Latin equivalent
registerJar(String jar file)	jarfile is the JAR to register.	register jarfile;
registerUDF(String udf file, String namespace)	udffile is the UDF file to register. namespace is the namespace to place the UDF in.	register udffile using jython as name space;
define(String alias, String definition)	alias is the name of the definition. definition is the string being aliased.	define alias defini tion;
set(String variable, String value)	variable is the variable to set. value is the value to set the variable to.	set variable value;

Once a script has been bound and a BoundScript returned, in addition to running the script you can also call describe, explain, or illustrate. These do exactly what they would if they were in a nonembedded Pig Latin script. However, they do not return the resulting output to your script; instead, it is dumped to the standard out. (These operators are intended for use in debugging rather than for returning data directly to your script.)

## CHAPTER 10

Writing Evaluation and Filter Functions

It is time to turn our attention to how you can extend Pig. So far we have looked at the operators and functions Pig provides. But Pig also makes it easy for you to add your own processing logic via User Defined Functions (UDFs). These are written in Java and, starting with version 0.8, in Python.* This chapter will walk through how you can build *evaluation functions*, UDFs that operate on single elements of data or collections of data. It will also cover how to write *filter functions*, UDFs that can be used as part of `filter` statements.

UDFs are powerful tools, and thus the interfaces are somewhat complex. In designing Pig, our goal was to make easy things easy and hard things possible. So, the simplest UDFs can be implemented in a single method, but you will have to implement a few more methods to take advantage of more advanced features. We will cover both cases in this chapter.

Throughout this chapter we will use several running examples of UDFs. Some of these are built-in Pig UDFs, which can be found in your Pig distribution at *src/org/apache/pig/builtin/*. The others can be found on GitHub with the other example UDFs, in the directory *udfs*.

Writing an Evaluation Function in Java

Pig and Hadoop are implemented in Java, and so it is natural to implement UDFs in Java. This allows UDFs access to the Hadoop APIs and to many of Pig's facilities.

Before diving into the details, it is worth considering names. Pig locates a UDF by looking for a Java class that exactly matches the UDF name in the script. For details on where it looks, see "Registering UDFs" on page 51 and "define and UDFs" on page 53. There is not an accepted standard on whether UDF names should be all uppercase, camelCased (e.g., MyUdf), or all lowercase. Even the built-in UDFs

---

* In 0.9, eval funcs can also be written in JavaScript, though this is experimental and has not yet been fully tested.

provided by Pig vary in this regard. Keep in mind that, whatever you choose, you and all of the users of your UDF will have a better user experience if you make the name short, easy to remember, and easy to type.

Where Your UDF Will Run

Writing code that will run in a parallel system presents challenges. A separate instance of your UDF will be constructed and run in each map or reduce task. It is not possible to share state across these instances because they may not all be running at the same time. There will be only one instance of your UDF per map or reduce task, so you can share state within that context.[†]

When writing code for a parallel system, you must remember the power of parallelism. Operations that are acceptable in serial programs may no longer be advisable. Consider a UDF that, when it first starts, connects to a database server to download a translation table. In a serial or low-parallelism environment, this is a reasonable approach. But if you have 10,000 map tasks in your job and they all connect to your database at once, you will most likely hear from your DBA, and the conversation is unlikely to be pleasant.

In addition to an instance in each task, Pig will construct an instance of your UDF on the frontend during the planning stage. It does this for a couple of reasons. One, it wants to test early that it can construct your UDF; it would rather fail during planning than at runtime. Two, as we will cover later in this chapter, it will ask your UDF some questions about schemas and types it accepts as part of the execution planning. It will also give your UDF a chance to store information it wants to make available to the instances of itself that will be run in the backend.

Evaluation Function Basics

All evaluation functions extend the Java class `org.apache.pig.EvalFunc`. This class uses Java generics. It is parameterized by the return type of your UDF. The core method in this class is `exec`. It takes one record and returns one result, which will be invoked for every record that passes through your execution pipeline. As input it takes a tuple, which contains all of the fields the script passes to your UDF. It returns the type by which you parameterized `EvalFunc`. For simple UDFs, this is the only method you need to implement. The following code gives an example of a UDF that raises an integer to an integral power and returns a long result:

```
// java/com/acme/math/Pow.java
/**
 * A simple UDF that takes a value and raises it to the power of a second
 * value.  It can be used in a Pig Latin script as Pow(x, y), where x and y
 * are both expected to be ints.
 */
```

---

† Assuming there is one instance of your UDF in the script. Each reference to a UDF in a script becomes a separate instance on the backend, even if they are placed in the same map or reduce task.

```
public class Pow extends EvalFunc<Long> {

    public Long exec(Tuple input) throws IOException {
        try {
            /* Rather than give you explicit arguments, UDFs are always handed
             * a tuple.  The UDF must know the arguments it expects and pull
             * them out of the tuple.  These next two lines get the first and
             * second fields out of the input tuple that was handed in.  Since
             * Tuple.get returns Objects, we must cast them to Integers.  If
             * the case fails, an exception will be thrown.
             */
            int base = (Integer)input.get(0);
            int exponent = (Integer)input.get(1);
            long result = 1;

            /* Probably not the most efficient method...*/
            for (int i = 0; i < exponent; i++) {
                long preresult = result;
                result *= base;
                if (preresult > result) {
                    // We overflowed.  Give a warning, but do not throw an
                    // exception.
                    warn("Overflow!", PigWarning.TOO_LARGE_FOR_INT);
                    // Returning null will indicate to Pig that we failed but
                    // we want to continue execution.
                    return null;
                }
            }
            return result;
        } catch (Exception e) {
            // Throwing an exception will cause the task to fail.
            throw new IOException("Something bad happened!", e);
        }
    }
}
```

EvalFunc is also used to implement aggregation functions. Because the group operator
returns a record for each group, with a bag containing all the records in that group,
your eval func still takes one record and returns one record. As an example of this, let's
take a look at the implementation of exec in Pig's COUNT function. Some of the error-
handling code has been removed for ease of reading:

```
// src/org/apache/pig/builtin/COUNT.java
public Long exec(Tuple input) throws IOException {
    try {
        // The data bag is passed to the UDF as the first element of the
        // tuple.
        DataBag bag = (DataBag)input.get(0);
        Iterator it = bag.iterator();
        long cnt = 0;
        while (it.hasNext()){
            Tuple t = (Tuple)it.next();
            // Don't count nulls or empty tuples
            if (t != null && t.size() > 0 &&
                t.get(0) != null) {
```

```
            cnt++;
        }
    }
    return cnt;
} catch (Exception e) {
    ...
}
}
```

Just as UDFs can take complex types as input, they also can return complex types as output. You could, for example, create a `SetIntersection` UDF that took two bags as input and returned a bag as output.

UDFs can also be handed the entire record by passing * to the UDF. You might expect that in this case the input `Tuple` argument passed to the UDF would contain all the fields passed into the operator the UDF is in. But it does not. Instead, it contains one field, which is a tuple that contains all those fields. Consider a Pig Latin script like this:

```
data      = load 'input' as (x, y, z);
processed = foreach data generate myudf(*);
```

In this case, `myudf.exec` will get a tuple with one field, which will be a tuple that will have three fields: `x`, `y`, and `z`. To access the `y` field of `data`, you will need to call `t.get(0).get(1)`.

Interacting with Pig values

Evaluation functions and other UDFs are exposed to the internals of how Pig represents data types. This means that when you read a field and expect it to be an integer, you need to know that it will be an instance of `java.lang.Integer`. For a complete list of Pig types and how they are represented in Java, see "Types" on page 23. For most of these types, you construct the appropriate Java objects in the normal way. However, this is not the case for tuples and bags. These are interfaces, and they do not have direct constructors. Instead, you must use factory classes for each of these. This was done so that users and developers could build their own implementations of tuple and bag and instruct Pig to use them.

`TupleFactory` is an abstract singleton class that you must use to create tuples. You can also configure which `TupleFactory` is used, since users who provide their own tuples will need to provide their own factory to produce them. To get an instance of `Tuple Factory` to construct tuples, call the static method `TupleFactory.getInstance()`.

You can now create new tuples with either `newTuple()` or `newTuple(int size)`. Whenever possible you should use the second method, which preallocates the tuple with the right number of fields. This avoids the need to dynamically grow the tuple later and is much more efficient. The method creates a tuple with `size` number of fields, all of which are null. You can now set the fields using the `Tuple`'s `set(int fieldNum, Object val)` method. As an example, we can look at how the example load function we will build in the next chapter creates tuples:

```
// JsonLoader.java
private TupleFactory tupleFactory = TupleFactory.getInstance();

private Object readField(JsonParser p,
                        ResourceFieldSchema field,
                        int fieldnum) throws IOException {
    ...
    ResourceSchema s = field.getSchema();
    ResourceFieldSchema[] fs = s.getFields();
    Tuple t = tupleFactory.newTuple(fs.length);

    for (int j = 0; j < fs.length; j++) {
        t.set(j, readField(p, fs[j], j));
    }
    ...
}
```

If you do not know the number of fields in the tuple when it is constructed, you can use newTuple(). You can then add fields using Tuple's append(Object val) method, which will append the field to the end of the tuple.

To read data from tuples, use the get(int fieldNum) method. This returns a Java Object because the tuple does not have a schema instance and does not know what type this field is. You must either cast the result to the appropriate type or use the utility methods in org.apache.pig.data.DataType to determine the type.

Similar to tuples, BagFactory must be used to construct bags. You can get an instance using BagFactory.getInstance(). To get a new, empty bag, call newDefaultBag(). You can then add tuples to it as you construct them using DataBag's add(Tuple t) method. You should do this rather than constructing a list of tuples and then passing it using newDefaultBag(List<Tuple> listOfTuples), because bags know how to spill to disk when they grow so large that they cannot fit into memory. Again we can look at Json Loader to see an example of constructing bags:

```
// JsonLoader.java
private BagFactory bagFactory = BagFactory.getInstance();

private Object readField(JsonParser p,
                        ResourceFieldSchema field,
                        int fieldnum) throws IOException {
    ...
    DataBag bag = bagFactory.newDefaultBag();

    JsonToken innerTok;
    while ((innerTok = p.nextToken()) != JsonToken.END_ARRAY) {

        t = tupleFactory.newTuple(fs.length);
        for (int j = 0; j < fs.length; j++) {
            t.set(j, readField(p, fs[j], j));
        }

        p.nextToken(); // read end of object
        bag.add(t);
```

```
        }
    ...
}
```

To read data from a bag, use the iterator provided by `iterator()`. This also implements Java's `Iterable`, so you can use the construct `for (Tuple t : bag)`.

 Bags make the assumption that once data is being read from them, no new data will be written to them. Their implementation of how they spill and reread data depends on this assumption. So once you call `iterator`, you should never call `add` again on the same bag.

Input and Output Schemas

Pig typechecks a script before running it. `EvalFunc` includes a method to allow you to turn on type checking for your UDF as well, both for input and output.

When your UDF returns a simple type, Pig uses Java reflection to determine the return type. However, because `exec` takes a tuple, Pig has no way to determine what input you expect your UDF to take. You can check this at runtime, of course, but your development and testing will go more smoothly if you check it at compile time instead. For example, we could use the `Pow` UDF example in the previous section like this:

```
register 'acme.jar';
A = load 'input' as (x:chararray, y :int);
B = foreach A generate y, com.acme.math.Pow(x, 2);
dump B;
```

Pig will start a job and run your tasks. All the tasks will fail, and you will get an error message `ERROR 2078: Caught error from UDF: com.acme.math.Pow [Something bad hap pened!]`. Runtime exceptions like this are particularly expensive in Hadoop, both because scheduling can take a while on a busy cluster and because each task is tried three times before the whole job is declared a failure. Let's fix this UDF so it checks up front that it was given reasonable input.

The method to declare the input your UDF expects is `outputSchema`. The method is called this because it returns the schema that describes the UDF's output. If your UDF does not override this method, Pig will attempt to ascertain your return type from the return type of your implementation of `EvalFunc`, and pass your UDF whatever input the script indicates. If your UDF does implement this method, Pig will pass it the schema of the input that the script has indicated to pass into the UDF. This is also your UDF's opportunity to throw an error if it receives an input schema that does not match its expectations. An implementation of this method for `Pow` looks like this:

```
// java/com/acme/math/Pow.java
public Schema outputSchema(Schema input) {
    // Check that we were passed two fields
    if (input.size() != 2) {
        throw new RuntimeException(
            "Expected (int, int), input does not have 2 fields");
```

```
    }

    try {
        // Get the types for both columns and check them.  If they are
        // wrong, figure out what types were passed and give a good error
        // message.
        if (input.getField(0).type != DataType.INTEGER ||
                input.getField(1).type != DataType.INTEGER) {
            String msg = "Expected input (int, int), received schema (";
            msg += DataType.findTypeName(input.getField(0).type);
            msg += ", ";
            msg += DataType.findTypeName(input.getField(1).type);
            msg += ")";
            throw new RuntimeException(msg);
        }
    } catch (Exception e) {
        throw new RuntimeException(e);
    }

    // Construct our output schema, which is one field that is a long
    return new Schema(new FieldSchema(null, DataType.LONG));
}
```

With this method added to Pow, when we invoke the previous script that mistakenly tries to pass a chararray to Pow, it now fails almost immediately with java.lang.Runti meException: Expected input of (int, int), but received schema (chararray, int).

Pig's Schema is a complicated class, and we will not delve into all its complexities here. The following summary will be enough to help you build your own schemas for out putSchema. At its core, Schema is a list of FieldSchemas and a mapping of aliases to FieldSchemas. Each FieldSchema contains an alias and a type. The types are stored as Java bytes, with constants for each type defined in the class org.apache.pig.data.Data Type. Schema is a recursive structure. Each FieldSchema also has a Schema member. This member is nonnull only when the type is complex. In the case of tuples, it defines the schema of the tuple. In the case of bags, it defines the schema of the tuples in the bag. Starting in 0.9, if a schema is present for a map, it indicates the data type of values in the map. Before 0.9, maps did not have schemas:

```
public class Schema implements Serializable, Cloneable {

    // List of all fields in the schema.
    private List<FieldSchema> mFields;

    // Map of alias names to field schemas, so that lookup can be done by alias.
    private Map<String, FieldSchema> mAliases;

    // A FieldSchema represents a schema for one field.
    public static class FieldSchema implements Serializable, Cloneable {

        // Alias for this field.
        public String alias;

        // Datatype, using codes from org.apache.pig.data.DataType.
```

```
        public byte type;

        // If this is a tuple itself, it can have a schema. Otherwise, this field
        // must be null.
        public Schema schema;

        /**
         * Constructor for any type.
         * @param a Alias, if known. If unknown, leave null.
         * @param t Type, using codes from org.apache.pig.data.DataType.
         */
        public FieldSchema(String a, byte t) { ... }
    }

    /**
     * Create a schema with more than one field.
     * @param fields List of field schemas that describes the fields.
     */
    public Schema(List<FieldSchema> fields) { ... }

    /**
     * Create a schema with only one field.
     * @param fieldSchema field to put in this schema.
     */
    public Schema(FieldSchema fieldSchema) { ... }

    /**
     * Given an alias name, find the associated FieldSchema.
     * @param alias Alias to look up.
     * @return FieldSchema, or null if no such alias is in this tuple.
     */
    public FieldSchema getField(String alias) throws FrontendException {
        // some error checking omitted.
        return mAliases.get(alias);
    }

    /**
     * Given a field number, find the associated FieldSchema.
     *
     * @param fieldNum Field number to look up.
     * @return FieldSchema for this field.
     */
    public FieldSchema getField(int fieldNum) throws FrontendException {
        // some error checking omitted.
        return mFields.get(fieldNum);
    }
}
```

As mentioned earlier, when your UDF returns a scalar type, Pig can use reflection to figure out that return type. When your UDF returns a bag or a tuple, however, you will need to implement outputSchema if you want Pig to understand the contents of that bag or tuple.

Error Handling and Progress Reporting

Our previous examples have given some hints of how to deal with errors. When your UDF encounters an error, you have a couple of choices on how to handle it. The most common case is to issue a warning and return a null. This tells Pig that your UDF failed and its output should be viewed as unknown.[‡] We saw an example of this when the `Pow` function detected overflow:

```
for (int i = 0; i < exponent; i++) {
    long preresult = result;
    result *= base;
    if (preresult > result) {
        // We overflowed.  Give a warning, but do not throw an
        // exception.
        warn("Overflow!", PigWarning.TOO_LARGE_FOR_INT);
        // Returning null will indicate to Pig that we failed but
        // we want to continue execution.
        return null;
    }
}
```

`warn`, a method of `EvalFunc`, takes a message that you provide as well as a warning code. The warning codes are in `org.apache.pig.PigWarning`, including several user-defined codes that you can use if none of the provided codes matches your situation. These warnings are aggregated by Pig and reported to the user at the end of the job.

Warning and returning null is convenient because it allows your job to continue. When you are processing billions of records, you do not want your job to fail because one record out of all those billions had a chararray where you expected an int. Given enough data, the odds are overwhelming that a few records will be bad, and most calculations will be fine if a few data points are missing.

For errors that are not tolerable, your UDF can throw an exception. If Pig catches an exception, it will assume that you are asking to stop everything, and it will cause the task to fail. Hadoop will then restart your task. If any particular task fails three times, Hadoop will not restart it again. Instead, it will kill all the other tasks and declare the job a failure.

When you have concluded that you do need an exception, you should also issue a log message so that you can read the task logs later and get more context to determine what happened. `EvalFunc` has a member `log` that is an instance of `org.apache.commons.log ging.Log`. Hadoop prints any log messages into logfiles on the task machine, which are available from the JobTracker UI. See "MapReduce Job Status" on page 92 for details. You can also print info messages into the log to help you with debugging.

In addition to error reporting, some UDFs will need to report progress. Hadoop listens to its tasks to make sure they are making progress. If it does not hear from a task for

---

‡ Recall that in Pig null means that the value is unknown, not that it is 0 or unset.

five minutes, it concludes that the task died or went into an infinite loop. It then kills the task if it is still running, cleans up its resources, and restarts the task elsewhere. Pig reports progress to Hadoop on a regular basis. However, if you have a UDF that is very compute-intensive and a single invocation of it might run for more than five minutes, you should also report progress. To do this, `EvalFunc` provides a member `reporter`. By invoking `report.progress()` or `report.progress(String msg)` (where `msg` can say whatever you want) at least every five minutes, your UDF will avoid being viewed as a timeout.

Constructors and Passing Data from Frontend to Backend

Our discussion so far assumes that your UDF knows everything it needs to know at development time. This is not always the case. Consider a UDF that needs to read a lookup table from HDFS. You would like to be able to declare the filename when you use the UDF. You can do that by defining a nondefault constructor for your UDF.

By default, `EvalFuncs` have a no-argument constructor, but you can provide a constructor that takes one or more `String` arguments. This alternate constructor is then referenced in Pig Latin by using the `define` statement to define the UDF; see "define and UDFs" on page 53 for details.

As an example, we will look at a new UDF, `MetroResolver`. This UDF takes a city name as input and returns the name of the larger metropolitan area that city is part of. For example, given Pasadena, it will return Los Angeles. Based on which country the input cities are in, a different lookup table will be needed. The name of a file in HDFS that contains this lookup table can be provided as a constructor argument. The class declaration, members, and constructor for our UDF look like this:

```
// java/com/acme/marketing/MetroResolver.java
/**
 * A lookup UDF that maps cities to metropolitan areas.
 */
public class MetroResolver extends EvalFunc<String> {

    String lookupFile;
    HashMap<String, String> lookup = null;

    /*
     * @param file - File that contains a lookup table mapping cities to metro
     * areas.  The file must be located on the filesystem where this UDF will
     * run.
     */
    public MetroResolver(String file) {
        // Just store the filename. Don't load the lookup table, since we may
        // be on the frontend or the backend.
        lookupFile = file;
    }
}
```

The UDF can now be invoked in a Pig Latin script like this:

```
register 'acme.jar';
define MetroResolver com.acme.marketing.MetroResolver('/user/you/cities/us');
A = load 'input' as (city:chararray);
B = foreach A generate city, MetroResolver(city);
dump B;
```

The filename */user/you/cities/us* will be passed to `MetroResolver` every time Pig constructs it. However, our UDF is not yet complete because we have not constructed the lookup table. In fact, we explicitly set it to null. It does not make sense to construct it in the constructor, because the constructor will be invoked on both the frontend and backend. There are forms of dark magic that will allow the UDF to figure out whether it is being invoked on the frontend or backend, but I cannot recommend them, because they are not guaranteed to work the same between releases. It is much better to do the lookup table construction in a method that we know will be called only in the backend.

`EvalFunc` does not provide an initialize method that it calls on the backend before it begins processing. You can work around this by keeping a flag to determine whether you have initialized your UDF in a given task. The `exec` function for `MetroResolver` does this by tracking whether `lookup` is null:

```
public String exec(Tuple input) throws IOException {
    if (lookup == null) {
        // We have not been initialized yet, so do it now.

        lookup = new HashMap<String, String>();
        // Get an instance of the HDFS FileSystem class so
        // we can read a file from HDFS.  We need a copy of
        // our configuration to do that.
        // Read the configuration from the UDFContext.
        FileSystem fs = FileSystem.get(UDFContext.getUDFContext().getJobConf());
        DataInputStream in = fs.open(new Path(lookupFile));
        String line;
        while ((line = in.readLine()) != null) {
            String[] toks = new String[2];
            toks = line.split(":", 2);
            lookup.put(toks[0], toks[1]);
        }
        in.close();
    }
    return lookup.get((String)input.get(0));
}
```

This initialization section handles opening the file and reading it. In order to open the file, it must first connect to HDFS. This is accomplished by `FileSystem.get`. This method in turn needs a `JobConf` object, which is where Hadoop stores all its job information. The `JobConf` object can be obtained using `UDFContext`, which we will cover in more detail later. Note that obtaining `JobConf` in this way works only on the backend, as no job configuration exists on the frontend.

Once we are connected to HDFS, we open the file and read it as we would any other file. It is parsed into two fields and put into the hash table. All subsequent calls to `exec` will just be lookups in the hash table.

Loading the distributed cache

Our `MetroResolver` UDF opens and reads its lookup file from HDFS, which you will often want. However, having hundreds or thousands of map tasks open the same file on HDFS at the same time puts significant load on the NameNode and the DataNodes that host the file's blocks. To avoid this situation, Hadoop provides the distributed cache, which allows users to preload HDFS files locally onto the nodes their tasks will run on. For details, see "Distributed Cache" on page 192.

Let's write a second version of `MetroResolver` that uses the distributed cache. Beginning in version 0.9, `EvalFunc` provides a method `getCacheFiles` that is called on the frontend. Your UDF returns a list of files from this method that it wants in the distributed cache. The format of each file is *client_file#task_file*, where *client_file* is the path to the file on your client, and *task_file* is the name the file will be given on your task node. *task_file* is relative to your UDF's working directory on the backend. You should place any files in your working directory rather than using an absolute path. *task_file* will be a local file on the task node and should be read using standard Java file utilities. It should not be read using HDFS's `FileSystem`:

```
// java/com/acme/marketing/MetroResolverV2.java
/**
 * A lookup UDF that maps cities to metropolatin areas, this time using the
 * Distributed Cache.
 */
public class MetroResolverV2 extends EvalFunc<String> {

    String lookupFile;
    HashMap<String, String> lookup = null;

    /*
     * @param file - File that contains a lookup table mapping cities to metro
     * areas.  The file must be located on the filesystem where this UDF will
     * run.
     */
    public MetroResolverV2(String file) {
        // Just store the filename. Don't load the lookup table, since we may
        // be on the frontend or the backend.
        lookupFile = file;
    }

    public String exec(Tuple input) throws IOException {
        if (lookup == null) {
            // We have not been initialized yet, so do it now.
            lookup = new HashMap<String, String>();

            // Open the file as a local file.
            FileReader fr = new FileReader("./mrv2_lookup");
            BufferedReader d = new BufferedReader(fr);
            String line;
            while ((line = d.readLine()) != null) {
                String[] toks = new String[2];
                toks = line.split(":", 2);
```

```
            lookup.put(toks[0], toks[1]);
        }
        fr.close();
    }
    return lookup.get((String)input.get(0));
}

public List<String> getCacheFiles() {
    List<String> list = new ArrayList<String>(1);
    // We were passed the name of the file on HDFS.  Append a
    // name for the file on the task node.
    list.add(lookupFile + "#mrv2_lookup");
    return list;
}
}
```

UDFContext

Constructor arguments work as a way to pass information into your UDF, if you know the data at the time the script is written. You can extend this using parameter substitution (see "Parameter Substitution" on page 77) so that data can be passed when the script is run. But some information you want to pass from frontend to backend cannot be known when the script is run, or it might not be accessible in String form on the command line. An example is collecting properties from the environment and passing them.

To allow UDFs to pass data from the frontend to the backend, starting in version 0.8, Pig provides a singleton class, UDFContext. Your UDF obtains a reference to it by calling getUDFContext. We have already seen that UDFs can use UDFContext to obtain a copy of the JobConf. Beginning in version 0.9, UDFContext also captures the System properties on the client and carries them to the backend. Your UDF can then obtain them by calling getClientSystemProperties.

UDFContext also provides mechanisms for you to pass a properties object explicitly for your UDF. You can either pass a properties object for all UDFs of the same class or pass a specific object for each instance of your UDF. To use the same one for all instances of your UDF, call getUDFProperties(this.getClass()). This will return a Prop erties object that is a reference to a properties object kept by UDFContext. UDFContext will capture and transmit to the backend any changes made in this object. You can call this in outputSchema, which is guaranteed to be called in the frontend. When you want to read the data, call the same method again in your exec method. When using the object in the exec method, keep in mind that any changes made to the returned Prop erties will not be transmitted to other instances of the UDF on the backend, unless you happen to have another instance of the same UDF in the same task. This is a mechanism for sending information from the frontend to the backend, not between instances in the backend.

Sometimes you will want to transmit different data to different instances of the same UDF. By different instances I mean different invocations in your Pig Latin script, not different instantiations in various map and reduce tasks. To support this, `UDFContext` provides `getUDFProperties(Class, String[])`. The constructor arguments to your UDF are a good candidate to be passed as the array of `String`. This allows each instance of the UDF to differentiate itself. If your UDF does not take constructor arguments, or all arguments have the same value, you can add one unused argument that is solely to distinguish separate instances of the UDF.

Consider a UDF that has its own properties file, which might be useful if you want to pass different properties to different UDFs, or if you have many UDF-specific properties that you want to change without changing your Pig properties file. Let's write a second version of the stock analyzer UDF that we used in Chapter 6:

```
// java/com/acme/financial/AnalyzeStockV2.java
/**
 * This UDF takes a bag of information about a stock and
 * produces a floating-point score between 1 and 100,
 * 1 being sell, 100 being buy.
 */
public class AnalyzeStockV2 extends EvalFunc<Float> {

    Random r = new Random();
    Properties myProperties = null;

    @Override
    public Float exec(Tuple input) throws IOException {
        if (myProperties == null) {
            // Retrieve our class-specific properties from UDFContext.
            myProperties =
                UDFContext.getUDFContext().getUDFProperties(this.getClass());
        }

        // Make sure the input isn't null and is of the right size.
        if (input == null || input.size() != 1) return null;

        DataBag b = (DataBag)input.get(0);
        for (Tuple t : b) {
            // Do some magic analysis, using properites from myProperties to
            // decide how ...
        }
        return r.nextFloat() * 100;
    }
    @Override
    public Schema outputSchema(Schema input) {
        try {
            // Read our properties file.
            Properties prop = new Properties();
            prop.load(new FileInputStream("/tmp/stock.properties"));
            // Get a properties object specific to this UDF class.
            UDFContext context = UDFContext.getUDFContext();
            Properties udfProp = context.getUDFProperties(this.getClass());
            // Copy our properties into it.  There is no need to pass it
            // back to UDFContext.
            for (Map.Entry<Object, Object> e : prop.entrySet()) {
                udfProp.setProperty((String)e.getKey(), (String)e.getValue());
```

```
        }
    } catch (Exception e) {
        throw new RuntimeException(e);
    }

    return new Schema(new Schema.FieldSchema(null, DataType.FLOAT));
    }

}
```

Overloading UDFs

Sometimes you want different UDF implementations depending on the data type the UDF is processing. For example, MIN(long) should return a long, whereas MIN(int) should return an int. To enable this, EvalFunc provides the method getArgToFuncMap ping. If this method returns a null, Pig will use the current UDF. To provide a list of alternate UDFs based on the input types, this function returns a list of FuncSpecs. A FuncSpec is a Pig class that describes a UDF. Each of these FuncSpecs describes a set of expected input arguments and the UDF, as a Java class, that should be used to handle them. Pig's typechecker will use this list to determine which Java class to place in the execution pipeline (more on this later). The getArgToFuncMapping of Pig's built-in MIN function looks like this:

```
// src/org/apache/pig/builtin/MIN.java
public List<FuncSpec> getArgToFuncMapping()
throws FrontendException {
  List<FuncSpec> funcList = new ArrayList<FuncSpec>();

  // The first element in the list is this class itself, which is built to
  // handle the case where the input is a bytearray.  So we return our own
  // classname and a schema that indicates this function expects a BAG with
  // tuples that have one field, which is a bytearray.  generateNestedSchema is a
  // helper method that generates schemas of bags that have tuples with one
  // field.
  funcList.add(new FuncSpec(this.getClass().getName(),
      Schema.generateNestedSchema(DataType.BAG, DataType.BYTEARRAY)));

  // If our input schema is a bag with tuples with one field that is a double,
  // then we use the class DoubleMin instead of MIN to implement min.
  funcList.add(new FuncSpec(DoubleMin.class.getName(),
      Schema.generateNestedSchema(DataType.BAG, DataType.DOUBLE)));

  // and so on...
  funcList.add(new FuncSpec(FloatMin.class.getName(),
      Schema.generateNestedSchema(DataType.BAG, DataType.FLOAT)));

  funcList.add(new FuncSpec(IntMin.class.getName(),
      Schema.generateNestedSchema(DataType.BAG, DataType.INTEGER)));

  funcList.add(new FuncSpec(LongMin.class.getName(),
      Schema.generateNestedSchema(DataType.BAG, DataType.LONG)));
```

```
    funcList.add(new FuncSpec(StringMin.class.getName(),
        Schema.generateNestedSchema(DataType.BAG, DataType.CHARARRAY)));

    return funcList;
}
```

Pig's typechecker goes through a set of steps to determine which `FuncSpec` is the closest match, and thus which Java class it should place in this job's execution pipeline. At each step, if it finds a match, it uses that match. If it finds more than one match at a given step, it will return an error that gives all the matching possibilities. If it finds no match in the whole list, it will also give an error. As an example of this, let's consider another version of the `Pow` UDF we built above. We will call this one `PowV2`. It takes either two longs or two doubles as input. Its `getArgToFuncMapping` looks like the following:

```
// java/com/acme/math/PowV2.java
public List<FuncSpec> getArgToFuncMapping() throws FrontendException {
    List<FuncSpec> funcList = new ArrayList<FuncSpec>();
    Schema s = new Schema();
    s.add(new Schema.FieldSchema(null, DataType.DOUBLE));
    s.add(new Schema.FieldSchema(null, DataType.DOUBLE));
    funcList.add(new FuncSpec(this.getClass().getName(), s));
    s = new Schema();
    s.add(new Schema.FieldSchema(null, DataType.LONG));
    s.add(new Schema.FieldSchema(null, DataType.LONG));
    funcList.add(new FuncSpec(LongPow.class.getName(), s));
    return funcList;
}
```

In the typechecker's search for the best UDF to use, step one is to look for an exact match, where all of the expected input declared by the UDF is matched by the actual input passed in Pig Latin. `Pow(2.0, 3.1415)` passes two doubles, so Pig Latin will choose `PowV2`. `Pow(2L, 3L)` passes two longs, so `LongPow` will be used.

Step two is to look for bytearrays that are passed into the UDF and see whether a match can be made by inserting casts for those bytearrays. For example, Pig will rewrite `Pow(x, 2L)`, where `x` is a bytearray, as `Pow((long)x, 2L)` and use `LongPow`. This rule can confuse Pig when all arguments are bytearrays, because bytearrays can be cast to any type. `Pow(x, y)`, where both `x` and `y` are bytearrays, results in an error message:

```
Multiple matching functions for com.acme.math.PowV2 with input schema:
    ({double,double}, {long,long}). Please use an explicit cast.
```

Step three is to look for an implicit cast that will match one of the provided schemas. The implicit cast that is "closest" will be used. Implicit casting of numeric types goes from int to long to float to double, and by closest I mean the cast that requires the least steps in that list. So, `Pow(2, 2)` will use `LongPow`, whereas `Pow(2.0, 2)` will use `PowV2`.

Step four is to look for a working combination of steps two and three, bytearray casts plus implicit casts. `Pow(x, 3.14f)`, where `x` is a bytearray, will use `PowV2` by promoting `3.14f` to a double and casting `x` to a double.

If after all these steps Pig still has not found a suitable method, it will fail and say it cannot determine which method to use. `Pow('hello', 2)` gives an error message:

```
Could not infer the matching function for com.acme.math.PowV2 as multiple or none of
them fit. Please use an explicit cast.
```

Memory Issues in Eval Funcs

Some operations you will perform in your UDFs will require more memory than is available. As an example, you might want to build a UDF that calculates the cumulative sum of a set of inputs. This will return a bag of values because, for each input, it needs to return the intermediate sum at that input.

Pig's bags handle spilling data to disk automatically when they pass a certain size threshold or when only a certain amount of heap space remains. Spilling to disk is expensive and should be avoided whenever possible. But if you must store large amounts of data in a bag, Pig will manage it.

Bags are the only Pig data type that know how to spill. Tuples and maps must fit into memory. Bags that are too large to fit in memory can still be referenced in a tuple or a map; this will not be counted as those tuples or maps not fitting into memory.

Algebraic Interface

I have already mentioned in a number of other places that there are significant advantages to using Hadoop's combiner whenever possible. It lowers skew in your reduce tasks, as well as the amount of data sent over the network between map and reduce tasks. For details on the combiner and when it is run, see "Combiner Phase" on page 190.

Use of the combiner is interesting when you are working with sets of data, usually sets you intend to aggregate and then compute a single or small set of values for. There are two classes of functions that fit nicely into the combiner: *distributive* and *algebraic*. A function is distributive if the same result is obtained by 1) dividing its input set into subsets, applying the function to those subsets, and then applying the function to those results; or 2) applying the function to the original set. SUM is an example of this. A function is said to be algebraic if it can be divided into initial, intermediate, and final functions (possibly different from the initial function), where the initial function is applied to subsets of the input set, the intermediate function is applied to results of the initial function, and the final function is applied to all of the results of the intermediate function. COUNT is an example of an algebraic function, with count being used as the initial function and sum as the intermediate and final functions. A distributive function is a special case of an algebraic function, where the initial, intermediate, and final functions are all identical to the original function.

An `EvalFunc` can declare itself to be algebraic by implementing the Java interface `Alge`
`braic`. `Algebraic` provides three methods that allow your UDF to declare Java classes
that implement its initial, intermediate, and final functionality. These classes must extend `EvalFunc`:

```
// src/org/apache/pig/Algebraic.java
public interface Algebraic{

    /**
     * Get the initial function.
     * @return A function name of f_init. f_init should be an eval func.
     */
    public String getInitial();

    /**
     * Get the intermediate function.
     * @return A function name of f_intermed. f_intermed should be an eval func.
     */
    public String getIntermed();

    /**
     * Get the final function.
     * @return A function name of f_final. f_final should be an eval func
     * parameterized by the same datum as the eval func implementing this interface.
     */
    public String getFinal();
}
```

Each of these methods returns a name of a Java class, which should itself implement
`EvalFunc`. Pig will use these UDFs to rewrite the execution of your script. Consider the
following Pig Latin script:

```
input = load 'data' as (x, y);
grpd  = group input by x;
cnt   = foreach grpd generate group, COUNT(input);
store cnt into 'result';
```

The execution pipeline for this script would initially look like:

Map
    load

Reduce
    foreach(group, COUNT), store

After being rewritten to use the combiner, it would look like:

Map
    load

    foreach(group, COUNT.Initial)

Combine
    foreach(group, COUNT.Intermediate)

Reduce
```
foreach(group, COUNT.Final), store
```

As an example, we will walk through the implementation for COUNT. Its algebraic functions look like this:

```
// src/org/apache/pig/builtin/COUNT.java
public String getInitial() {
    return Initial.class.getName();
}

public String getIntermed() {
    return Intermediate.class.getName();
}

public String getFinal() {
    return Final.class.getName();
}
```

Each of these referenced classes is a static internal class in COUNT. The implementation of Initial is:

```
// src/org/apache/pig/builtin/COUNT.java
static public class Initial extends EvalFunc<Tuple> {

    public Tuple exec(Tuple input) throws IOException {
        // Since Initial is guaranteed to be called
        // only in the map, it will be called with an
        // input of a bag with a single tuple - the
        // count should always be 1 if bag is nonempty,
        DataBag bag = (DataBag)input.get(0);
        Iterator it = bag.iterator();
        if (it.hasNext()){
            Tuple t = (Tuple)it.next();
            if (t != null && t.size() > 0 && t.get(0) != null)
                return mTupleFactory.newTuple(Long.valueOf(1));
        }
        return mTupleFactory.newTuple(Long.valueOf(0));
    }
}
```

Even though the initial function is guaranteed to receive only one record in its input, that record will match the schema of the original function. So, in the case of COUNT, it will be a bag. Thus, this initial method determines whether there is a nonnull record in that bag. If so, it returns one; otherwise, it returns zero. The return type of the initial function is a tuple. The contents of that tuple are entirely up to you as the UDF implementer. In this case, the initial returns a tuple with one long field.

COUNT's Intermediate class sums the counts seen so far:

```
// src/org/apache/pig/builtin/COUNT.java
static public class Intermediate extends EvalFunc<Tuple> {

    public Tuple exec(Tuple input) throws IOException {
        try {
```

```
            return mTupleFactory.newTuple(sum(input));
        } catch (ExecException ee) {
            ...
        }
    }
}

static protected Long sum(Tuple input)
throws ExecException, NumberFormatException {
    DataBag values = (DataBag)input.get(0);
    long sum = 0;
    for (Iterator<Tuple> it = values.iterator(); it.hasNext();) {
        Tuple t = it.next();
        sum += (Long)t.get(0);
    }
    return sum;
}
```

The input to the intermediate function is a bag of tuples that were returned by the initial function. The intermediate function may be called zero, one, or many times. So, it needs to output tuples that match the input tuples it expects. The framework will handle placing those tuples in bags. COUNT's intermediate function returns a tuple with a long. As we now want to sum the previous counts, this function implements SUM rather than COUNT.

The final function is called in the reducer and is guaranteed to be called only once. Its input type is a bag of tuples that both the initial and intermediate implementations return. Its return type needs to be the return type of the original UDF, which in this case is long. In COUNT's case, this is the same operation as the intermediate because it sums the intermediate sums:

```
// src/org/apache/pig/builtin/COUNT.java
static public class Final extends EvalFunc<Long> {
    public Long exec(Tuple input) throws IOException {
        try {
            return sum(input);
        } catch (Exception ee) {
            ...
        }
    }
}
```

Implementing Algebraic does not guarantee that the algebraic implementation will always be used. Pig chooses the algebraic implementation only if all UDFs in the same foreach statement are algebraic. This is because our testing has shown that using the combiner with data that cannot be combined significantly slows down the job. And there is no way in Hadoop to route some data to the combiner (for algebraic functions) and some straight to the reducer (for nonalgebraic). This means that your UDF must always implement the exec method, even if you hope it will always be used in algebraic mode. An additional motivation is to implement algebraic mode for your UDFs when possible.

Accumulator Interface

Some calculations cannot be done in an algebraic manner. In particular, any function that requires its records to be sorted before beginning is not algebraic. But many of these methods still do not need to see their entire input at once; they can work on subsets of the data as long as they are guaranteed it is all available. This means Pig does not have to read all of the records into memory at once. Instead, it can read a subset of the records and pass them to the UDF. To handle these cases, Pig provides the `Accumulator` interface. Rather than calling a UDF once with the entire input set in one bag, Pig will call it multiple times with a subset of the records. When it has passed all the records in, it will then ask for a result. Finally, it will give the UDF a chance to reset its state before passing it records for the next group:

```
// src/org/apache/pig/Accumulator.java
public interface Accumulator <T> {
    /**
     * Pass tuples to the UDF.
     * @param b A tuple containing a single field, which is a bag.  The bag will
     * contain the set of tuples being passed to the UDF in this iteration.
     */
    public void accumulate(Tuple b) throws IOException;

    /**
     * Called when all tuples from current key have been passed to accumulate.
     * @return the value for the UDF for this key.
     */
    public T getValue();

    /**
     * Called after getValue() to prepare processing for next key.
     */
    public void cleanup();
}
```

As an example, let's look at COUNT's implementation of the accumulator:

```
// src/org/apache/pig/builtin/COUNT.java
private long intermediateCount = 0L;

public void accumulate(Tuple b) throws IOException {
    try {
        DataBag bag = (DataBag)b.get(0);
        Iterator it = bag.iterator();
        while (it.hasNext()){
            Tuple t = (Tuple)it.next();
            if (t != null && t.size() > 0 && t.get(0) != null) {
                intermediateCount += 1;
            }
        }
    } catch (Exception e) {
        ...
    }
}
```

```
public void cleanup() {
    intermediateCount = 0L;
}

public Long getValue() {
    return intermediateCount;
}
```

By default, Pig passes `accumulate` 20,000 records at once. You can modify this value by setting the property `pig.accumulative.batchsize` either on the command line or using `set` in your script.

As mentioned earlier, one major class of methods that can use the accumulator are those that require sorted input, such as session analysis. Usually such a UDF will want records within the group sorted by timestamp. As an example, let's say you have log data from your web servers that includes the user ID, timestamp, and the URL the user viewed, and you want to do session analysis on this data:

```
logs    = load 'serverlogs' as (id:chararray, ts: long, url: chararray);
byuser  = group logs by id;
results = foreach byuser {
                sorted = order logs by ts;
                generate group, SessionAnalysis(sorted);
};
```

Pig can move the sort done by the `order` statement to Hadoop, to be done as part of the shuffle phase. Thus, Pig is still able to read a subset of records at a time from Hadoop and pass those directly to `SessionAnalysis`. This important optimization allows accumulator UDFs to work with sorted data.

Whenever possible, Pig will choose to use the algebraic implementation of a UDF over the accumulator. This is because the accumulator helps avoid spilling records to disk, but it does not reduce network cost or help balance the reducers. If all UDFs in a `foreach` implement `Accumulator` and at least one does not implement `Algebraic`, Pig will use the accumulator. If at least one does not use the accumulator, Pig will not use the accumulator. This is because Pig already has to read the entire bag into memory to pass to the UDF that does not implement the accumulator, so there is no longer any value in the accumulator.

Python UDFs

Pig and Hadoop are implemented in Java, so Java is a natural choice for UDFs as well. But not being forced into Java would be nice. For simple UDFs of only a few lines, the cycle of write, compile, package into a JAR, and deploy is an especially heavyweight process. To allow users to write UDFs in scripting languages, we added support for UDFs in Python to Pig 0.8. We did it in such a way that supporting any scripting language that compiles down to the JVM requires only a few hundred lines of code. We hope to keep expanding the supported languages in the future.

Python UDFs consist of a single function that is used in place of the exec method of a Java function. They can be annotated to indicate their schema. The more advanced features of evaluation functions—such as overloading, constructor arguments, and algebraic and accumulator interfaces—are not available yet.

Python UDFs are executed using the Jython framework. The benefit is that Python UDFs can be compiled to Java bytecode and run with relatively little performance penalty. The downside is that Jython is compatible with version 2.5 of Python, so Python 3 features are not available to UDF writers.

To register and define your Python UDFs in Pig Latin, see "Registering Python UDFs" on page 52. In this section we will focus on writing the UDFs themselves. Let's take a look at the production UDF we used in that earlier section:

```
# production.py
@outputSchema("production:float")
def production(slugging_pct, onbase_pct):
    return slugging_pct + onbase_pct
```

The code is self-explanatory. The annotation of @outputSchema tells Pig that this UDF will return a float and that the name of the field is "production". The output schema annotation can specify any Pig type. The syntax for tuples and bags matches the syntax for declaring a field to be a tuple or a bag in load; see "Schemas" on page 27 for details.

Sometimes schemas are variable and not statically expressible. For these cases you can provide a schema function that will define your schema. Let's write a Python UDF that squares a number, always returning a number of the same type:

```
# square.py
@outputSchemaFunction("schema")
def square(num):
    return num * num


@schemaFunction("schema")
def schema(input):
    # Return whatever type we were handed
    return input
```

The input to the schema function is in the same format as the one specified in @output Schema: *colname:type*. Its output is expected to be in the same format.

If neither @outputSchema nor @outputSchemaFunction is provided for a Python function, it will be assumed to return a single bytearray value. Because there will be no load function for the value, Pig will not be able to cast it to any other type, so it will be worthless for anything but store or dump.

In order to pass data between Java and Python, Pig must define a mapping of types. Table 10-1 describes the mapping between Pig and Python types.

Table 10-1. Pig-Python type translations

Pig type	Python type
int	number
long	number
float	number
double	number
chararray	string
bytearray	string
map	dictionary
tuple	tuple
bag	list of tuples

Any value that is null in Pig will be translated to the None object in Python. Similarly, any time the None object is returned by Python, Pig will map it to a null of the expected type.

One issue that Pig does not handle for your Python UDFs is bringing along dependent modules. If your Python file imports other modules, you will need to wrap those in a JAR and register that file as part of your Pig script.§

One last issue to consider is performance. What is the cost of using Python instead of Java? Of course it depends on your script, the computation you are doing, and your data. And because Python UDFs do not yet support advanced features such as algebraic mode, it can be harder to optimize them. Given all those caveats, tests have shown that Jython functions have a higher instantiation overhead. Once that is paid, they take about 1.2 times the amount of time as the equivalent Java functions. Due to the instantiation overhead, tests with few input lines (10,000 or so) took twice as long as their Java equivalents. These tests were run on simple functions that did almost no processing, so it is not a measure of Jython versus Java, but rather of Pig's overhead in working with Jython.

Writing Filter Functions

Filter functions are evaluation functions that return a Boolean value. Pig does not support Boolean as a full-fledged type, so filter functions cannot appear in statements such as `foreach` where the results are output to another operator. However, filter functions can be used in `filter` statements. Consider a "nearness" function that, given two zip

---

§ Code has been checked in that allows Pig to determine the dependency tree for your Python code, fetch all the needed modules, and ship them as part of the job. As of this writing, it has not yet been released. See PIG-1824 (*https://issues.apache.org/jira/browse/PIG-1824*) for details.

codes, returns true or false depending on whether those two zip codes are within a certain distance of each other:

```
/**
 * A filter UDF that determines whether two zip codes are within a given distance.
 */
public class CloseEnough extends FilterFunc {

    int distance;
    Random r = new Random();

    /*
     * @param miles - Distance in miles that two zip codes can be apart and
     * still be considered close enough.
     */
    public CloseEnough(String miles) {
        // UDFs can only take strings; convert to int here.
        distance = Integer.valueOf(miles);
    }

    public Boolean exec(Tuple input) throws IOException {
        // expect two strings
        String zip1 = (String)input.get(0);
        String zip2 = (String)input.get(1);
        // do some lookup on zip code tables
        return r.nextBoolean();
    }
}
```

## CHAPTER 11

Writing Load and Store Functions

We will now consider some of the more complex and most critical parts of Pig: data input and output. Operating on huge data sets is inherently I/O-intensive. Hadoop's massive parallelism and movement of processing to the data mitigates but does not remove this. Having efficient methods to load and store data is therefore critical. Pig provides default load and store functions for text data and for HBase, but many users find they need to write their own load and store functions to handle the data formats and storage mechanisms they use.

As with evaluation functions, the design goal for load and store functions was to make easy things easy and hard things possible. Also, we wanted to make load and store functions a thin wrapper over Hadoop's `InputFormat` and `OutputFormat`. The intention is that once you have an input format and output format for your data, the additional work of creating and storing Pig tuples is minimal. In the same way evaluation functions were implemented, more complex features such as schema management and projection push down are done via separate interfaces to avoid cluttering the base interface. Pig's load and store functions were completely rewritten between versions 0.6 and 0.7. This chapter will cover only the interfaces for 0.7 and later releases.

One other important design goal for load and store functions is to not assume that the input sources and output sinks are HDFS. In the examples throughout this book, `A = load 'foo';` has implied that `foo` is a file, but there is no need for that to be the case. `foo` is a resource locator that makes sense to your load function. It could be an HDFS file, an HBase table, a database JDBC connection string, or a web service URL. Because reading from HDFS is the most common case, many defaults and helper functions are provided for this case.

In this chapter we will walk through writing a load function and a store function for JSON data on HDFS, `JsonLoader` and `JsonStorage`, respectively. These are located in the example code in *udfs/java/com/acme/io*. They use the Jackson JSON library, which is included in your Pig distribution. However, the Jackson JAR is not shipped to the backend by Pig, so when using these UDFs in your script, you will need to register the Jackson JAR in addition to the acme examples JAR:

```
register 'acme.jar';
register 'src/pig/trunk/build/ivy/lib/Pig/jackson-core-asl-1.6.0.jar';
```

These UDFs will serve as helpful examples, but they will not cover all of the functionality of load and store functions. For those sections not shown in these examples, we will look at other existing load and store functions.

Load Functions

Pig's load function is built on top of a Hadoop `InputFormat`, the class that Hadoop uses to read data. `InputFormat` serves two purposes: it determines how input will be split between map tasks, and it provides a `RecordReader` that produces key-value pairs as input to those map tasks. The load function takes these key-value pairs and returns a Pig `Tuple`.

The base class for the load function is `LoadFunc`. This is an abstract class, which allows it to provide helper functions and default implementations. Many load functions will only need to extend `LoadFunc`.

Load functions' operations are split between Pig's frontend and backend. On the frontend, Pig does job planning and optimization, and load functions participate in this in several ways that we will discuss later. On the backend, load functions get each record from the `RecordReader`, convert it to a tuple, and pass it on to Pig's map task. Load functions also need to be able to pass data between the frontend and backend invocations so they can maintain state.

Frontend Planning Functions

For all load functions, Pig must do three things as part of frontend planning: 1) it needs to know the input format it should use to read the data; 2) it needs to be sure that the load function understands where its data is located; and 3) it needs to know how to cast bytearrays returned from the load function.

Determining InputFormat

Pig needs to know which `InputFormat` to use for reading your input. It calls `getInput Format` to get an instance of the input format. It gets an instance rather than the class itself so that your load function can control the instantiation: any generic parameters, constructor arguments, etc. For our example load function, this method is very simple. It uses `TextInputFormat`, an input format that reads text data from HDFS files:

```
// JsonLoader.java
public InputFormat getInputFormat() throws IOException {
    return new TextInputFormat();
}
```

Determining the location

Pig communicates the location string provided by the user to the load function via `setLocation`. So, if the load operator in Pig Latin is `A = load 'input';`, "input" is the location string. This method is called on both the frontend and backend, possibly multiple times. Thus you need to take care that this method does not do anything that will cause problems if done more than one time. Your load function should communicate the location to its input format. For example, `JsonLoader` passes the filename via a helper method on `FileInputFormat` (a superclass of `TextInputFormat`):

```
// JsonLoader.java
public void setLocation(String location, Job job) throws IOException {
    FileInputFormat.setInputPaths(job, location);
}
```

The Hadoop `Job` is passed along with the location because that is where input formats usually store their configuration information.

`setLocation` is called on both the frontend and backend because input formats store their location in the `Job` object, as shown in the preceding example. For MapReduce jobs, which always have only one input, this works. For Pig jobs, where the same input format might be used to load multiple different inputs (such as in the join or union case), one instance of the input path will overwrite another in the `Job` object. To work around this, Pig remembers the location in an input-specific parameter and calls `set Location` again on the backend so that the input format can get itself set up properly before reading.

For files on HDFS, the location provided by the user might be relative rather than absolute. To deal with this, Pig needs to resolve these to absolute locations based on the current working directory at the time of the load. Consider the following Pig Latin:

```
cd /user/joe;
input1 = load 'input';
cd /user/fred;
input2 = load 'input';
```

These two `load` statements should load different files. But Pig cannot assume it understands how to turn a relative path into an absolute path, because it does not know what that input is. It could be an HDFS path, a database table name, etc. So it leaves this to the load function. Before calling `setLocation`, Pig passes the location string to `relative ToAbsolutePath` to do any necessary conversion. Because most loaders are reading from HDFS, the default implementation in `LoadFunc` handles the HDFS case. If your loading will never need to do this conversion, it should override this method and return the location string passed to it.

Getting the casting functions

Some Pig functions, such as `PigStorage` and `HBaseStorage`, load data by default without understanding its type information, and place the data unchanged in `DataByteArray` objects. At a later time, when Pig needs to cast that data to another type, it does not know how to because it does not understand how the data is represented in the byte-array. Therefore, it relies on the load function to provide a method to cast from byte-array to the appropriate type.

Pig determines which set of casting functions to use by calling getLoadCaster on the load function. This should return either null, which indicates that your load function does not expect to do any bytearray casts, or an implementation of the LoadCaster interface, which will be used to do the casts. We will look at the methods of LoadCas ter in "Casting bytearrays" on page 156.

Our example loader returns null because it provides typed data based on the stored schema and, therefore, does not expect to be casting data. Any bytearrays in its data are binary data that should not be cast.

Passing Information from the Frontend to the Backend

As with evaluation functions, load functions can make use of UDFContext to pass in-formation from frontend invocations to backend invocations. For details on UDFCon text, see "UDFContext" on page 131. One significant difference between using UDF Context in evaluation and load functions is determining the instance-specific signature of the function. In evaluation functions, constructor arguments were suggested as a way to do this. For load functions, the input location usually will be the differentiating factor. However, LoadFunc does not guarantee that it will call setLocation before other methods where you might want to use UDFContext. To work around this, setUDFCon textSignature is provided. It provides an instance-unique signature that you can use when calling getUDFProperties. This method is guaranteed to be called before any other methods on LoadFunc in both the frontend and backend. Your UDF can then store this signature and use it when getting its property object:

```
// JsonLoader.java
private String udfcSignature = null;

public void setUDFContextSignature(String signature) {
    udfcSignature = signature;
}
```

setLocation is the only method in the load function that is guaranteed to be called on the frontend. It is therefore the best candidate for storing needed information to UDF Context. You might need to check that the data you are writing is available and nonnull to avoid overwriting your values when setLocation is called on the backend.

Backend Data Reading

On the backend, your load function takes the key-value pairs produced by its input format and produces Pig Tuples.

Getting ready to read

Before reading any data, Pig gives your load function a chance to set itself up by calling prepareToRead. This is called in each map task and passes a copy of the RecordReader, which your load function will need later to read records from the input. RecordReader is a class that InputFormat uses to read records from an input split. Pig obtains the record reader it passes to prepareToRead by calling getRecordReader on the input format that your store function returned from getInputFormat. Pig also passes an instance of the PigSplit that contains the Hadoop InputSplit corresponding to the partition of input this instance of your load function will read. If you need split-specific information, you can get it from here.

Our example loader, beyond storing the record reader, also reads the schema file that was stored into UDFContext in the frontend so that it knows how to parse the input file. Notice how it uses the signature passed in setUDFContextSignature to access the appropriate properties object. Finally, it creates a JsonFactory object that is used to generate a parser for each line:

```
// JsonLoader.java
public void prepareToRead(RecordReader reader, PigSplit split)
throws IOException {
    this.reader = reader;

    // Get the schema string from the UDFContext object.
    UDFContext udfc = UDFContext.getUDFContext();
    Properties p =
        udfc.getUDFProperties(this.getClass(), new String[]{udfcSignature});
    String strSchema = p.getProperty("pig.jsonloader.schema");
    if (strSchema == null) {
        throw new IOException("Could not find schema in UDF context");
    }

    // Parse the schema from the string stored in the properties object.
    ResourceSchema schema =
        new ResourceSchema(Utils.getSchemaFromString(strSchema));
    fields = schema.getFields();

    jsonFactory = new JsonFactory();
}
```

Reading records

Now we have reached the meat of your load function, reading records from its record reader and returning tuples to Pig. Pig will call getNext and place the resulting tuple into its processing pipeline. It will keep doing this until getNext returns a null, which indicates that the input for this split has been fully read.

Pig does not copy the tuple that results from this method, but instead feeds it directly to its pipeline to avoid the copy overhead. This means this method cannot reuse objects, and instead must create a new tuple and contents for each record it reads. On the other hand, record readers may choose to reuse their key and value objects from record to record; most standard implementations do. So, before writing a loader that tries to be efficient and wraps the keys and values from the record reader directly into the tuple to avoid a copy, you must make sure you understand how the record reader is managing its data.

For information on creating the appropriate Java objects when constructing tuples for Pig, see "Interacting with Pig values" on page 122.

Our sample load function's implementation of getNext reads the value from the Hadoop record (the key is ignored), constructs a JsonParser to parse it, parses the fields, and returns the resulting tuple. If there are parse errors, it does not throw an exception. Instead, it returns a tuple with null fields where the data could not be parsed. This prevents bad lines from causing the whole job to fail. Warnings are issued so that users can see which records were ignored:

```java
// JsonLoader.java
public Tuple getNext() throws IOException {
    Text val = null;
    try {
        // Read the next key-value pair from the record reader.  If it's
        // finished, return null.
        if (!reader.nextKeyValue()) return null;

        // Get the current value.  We don't use the key.
        val = (Text)reader.getCurrentValue();
    } catch (InterruptedException ie) {
        throw new IOException(ie);
    }
    // Create a parser specific for this input line.  This might not be the
    // most efficient approach.
    ByteArrayInputStream bais = new ByteArrayInputStream(val.getBytes());
    JsonParser p = jsonFactory.createJsonParser(bais);

    // Create the tuple we will be returning.  We create it with the right
    // number of fields, as the Tuple object is optimized for this case.
    Tuple t = tupleFactory.newTuple(fields.length);

    // Read the start object marker.  Throughout this file if the parsing
    // isn't what we expect, we return a tuple with null fields rather than
    // throwing an exception.  That way a few mangled lines don't fail the job.
    if (p.nextToken() != JsonToken.START_OBJECT) {
        log.warn("Bad record, could not find start of record " + val.toString());
        return t;
    }

    // Read each field in the record.
    for (int i = 0; i < fields.length; i++) {
        t.set(i, readField(p, fields[i], i));
    }

    if (p.nextToken() != JsonToken.END_OBJECT) {
        log.warn("Bad record, could not find end of record " +
            val.toString());
```

```
            return t;
        }
    p.close();
    return t;
}

private Object readField(JsonParser p,
                         ResourceFieldSchema field,
                         int fieldnum) throws IOException {
    // Read the next token.
    JsonToken tok = p.nextToken();
    if (tok == null) {
        log.warn("Early termination of record, expected " + fields.length
            + " fields bug found " + fieldnum);
        return null;
    }

    // Check to see if this value was null.
    if (tok == JsonToken.VALUE_NULL) return null;

    // Read based on our expected type.
    switch (field.getType()) {
    case DataType.INTEGER:
        // Read the field name.
        p.nextToken();
        return p.getValueAsInt();

    case DataType.LONG:
        p.nextToken();
        return p.getValueAsLong();

    case DataType.FLOAT:
        p.nextToken();
        return (float)p.getValueAsDouble();

    case DataType.DOUBLE:
        p.nextToken();
        return p.getValueAsDouble();

    case DataType.BYTEARRAY:
        p.nextToken();
        byte[] b = p.getBinaryValue();
        // Use the DBA constructor that copies the bytes so that we own
        // the memory.
        return new DataByteArray(b, 0, b.length);

    case DataType.CHARARRAY:
        p.nextToken();
        return p.getText();

    case DataType.MAP:
        // Should be a start of the map object.
        if (p.nextToken() != JsonToken.START_OBJECT) {
            log.warn("Bad map field, could not find start of object, field "
                + fieldnum);
```

```java
            return null;
        }
        Map<String, String> m = new HashMap<String, String>();
        while (p.nextToken() != JsonToken.END_OBJECT) {
            String k = p.getCurrentName();
            String v = p.getText();
            m.put(k, v);
        }
        return m;

    case DataType.TUPLE:
        if (p.nextToken() != JsonToken.START_OBJECT) {
            log.warn("Bad tuple field, could not find start of object, "
                + "field " + fieldnum);
            return null;
        }

        ResourceSchema s = field.getSchema();
        ResourceFieldSchema[] fs = s.getFields();
        Tuple t = tupleFactory.newTuple(fs.length);

        for (int j = 0; j < fs.length; j++) {
            t.set(j, readField(p, fs[j], j));
        }

        if (p.nextToken() != JsonToken.END_OBJECT) {
            log.warn("Bad tuple field, could not find end of object, "
                + "field " + fieldnum);
            return null;
        }
        return t;

    case DataType.BAG:
        if (p.nextToken() != JsonToken.START_ARRAY) {
            log.warn("Bad bag field, could not find start of array, "
                + "field " + fieldnum);
            return null;
        }

        s = field.getSchema();
        fs = s.getFields();
        // Drill down the next level to the tuple's schema.
        s = fs[0].getSchema();
        fs = s.getFields();

        DataBag bag = bagFactory.newDefaultBag();

        JsonToken innerTok;
        while ((innerTok = p.nextToken()) != JsonToken.END_ARRAY) {
            if (innerTok != JsonToken.START_OBJECT) {
                log.warn("Bad bag tuple field, could not find start of "
                    + "object, field " + fieldnum);
                return null;
            }
```

```
                t = tupleFactory.newTuple(fs.length);
                for (int j = 0; j < fs.length; j++) {
                    t.set(j, readField(p, fs[j], j));
                }

                if (p.nextToken() != JsonToken.END_OBJECT) {
                    log.warn("Bad bag tuple field, could not find end of "
                        + "object, field " + fieldnum);
                    return null;
                }
                bag.add(t);
            }
            return bag;

        default:
            throw new IOException("Unknown type in input schema: " +
                field.getType());
        }

    }
```

Additional Load Function Interfaces

Your load function can provide more complex features by implementing additional
interfaces. (Implementation of these interfaces is optional.)

Loading metadata

Many data storage mechanisms can record the schema along with the data. Pig does
not assume the ability to store schemas, but if your storage can hold the schema, it can
be very useful. This frees script writers from needing to specify the field names and
types as part of the load operator in Pig Latin. This is user-friendly and less error-prone,
and avoids the need to rewrite scripts when the schema of your data changes.

Some types of data storage also partition the data. If Pig understands this partitioning,
it can load only those partitions that are needed for a particular script. Both of these
functions are enabled by implementing the LoadMetadata interface.

getSchema in the LoadMetadata interface gives your load function a chance to provide a
schema. It is passed the location string the user provides as well as the Hadoop Job
object, in case it needs information in this object to open the schema. It is expected to
return a ResourceSchema, which represents the data that will be returned. Resource
Schema is very similar to the Schema class used by evaluation functions. (See "Input and
Output Schemas" on page 124 for details.) There is one important difference, however.
In ResourceFieldSchema, the schema object associated with a bag always has one field,
which is a tuple. The schema for the tuples in the bag is described by that tuple's
ResourceFieldSchema.

Our example load and store functions keep the schema in a side file* named _schema in HDFS. Our implementation of getSchema reads this file and also serializes the schema into UDFContext so that it is available on the backend:

```
// JsonLoader.java
public ResourceSchema getSchema(String location, Job job)
throws IOException {
    // Open the schema file and read the schema.
    // Get an HDFS handle.
    FileSystem fs = FileSystem.get(job.getConfiguration());
    DataInputStream in = fs.open(new Path(location + "/_schema"));
    String line = in.readLine();
    in.close();

    // Parse the schema.
    ResourceSchema s = new ResourceSchema(Utils.getSchemaFromString(line));
    if (s == null) {
        throw new IOException("Unable to parse schema found in file " +
            location + "/_schema");
    }

    // Now that we have determined the schema, store it in our
    // UDFContext properties object so we have it when we need it on the
    // backend.
    UDFContext udfc = UDFContext.getUDFContext();
    Properties p =
        udfc.getUDFProperties(this.getClass(), new String[]{udfcSignature});
    p.setProperty("pig.jsonloader.schema", line);

    return s;
}
```

Once your loader implements getSchema, load statements that use your loader do not need to declare their schemas in order for the field names to be used in the script. For example, if we had data with a schema of user:chararray, age:int, gpa:double, the following Pig Latin will compile and run:

```
register 'acme.jar';
register 'src/pig/trunk/build/ivy/lib/Pig/jackson-core-asl-1.6.0.jar';

A = load 'input' using com.acme.io.JsonLoader();
B = foreach A generate user;
dump B;
```

LoadMetadata also includes a getStatistics method. Pig does not yet make use of statistics in job planning; this method is for future use.

---

* A file in the same directory that is not a part file. Side files start with an underscore character. MapReduce's FileInputFormat knows to ignore them when reading input for a job.

Using partitions

Some types of storage partition their data, allowing you to read only the relevant sections for a given job. The `LoadMetadata` interface also provides methods for working with partitions in your data. In order for Pig to request the relevant partitions, it must know how the data is partitioned. Pig determines this by calling `getPartitionKeys`. If this returns a `null` or the `LoadMetadata` interface is not implemented by your loader, Pig will assume it needs to read the entire input.

Pig expects `getPartitionKeys` to return an array of strings, where each string represents one field name. Those fields are the keys used to partition the data. Pig will look for a `filter` statement immediately following the `load` statement that includes one or more of these fields. If such a statement is found, it will be passed to `setPartitionFilter`. If the `filter` includes both partition and nonpartition keys and it can be split,[†] Pig will split it and pass just the partition-key-related expression to `setPartitionFilter`. As an example, consider an HCatalog[‡] table *web_server_logs* that is partitioned by two fields, date and colo:

```
logs    = load 'web_server_logs' using HCatLoader();
cleaned = filter logs by date = '20110614' and NotABot(user_id);
...
```

Pig will call `getPartitionKeys`, and `HCatLoader` will return two key names, `date` and `colo`. Pig will find the `date` field in the `filter` statement and rewrite the filter as shown in the following example, pushing down the `date = '20110614'` predicate to `HCatLoader` via `setPartitionFilter`:

```
logs    = load 'web_server_logs' using HCatLoader();
cleaned = filter logs by NotABot(user_id);
...
```

It is now up to HCatalog loader to assure that it only returns data from *web_server_logs* where `date` is `20110614`.

The one exception to this is fields used in eval funcs or filter funcs. Pig assumes that loaders do not understand how to invoke UDFs, so Pig will not push these expressions.

Our example loader works on file data, so it does not implement `getPartitionKeys` or `setPartitionFilter`. For an example implementation of these methods, see the HCatalog code at *http://svn.apache.org/viewvc/incubator/hcatalog/trunk/src/java/org/apache/hcatalog/pig/HCatLoader.java?view=markup*.

---

† Meaning that the filter can be broken into two filters—one that contains the partition keys and one that does not—and produce the same end result. This is possible when the expressions are connected by **and** but not when they are connected by **or**.

‡ HCatalog is a table-management service for Hadoop. It includes Pig load and store functions. See "Metadata in Hadoop" on page 169 for more information on HCatalog.

Casting bytearrays

If you need to control how binary data that your loader loads is cast to other data types, you can implement the `LoadCaster` interface. Because this interface contains a lot of methods, implementers often implement it as a separate class. This also allows load functions to share implementations of `LoadCaster`, since Java does not support multiple inheritance.

The interface consists of a series of methods: `bytesToInteger`, `bytesToLong`, etc. These will be called to convert a bytearray to the appropriate type. Starting in 0.9, there are two `bytesToMap` methods. You should implement the one that takes a `ResourceField Schema`; the other one is for backward-compatibility. The `bytesToBag`, `bytesToTuple`, and `bytesToMap` methods take a `ResourceFieldSchema` that describes the field being converted. Calling `getSchema` on this object will return a schema that describes this bag, tuple, or map, if one exists. If Pig does not know the intended structure of the object, `get Schema` will return null. Keep in mind that the schema of the bag will be one field, a tuple, which in turn will have a schema describing the contents of that tuple.

A default load caster, `Utf8StorageConverter`, is provided. It handles converting UTF8-encoded text to Pig types. Scalar conversions are done in a straightforward way. Maps are expected to be surrounded by [] (square brackets), with keys separated by values with # (hash) and key-value pairs separated by , (commas). Tuples are surrounded by () (parentheses) and have fields separated by , (commas). Bags are surrounded by {} (braces) and have tuples separated by , (commas). There is no ability to escape these special characters.

Pushing down projections

Often a Pig Latin script will need to read only a few fields in the input. Some types of storage formats store their data by fields instead of by records (for example, Hive's *RCFile*). For these types of formats, there is a significant performance gain to be had by loading only those fields that will be used in the script. Even for record-oriented storage formats, it can be useful to skip deserializing fields that will not be used.

As part of its optimizations, Pig analyzes Pig Latin scripts and determines what fields in an input it needs at each step in the script. It uses this information to aggressively drop fields it no longer needs. If the loader implements the `LoadPushDown` interface, Pig can go a step further and provide this information to the loader.

Once Pig knows the fields it needs, it assembles them in a `RequiredFieldList` and passes that to `pushProjection`. In the load function's reply, it indicates whether it can meet the request. It responds with a `RequiredFieldResponse`, which is a fancy wrapper around a Boolean. If the Boolean is true, Pig will assume that only the required fields are being returned from `getNext`. If it is false, Pig will assume that all fields are being returned by `getNext`, and it will handle dropping the extra ones itself.

The RequiredField class used to describe which fields are required is slightly complex. Beyond allowing a user to specify whether a given field is required, it provides the ability to specify which subfields of that field are required. For example, for maps, certain keys can be listed as required. For tuples and bags, certain fields can be listed as required.

Load functions that implement LoadPushDown should not modify the schema object returned by getSchema. This should always be the schema of the full input. Pig will manage the translation between the schema having all of the fields and the results of getNext having only some.

Our example loader does not implement LoadPushDown. For an example of a loader that does, see HCatLoader at *http://svn.apache.org/viewvc/incubator/hcatalog/trunk/src/java/ org/apache/hcatalog/pig/HCatLoader.java?view=markup*.

Store Functions

Pig's store function is, in many ways, a mirror image of the load function. It is built on top of Hadoop's OutputFormat. It takes Pig Tuples and creates key-value pairs that its associated output format writes to storage.

StoreFunc is an abstract class, which allows it to provide default implementations for some methods. However, some functions implement both load and store functionality; PigStorage is one example. Because Java does not support multiple inheritance, the interface StoreFuncInterface is provided. These dual load/store functions can implement this interface rather than extending StoreFunc.

Store function operations are split between the frontend and backend of Pig. Pig does planning and optimization on the frontend. Store functions have an opportunity at this time to check that a valid schema is being used and set up the storage location. On the backend, store functions take a tuple from Pig, convert it to a key-value pair, and pass it to a Hadoop RecordWriter. Store functions can pass information from frontend invocations to backend invocations via UDFContext.

Store Function Frontend Planning

Store functions have three tasks to fulfill on the frontend:

- Instantiate the OutputFormat they will use to store data.
- Check the schema of the data being stored.
- Record the location where the data will be stored.

Determining OutputFormat

Pig calls getOutputFormat to get an instance of the output format that your store function will use to store records. This method returns an instance rather than the classname or the class itself. This allows your store function to control how the class is instantiated.

The example store function `JsonStorage` uses `TextOutputFormat`. This is an output format that stores text data in HDFS. We have to instantiate this with a key of `LongWritable` and a value of `Text` to match the expectations of `TextInputFormat`:

```
// JsonStorage.java
public OutputFormat getOutputFormat() throws IOException {
    return new TextOutputFormat<LongWritable, Text>();
}
```

Setting the output location

Pig calls `setStoreLocation` to communicate the location string the user provides to your store function. Given the Pig Latin `store Z into 'output';`, "output" is the location string. This method, called on both the frontend and the backend, could be called multiple times; consequently, it should not have any side effects that will cause a problem if this happens. Your store function will need to communicate the location to its output format. Our example store function uses the `FileOutputFormat` utility function `setOutputPath` to do this:

```
// JsonStorage.java
public void setStoreLocation(String location, Job job) throws IOException {
    FileOutputFormat.setOutputPath(job, new Path(location));
}
```

The Hadoop `Job` is passed to this function as well. Most output formats store the location information in the job.

Pig calls `setStoreLocation` on both the frontend and backend because output formats usually store their location in the job, as we see in our example store function. This works for MapReduce jobs, where a single output format is guaranteed. But due to the `split` operator, Pig can have more than one instance of the same store function in a job. If multiple instances of a store function call `FileOutputFormat.setOutputPath`, whichever instance calls it last will overwrite the others. Pig avoids this by keeping output-specific information and calling `setStoreLocation` again on the backend so that it can properly configure the output format.

For HDFS files, the user might provide a relative path. Pig needs to resolve these to absolute paths using the current working directory at the time the store is called. To accomplish this, Pig calls `relToAbsPathForStoreLocation` with the user-provided location string before calling `setStoreLocation`. This method translates between relative and absolute paths. For store functions writing to HDFS, the default implementation in `StoreFunc` handles the conversion. If you are writing a store function that does not use file paths (e.g., HBase), you should override this method to return the string it is passed.

Checking the schema

As part of frontend planning, Pig gives your store function a chance to check the schema of the data to be stored. If you are storing data to a system that expects a certain schema for the output (such as an RDBMS) or you cannot store certain data types, this is the place to perform those checks. Oddly enough, this method returns a void rather than a Boolean. So if you detect an issue with the schema, you must throw an IOException.

Our example store function does not have limitations on the schemas it can store. However, it uses this function as a place to serialize the schema into UDFContext so that it can be used on the backend when writing data:

```
// JsonStorage.java

public void checkSchema(ResourceSchema s) throws IOException {
    UDFContext udfc = UDFContext.getUDFContext();
    Properties p =
        udfc.getUDFProperties(this.getClass(), new String[]{udfcSignature});
    p.setProperty("pig.jsonstorage.schema", s.toString());
}
```

Store Functions and UDFContext

Store functions work with UDFContext exactly as load functions do, but with one exception: the signature for store functions is passed to the store function via setStoreFuncUDFContextSignature. See "Passing Information from the Frontend to the Backend" on page 148 for a discussion of how load functions work with UDFContext. Our example store function stores the signature in a member variable for later use:

```
// JsonStorage.java
public void setStoreFuncUDFContextSignature(String signature) {
    udfcSignature = signature;
}
```

Writing Data

During backend processing, the store function is first initialized, and then takes Pig tuples and converts them to key-value pairs to be written to storage.

Preparing to write

Pig calls your store function's prepareToWrite method in each map or reduce task before writing any data. This call passes a RecordWriter instance to use when writing data. RecordWriter is a class that OutputFormat uses to write individual records. Pig will get the record writer it passes to your store function by calling getRecordWriter on the output format your store function returned from getOutputFormat. Your store function will need to keep this reference so that it can be used in putNext.

The example store function JsonStorage also uses this method to read the schema out of the UDFContext. It will use this schema when storing data. Finally, it creates a Json Factory for use in putNext:

```
// JsonStorage.java
public void prepareToWrite(RecordWriter writer) throws IOException {
```

```
// Store the record writer reference so we can use it when it's time
// to write tuples.
this.writer = writer;

// Get the schema string from the UDFContext object.
UDFContext udfc = UDFContext.getUDFContext();
Properties p =
    udfc.getUDFProperties(this.getClass(), new String[]{udfcSignature});
String strSchema = p.getProperty("pig.jsonstorage.schema");
if (strSchema == null) {
    throw new IOException("Could not find schema in UDF context");
}

// Parse the schema from the string stored in the properties object.
ResourceSchema schema =
    new ResourceSchema(Utils.getSchemaFromString(strSchema));
fields = schema.getFields();

// Build a Json factory.
jsonFactory = new JsonFactory();
jsonFactory.configure(
    JsonGenerator.Feature.WRITE_NUMBERS_AS_STRINGS, false);
}
```

Writing records

putNext is the core method in the store function class. Pig calls this method for every
tuple it needs to store. Your store function needs to take these tuples and produce the
key-value pairs that its output format expects. For information on the Java objects in
which the data will be stored and how to extract them, see "Interacting with Pig values" on page 122.

JsonStorage encodes the contents of the tuple in JSON format and writes the resulting
string into the value field of TextOutputFormat. The key field is left null:

```
// JsonStorage.java
public void putNext(Tuple t) throws IOException {
    // Build a ByteArrayOutputStream to write the JSON into.
    ByteArrayOutputStream baos = new ByteArrayOutputStream(BUF_SIZE);
    // Build the generator.
    JsonGenerator json =
        jsonFactory.createJsonGenerator(baos, JsonEncoding.UTF8);

    // Write the beginning of the top-level tuple object.
    json.writeStartObject();
    for (int i = 0; i < fields.length; i++) {
        writeField(json, fields[i], t.get(i));
    }
    json.writeEndObject();
    json.close();

    // Hand a null key and our string to Hadoop.
    try {
        writer.write(null, new Text(baos.toByteArray()));
```

```
        } catch (InterruptedException ie) {
            throw new IOException(ie);
        }
}

private void writeField(JsonGenerator json,
                        ResourceFieldSchema field,
                        Object d) throws IOException {

    // If the field is missing or the value is null, write a null.
    if (d == null) {
        json.writeNullField(field.getName());
        return;
    }

    // Based on the field's type, write it out.
    switch (field.getType()) {
    case DataType.INTEGER:
        json.writeNumberField(field.getName(), (Integer)d);
        return;

    case DataType.LONG:
        json.writeNumberField(field.getName(), (Long)d);
        return;

    case DataType.FLOAT:
        json.writeNumberField(field.getName(), (Float)d);
        return;

    case DataType.DOUBLE:
        json.writeNumberField(field.getName(), (Double)d);
        return;

    case DataType.BYTEARRAY:
        json.writeBinaryField(field.getName(), ((DataByteArray)d).get());
        return;

    case DataType.CHARARRAY:
        json.writeStringField(field.getName(), (String)d);
        return;

    case DataType.MAP:
        json.writeFieldName(field.getName());
        json.writeStartObject();
        for (Map.Entry<String, Object> e : ((Map<String, Object>)d).entrySet()) {
            json.writeStringField(e.getKey(), e.getValue().toString());
        }
        json.writeEndObject();
        return;

    case DataType.TUPLE:
        json.writeFieldName(field.getName());
        json.writeStartObject();

        ResourceSchema s = field.getSchema();
```

```
        if (s == null) {
            throw new IOException("Schemas must be fully specified to use "
                + "this storage function.  No schema found for field " +
                field.getName());
        }
        ResourceFieldSchema[] fs = s.getFields();

        for (int j = 0; j < fs.length; j++) {
            writeField(json, fs[j], ((Tuple)d).get(j));
        }
        json.writeEndObject();
        return;

    case DataType.BAG:
        json.writeFieldName(field.getName());
        json.writeStartArray();
        s = field.getSchema();
        if (s == null) {
            throw new IOException("Schemas must be fully specified to use "
                + "this storage function.  No schema found for field " +
                field.getName());
        }
        fs = s.getFields();
        if (fs.length != 1 || fs[0].getType() != DataType.TUPLE) {
            throw new IOException("Found a bag without a tuple "
                + "inside!");
        }
        // Drill down the next level to the tuple's schema.
        s = fs[0].getSchema();
        if (s == null) {
            throw new IOException("Schemas must be fully specified to use "
                + "this storage function.  No schema found for field " +
                field.getName());
        }
        fs = s.getFields();
        for (Tuple t : (DataBag)d) {
            json.writeStartObject();
            for (int j = 0; j < fs.length; j++) {
                writeField(json, fs[j], t.get(j));
            }
            json.writeEndObject();
        }
        json.writeEndArray();
        return;
    }
}
```

Failure Cleanup

When jobs fail after execution has started, your store function may need to clean up partially stored results. Pig will call cleanupOnFailure to give your store function an opportunity to do this. It passes the location string and the job object so that your store function knows what it should clean up. In the HDFS case, the default implementation handles removing any output files created by the store function. You need to implement this method only if you are storing data somewhere other than HDFS.

Storing Metadata

If your storage format can store schemas in addition to data, your store function can implement the interface StoreMetadata. This provides a storeSchema method that is called by Pig as part of its frontend operations. Pig passes storeSchema a Resource Schema, the location string, and the job object so that it can connect to its storage. The ResourceSchema is very similar to the Schema class described in "Input and Output Schemas" on page 124. There is one important difference, however. In ResourceField Schema, the schema object associated with a bag always has one field, which is a tuple. The schema for the tuples in the bag is described by that tuple's ResourceFieldSchema.

The example store function JsonStorage stores the schema in a side file named _schema_ in the same directory as the data. The schema is stored as a string, using the toString method provided by the class:

```
// JsonStorage.java
public void storeSchema(ResourceSchema schema, String location, Job job)
throws IOException {
    // Store the schema in a side file in the same directory.  MapReduce
    // does not include files starting with "_" when reading data for a job.
    FileSystem fs = FileSystem.get(job.getConfiguration());
    DataOutputStream out = fs.create(new Path(location + "/_schema"));
    out.writeBytes(schema.toString());
    out.writeByte('\n');
    out.close();
}
```

StoreMetadata also has a storeStatistics function, but Pig does not use this yet.

## CHAPTER 12

Pig and Other Members of the Hadoop Community

The community of applications that run on Hadoop has grown significantly as the adoption of Hadoop has increased. Many (but not all) of these applications are Apache projects. Some are quite similar in functionality. It can be confusing, especially for those new to Hadoop, to understand how these different applications integrate, complement, and overlap. In this chapter we will look at the different projects from a Pig perspective, focusing on how they complement, integrate, or compete with Pig.

Pig and Hive

Apache *Hive* (*http://hive.apache.org*) provides a SQL layer on top of Hadoop. It takes SQL queries and translates them to MapReduce jobs, much in the same way that Pig translates Pig Latin. It stores data in tables and keeps metadata concerning those tables, such as partitions and schemas. Many view Pig and Hive as competitors. Since both provide a way for users to operate on data stored in Hadoop without writing Java code, this is a natural conclusion. However, as was discussed in "Comparing query and dataflow languages" on page 4, SQL and Pig Latin have different strengths and weaknesses. Because Hive provides SQL, it is a better tool for doing traditional data analytics. Most data analysts are already familiar with SQL, and business intelligence tools expect to speak to data sources in SQL. Pig Latin is a better choice when building a data pipeline or doing research on raw data.

Cascading

Another data-processing framework available for Hadoop is *Cascading*, available at *http://www.cascading.org*. The goal of Cascading is similar to Pig in that it enables users to build data flows on Hadoop. However, its approach differs significantly. Rather than presenting a new language, Cascading data flows are written in Java. A library of operators is provided so that users can string together data operators as well as implement their own. This allows users more control but requires more low-level coding.

NoSQL Databases

Over the last few years a number of *NoSQL* databases have arisen. These databases break one or more of the traditional rules of relational database systems. They do not expect data to be normalized. Instead, the data accessed by a single application lives in one large table so that few or no joins are necessary. Many of these databases do not implement full ACID semantics.[*]

Like MapReduce, these systems are built to manage terabytes of data. Unlike MapReduce, they are focused on random reads and writes of data. Where MapReduce and technologies built on top of it (such as Pig) are optimized for reading vast quantities of data very quickly, these NoSQL systems optimize for finding a few records very quickly. This different focus does not mean that Pig does not work with these systems. Users often want to analyze the data stored in these systems. Also, because these systems offer good random lookup, certain types of joins could benefit from having the data stored in these systems.

Two NoSQL databases have been integrated with Pig: HBase and Cassandra.

HBase

Apache *HBase* is a NoSQL database that uses HDFS to store its data. HBase presents its data to users in tables. Within each table, every row has a key. Reads in HBase are done by a key, a range of keys, or a bulk scan. Users can also update or insert individual rows by keys. In addition to a key, rows in HBase have column families, and all rows in a table share the same column families. Within each column family there are columns. There is no constraint that each row have the same columns as any other row in a given column family. Thus an HBase table T might have one column family F, which every row in that table would share, but a row with key x could have columns a, b, c in F, while another row with key y has columns a, b, d in F. Column values also have a version number. HBase keeps a configurable number of versions, so users can access the most recent version or previous versions of a column value. All keys and column values in HBase are arrays of bytes.

Pig provides `HBaseStorage` to read data from and write data to HBase tables. All these reads and writes are bulk operations. Bulk reads from HBase are slower than scans in HDFS. However, if the data is already in HBase, it is faster to read it directly than it is to extract it, place it in HDFS, and then read it.

---

[*] Atomicity, Consistency, Isolation, and Durability. See *http://en.wikipedia.org/wiki/ACID* for a discussion of these properties in relational databases.

When loading from HBase, you must tell Pig what table to read from and what column families and columns to read. You can read individual columns or, beginning in version 0.9, whole column families. Because column families contain a variable set of columns and their values, they must be cast to Pig's map type. As an example, let's say we have an HBase table users that stores information on users and their links to other users. It has two column families: user_info and links. The key for the table is the user ID. The user_info column family has columns such as name, email, etc. The links column family has a column for each user that the user is linked to. The column name is the linked user's ID, and the value of these columns is the type of the link—friend, relation, colleague, etc.:

```
user_links = load 'hbase://users'
             using org.apache.pig.backend.hadoop.hbase.HBaseStorage(
             'user_info:name, links:*', '-loadKey true -gt 10000')
             as (id, name:chararray, links:map[]);
```

The load location string is the HBase table name. The appropriate HBase client configuration must be present on your machine to allow the HBase client to determine how to connect to the HBase server. Two arguments are passed as constructor arguments to HBaseStorage. The first tells it which column families and columns to read, and the second passes a set of options.

In HBase, columns are referenced as *column_family:column*. In the preceding example, user_info:name indicates the column name in the column family user_info. When you want to extract a whole column family, you give the column family and an asterisk, for example, links:*. You can also get a subset of the columns in a column family. For example, links:100* would result in a map having all columns that start with "100". The map that contains a column family has the HBase column names as keys and the column values as values.

The options string allows you to configure HBaseStorage. This can be used to control whether the key is loaded, which rows are loaded, and other features. All of these options are placed in one string, separated by spaces. Table 12-1 describes each of these options.

Table 12-1. HBaseStorage options

Option	Valid values	Default	Description
loadKey	Boolean	false	If true, the key will be loaded as the first column in the input.
gt	Row key	None	Only loads rows with a key greater than the provided value.
gte	Row key	None	Only loads rows with a key greater than or equal to the provided value.
lt	Row key	None	Only loads rows with a key less than the provided value.
lte	Row key	None	Only loads rows with a key less than or equal to the provided value.
caching	Integer	100	The number of rows the scanners should cache.
limit	Integer	None	Read at most this many rows from each HBase region.

Option	Valid values	Default	Description
caster	Java classname	Utf8Storage Converter	The Java class to use to do casting between Pig types and the bytes that HBase stores. This class must implement Pig's LoadCaster and StoreCaster interfaces. The default Utf8StorageConverter can be used when the data stored in HBase is in UTF8 format and the numbers are stored as strings (rather than in binary). HBaseBinary Converter uses Java's Byte.toInt, Byte.toString, etc., methods. It is not possible to cast to maps using this converter, so you cannot read entire column families.

As of the time of this writing, Pig is able to read only the latest version of a column value. There have been discussions about what the best interface and data type mapping would be to enable Pig to read multiple versions. This feature will most likely be added at some point in the future.

HBaseStorage stores data into HBase as well. When storing data, you specify the table name as the location string, just as in load. The constructor arguments are also similar to the load case. The first describes the mapping of Pig fields to the HBase table, which uses the same *column_family:column* syntax as in load. Any Pig value can be mapped to a column. A Pig map can be mapped to a column family by saying *column_fam ily:** (again, only in 0.9 and later). The row key is not referenced in this argument, but it is assumed to be the first field in the Pig tuple. The only valid option in the optional second argument in the store case is -caster.

Assume at the end of processing that our Pig data has a schema of id: long, name:char array, email:chararray, links:map. Storing into our example HBase table we used earlier looks like this:

```
// Schema of user_links is (id, name, email, links).
// Notice how the id (key) field is omitted in the argument.
store user_links into 'hbase://users'
    using org.apache.pig.backend.hadoop.hbase.HBaseStorage(
    'user_info:name, user_info:email, links:*');
```

Cassandra

Apache *Cassandra* is another scalable database used for high-volume random reading and writing of data. It differs from HBase in its approach to distribution. Whereas HBase guarantees consistency between its servers, Cassandra has an eventual consistency model, meaning that servers might have different values for the same data for some period of time. For more information about Cassandra, see *Cassandra: The Definitive Guide*, by Eben Hewitt (O'Reilly).

Cassandra comes with support for Pig, which means that you can load data from and store data to Cassandra column families. This works just as it does with any other storage mechanism that is used with Pig, such as HDFS. This includes data locality for input splits.

Pig and Cassandra can be used together in a number of ways. Pig can be used to do traditional analytics while Cassandra performs real-time operations. Because Pig and MapReduce can be run on top of Cassandra, this can be done without moving data between Cassandra and HDFS. HDFS is still required for storing intermediate results; however, Pig can be used to do data exploration, research, testing, validation, and correction over Cassandra data as well. It can be used to populate the data store with new data as new tables or column families are added.

The Pygmalion project (*https://github.com/jeromatron/pygmalion*) was written to ease development when using Pig with data stored in Cassandra. It includes helpful UDFs to extract column values from the results, marshal the data back to a form that Cassandra accepts, and others.

In order to properly integrate Pig workloads with data stored in Cassandra, the Cassandra cluster needs to colocate the data with Hadoop task trackers. This allows the Hadoop job tracker to move the data processing to the nodes where the data resides. Traditionally, Cassandra is used for heavy writes and real-time, random-access queries. Heavy Hadoop analytic workloads can be performed on Cassandra without degrading the performance of real-time queries by splitting the cluster by workload type. A set of nodes is dedicated to handling analytic batch processing and another set is dedicated to handling real-time queries. Cassandra's cross-datacenter replication copies data transparently between these sections of the cluster so that manual copying of data is never required, and the analytic section always has updated data.

Metadata in Hadoop

Apache *HCatalog* provides a metadata and table management layer for Hadoop. It allows Hadoop users—whether they use MapReduce, Pig, Hive, or other tools—to view their data in HDFS as if it were in tables. These tables are partitioned and have consistent schemas. As a consequence of this abstraction, Pig users do not need to be concerned with where a file is located, which load and store function should be used, and whether the file is compressed. It also makes it much easier for Pig, MapReduce, and Hive users to share data because HCatalog provides a single schema and data type model for all of these tools. That data type model, taken from Hive, varies slightly from Pig's, but the load and store functions take care of mapping between the models. HCatalog uses Hive's metastore to store metadata. For full details of HCatalog, see *http://incubator.apache.org/hcatalog*.

HCatalog includes the load function `HCatLoader`. The location string for `HCatLoader` is the name of the table. It implements `LoadMetadata`, so you do not need to specify the schema as part of your `load` statement; Pig will get it from `HCatLoader`. Also, because it implements this interface, Pig can work with HCatalog's partitioning. If you place the `filter` statement that describes which partitions you want to read immediately after the load, Pig will push that into the load so that HCatalog returns only the relevant partitions.

HCatStorer is the store function for HCatalog. As with the load function, the location string indicates the table to store records to. The store function also requires a constructor argument to indicate the partition key values for this store. At this time (version 0.1) only one partition can be written to in a single store. There are plans to allow writing to multiple partitions in version 0.2. HCatStorer expects the schema of the alias being stored to match the schema of the table that records are being stored to.

As an example, let's consider a very simple data pipeline that reads in raw web logs from a table web_server_logs, does some processing, and stores them back into HCatalog in a table named processed_logs. web_server_log's schema is (userid:chararray, date:chararray, time:chararray, url:chararray), and processed_log's schema is (userid:chararray, user_ref:int, date:chararray, time:chararray, pageid:int, url:chararray). A Pig Latin script to do this processing would look like the following:

```
logs    = load 'web_server_logs' using HCatalogLoader();
-- use parameter substitution so script doesn't have to be rewritten every day
-- filter will be split and date portion pushed to the loader
today   = filter logs by date = '$DATE' and NotABot(user_id);
...
-- schema of output must exactly match HCatalog schema
-- of processed_logs, including field names
output = foreach rslvd generate userid, user_ref, date, time, pageid, url;
store output into 'processed_logs' using HCatStorer('date=$DATE');
```

Built-in User Defined Functions and Piggybank

This appendix covers UDFs that come as part of the Pig distribution, including built-in UDFs and user-contributed UDFs in Piggybank.

Built-in UDFs

Pig comes prepackaged with many UDFs that can be used directly in Pig without using `register` or `define`. These include load, store, evaluation, and filter functions.

Built-in Load and Store Functions

Pig's built-in load functions are listed in Table A-1; Table A-2 lists the store functions.

Table A-1. Load functions

Function	Location String indicates	Constructor arguments	Description
HBaseStorage	HBase table	The first argument is a string describing column family and column to Pig field mapping. The second is an option string (optional).	Load data from HBase (see "HBase" on page 166).
PigStorage	HDFS file	The first argument is a field separator (optional; defaults to Tab).	Load text data from HDFS (see "Load" on page 34).
TextLoader	HDFS file	None.	Reads lines of text, each line as a tuple with one chararray field.

Table A-2. Store functions

Function	Location String indicates	Constructor arguments	Description
HBaseStorage	HBase table	The first argument is a string describing Pig field to HBase column family and column mapping.	Store data to HBase (see "HBase" on page 166).
		The second is an option string (optional).	
PigStorage	HDFS file	The first argument is a field separator (optional; defaults to Tab).	Store text to HDFS in text format (see "Store" on page 36).

Built-in Evaluation and Filter Functions

The evaluation functions can be divided into math functions that mimic many of the Java math functions; aggregate functions that take a bag of values and produce a single result; functions that operate on or produce complex types; chararray and bytearray functions; filter functions; and miscellaneous functions.

Each of the built-in evaluation and filter functions is discussed in the following lists. In these lists, for brevity, a bag of tuples with a given type is specified by braces surrounding parentheses and a list of the tuples' fields. For example, a bag of tuples with one integer field is denoted as {(int)}.

Built-in math UDFs

double ABS(double *input*)

> *Parameter:*
>> input
>
> *Returns:*
>> Absolute value
>
> *Since version:*
>> 0.8

double ACOS(double *input*)

> *Parameter:*
>> input
>
> *Returns:*
>> Arc cosine
>
> *Since version:*
>> 0.8

double ASIN(double *input*)

> *Parameter:*
>> input

Returns:
        Arc sine
Since version:
        0.8

double ATAN(double *input*)

Parameter:
        input
Returns:
        Arc tangent
Since version:
        0.8

double CBRT(double *input*)

Parameter:
        input
Returns:
        Cube root
Since version:
        0.8

double CEIL(double *input*)

Parameter:
        input
Returns:
        Next-highest double value that is a mathematical integer
Since version:
        0.8

double COS(double *input*)

Parameter:
        input
Returns:
        Cosine
Since version:
        0.8

double COSH(double *input*)

Parameter:
        input
Returns:
        Hyperbolic cosine

Since version:
0.8

`double EXP(double `*`input`*`)`

Parameter:
input

Returns:
Euler's number (*e*) raised to the power of *input*

Since version:
0.8

`double FLOOR(double `*`input`*`)`

Parameter:
input

Returns:
Next-lowest double value that is a mathematical integer

Since version:
0.8

`double LOG(double `*`input`*`)`

Parameter:
input

Returns:
Natural logarithm of *input*

Since version:
0.8

`double LOG10(double `*`input`*`)`

Parameter:
input

Returns:
Logarithm base 10 of *input*

Since version:
0.8

`long ROUND(double `*`input`*`)`

Parameter:
input

Returns:
Long nearest to the value of *input*

Since version:
0.8

double SIN(double *input*)

> *Parameter:*
>> *input*
>
> *Returns:*
>> Sine
>
> *Since version:*
>> 0.8

double SINH(double *input*)

> *Parameter:*
>> *input*
>
> *Returns:*
>> Hyperbolic sine
>
> *Since version:*
>> 0.8

double SQRT(double *input*)

> *Parameter:*
>> *input*
>
> *Returns:*
>> Square root
>
> *Since version:*
>> 0.8

double TAN(double *input*)

> *Parameter:*
>> *input*
>
> *Returns:*
>> Tangent
>
> *Since version:*
>> 0.8

double TANH(double *input*)

> *Parameter:*
>> *input*
>
> *Returns:*
>> Hyperbolic tangent
>
> *Since version:*
>> 0.8

Built-in aggregate UDFs

int AVG({(*int*)} *input*)

> *Parameter:*
>> *input*
>
> *Returns:*
>> Average of all values in *input*; nulls are ignored
>
> *Since version:*
>> 0.2

long AVG({(long)} *input*)

> *Parameter:*
>> *input*
>
> *Returns:*
>> Average of all values in *input*; nulls are ignored
>
> *Since version:*
>> 0.2

float AVG({(float)} *input*)

> *Parameter:*
>> *input*
>
> *Returns:*
>> Average of all values in *input*; nulls are ignored
>
> *Since version:*
>> 0.2

double AVG({(double)} *input*)

> *Parameter:*
>> *input*
>
> *Returns:*
>> Average of all values in *input*; nulls are ignored
>
> *Since version:*
>> 0.2

double AVG({(bytearray)} *input*)

> *Parameter:*
>> *input*
>
> *Returns:*
>> Average of all bytearrays, cast to doubles, in *input*; nulls are ignored
>
> *Since version:*
>> 0.1

long COUNT
> A version of COUNT that matches SQL semantics for COUNT(col)

Parameter:
    input

Returns:
    Number of records in *input*, excluding null values

Since version:
    0.1

long COUNT_STAR

A version of COUNT that matches SQL semantics for COUNT(*)

Parameter:
    input

Returns:
    Number of all records in *input*, including null values

Since version:
    0.4

int MAX({(int)} *input*)

Parameter:
    input

Returns:
    Maximum value in *input*; nulls are ignored

Since version:
    0.2

long MAX({(long)} *input*)

Parameter:
    input

Returns:
    Maximum value in *input*; nulls are ignored

Since version:
    0.2

float MAX({(float)} *input*)

Parameter:
    input

Returns:
    Maximum value in *input*; nulls are ignored

Since version:
    0.2

double MAX({(double)} *input*)

Parameter:
    input

Returns:
Maximum value in *input*; nulls are ignored

Since version:
0.2

`chararray MAX`

Parameter:
input

Returns:
Maximum value in *input*; nulls are ignored

Since version:
0.2

`double MAX({(bytearray)} input)`

Parameter:
input

Returns:
Maximum of all bytearrays, cast to doubles, in *input*; nulls are ignored

Since version:
0.1

`int MIN({(int)} input)`

Parameter:
input

Returns:
Minimum value in *input*; nulls are ignored

Since version:
0.2

`long MIN({(long)} input)`

Parameter:
input

Returns:
Minimum value in *input*; nulls are ignored

Since version:
0.2

`float MIN({(float)} input)`

Parameter:
input

Returns:
Minimum value in *input*; nulls are ignored

Since version:
    0.2

`double MIN({(double)} `*`input`*`)`

Parameter:
    input

Returns:
    Minimum value in *input*; nulls are ignored

Since version:
    0.2

`chararray MIN`

Parameter:
    input

Returns:
    Minimum value in *input*; nulls are ignored

Since version:
    0.2

`double MIN({(bytearray)} `*`input`*`)`

Parameter:
    input

Returns:
    Minimum of all bytearrays, cast to doubles, in *input*; nulls are ignored

Since version:
    0.1

`long SUM({(int)} `*`input`*`)`

Parameter:
    input

Returns:
    Sum of all values in the bag; nulls are ignored

Since version:
    0.2

`long SUM({(long)} `*`input`*`)`

Parameter:
    input

Returns:
    Sum of all values in the bag; nulls are ignored

Since version:
    0.2

```
double SUM({(float)} input)
```

Parameter:
    input

Returns:
    Sum of all values in the bag; nulls are ignored

Since version:
    0.2

```
double SUM({(double)} input)
```

Parameter:
    input

Returns:
    Sum of all values in the bag; nulls are ignored

Since version:
    0.2

```
double SUM({(bytearray)} input)
```

Parameter:
    input

Returns:
    Sum of all bytearrays, cast to doubles, in *input*; nulls are ignored

Since version:
    0.1

Built-in chararray and bytearray UDFs

```
chararray CONCAT(chararray c1, chararray c2)
```

Parameters:
    c1

    c2

Returns:
    Concatenation of *c1* and *c2*

Since version:
    0.1

```
bytearray CONCAT(bytearray b1, bytearray b2)
```

Parameters:
    b1

    b2

Returns:
    Concatenation of *b1* and *b2*

Since version:
> 0.1

`int INDEXOF(chararray `*`source,`*` chararray `*`search`*`)`

> *Parameters:*
>> *source*: the chararray to search in
>>
>> *search*: the chararray to search for
>
> *Returns:*
>> Index of the first instance of *search* in *source*; -1 if *search* is not in *source*
>
> *Since version:*
>> 0.8

`int LAST_INDEX_OF(chararray `*`source,`*` chararray `*`search`*`)`

> *Parameters:*
>> *source*: the chararray to search in
>>
>> *search*: the chararray to search for
>
> *Returns:*
>> Index of the last instance of *search* in *source*; -1 if *search* is not in *source*
>
> *Since version:*
>> 0.8

`chararray LCFIRST(chararray `*`input`*`)`

> *Parameter:*
>> *input*
>
> *Returns:*
>> *input*, with the first character converted to lowercase
>
> *Since version:*
>> 0.8

`chararray LOWER(chararray `*`input`*`)`

> *Parameter:*
>> *input*
>
> *Returns:*
>> *input* with all characters converted to lowercase
>
> *Since version:*
>> 0.8

`chararray REGEX_EXTRACT(chararray `*`source,`*` chararray `*`regex,`*` int `*`n`*`)`

> *Parameters:*
>> *source*: the chararray to search in
>>
>> *regex*: the regular expression to search for
>>
>> *n*: take the *n*th match, counting from 0

Returns:
nth subset of the *source* matching *regex*; null if there are no matches

Since version:
0.8

(chararray) REGEX_EXTRACT_ALL(chararray *source*, chararray *regex*)

Parameters:
source: the chararray to search in

regex: the regular expression to search for

Returns:
Tuple containing all subsets of *source* matching *regex*; null if there are no matches

Since version:
0.8

chararray REPLACE(chararray *source*, chararray *toReplace*, chararray *newValue*)

Parameters:
source: the chararray to search in

toReplace: the chararray to be replaced

newValue: the new chararray to replace it with

Returns:
source with all instances of *toReplace* changed to *newValue*

Since version:
0.8

long SIZE(chararray *input*)

Parameter:
input

Returns:
Number of characters in *input*

Since version:
0.2

long SIZE(bytearray *input*)

Parameter:
input

Returns:
Number of bytes in *input*

Since version:
0.2

(chararray) STRSPLIT(chararray *source*)
Split a chararray by whitespace

Parameter:
    source: the chararray to split

Returns:
    Tuple with one field for each section of *source*

Since version:
    0.8

(chararray) STRSPLIT(chararray *source*, chararray *regex*)
Split a chararray by a regular expression

Parameters:
    source: the chararray to split

    regex: the regular expression to use as the delimiter

Returns:
    Tuple with one field for each section of *source*

Since version:
    0.8

(chararray) STRSPLIT(chararray *source*, chararray *regex*, int *maxsplits*)
Split a chararray by a regular expression

Parameters:
    source: the chararray to split

    regex: the regular expression to use as the delimiter

    max: the maximum number of splits

Returns:
    Tuple with one field for each section of *source*; if there are more than one *maxsplits* sections, only the first *maxsplits* sections will be in the tuple

Since version:
    0.8

chararray SUBSTRING(chararray *source*, int *start*, int *end*)

Parameters:
    source: the chararray to split

    start: the start position (inclusive), counting from 0

    end: the end position (exclusive), counting from 0

Returns:
    Subchararray; error if any input value has a length shorter than *start*

Since version:
    0.8

{(chararray)} TOKENIZE(chararray *input*)

Parameter:
    source: the chararray to split

Returns:

> *input* split on whitespace, with each resulting value being placed in its own tuple and all tuples placed in the bag

Since version:

> 0.1

`chararray TRIM(chararray input)`

Parameter:

> *input*

Returns:

> *input* with all leading and trailing whitespace removed

Since version:

> 0.8

`chararray UCFIRST(chararray input)`

Parameter:

> *input*

Returns:

> *input* with the first character converted to uppercase

Since version:

> 0.8

`chararray UPPER(chararray input)`

Parameter:

> *input*

Returns:

> *input* with all characters converted to uppercase

Since version:

> 0.8

Built-in complex type UDFs

`{(chararray, chararray, double)} COR({(double)} b1, {(double)} b2)`

> Calculate the correlation between two bags of doubles

Parameters:

> *b1*
>
> *b2*

Returns:

> First chararray is the name of *b1*, second chararray is the name of *b2*, double is the correlation between *b1* and *b2*

Since version:

> 0.8

`{(chararray, chararray, double)} COV({(double)} b1, {(double)} b2)`

Calculate the covariance of two bags of doubles

Parameters:

  b1

  b2

Returns:

First chararray is the name of *b1*, second chararray is the name of *b2*, double is the covariance of *b1* and *b2*

Since version:

  0.8

`bag DIFF(bag b1, bag b2)`

Parameters:

  b1

  b2

Returns:

All records from *b1* that are not in *b2*, and all records from *b2* that are not in *b1*

Since version:

  0.1

`long SIZE(map input)`

Parameter:

  input

Returns:

Number of key-value pairs in *input*

Since version:

  0.2

`long SIZE(tuple input)`

Parameter:

  input

Returns:

Number of fields in *input*

Since version:

  0.2

`long SIZE(bag input)`

Parameter:

  input

Returns:

Number of tuples in *input*

Since version:
    0.2

bag TOBAG(...)

Parameter:
    Variable

Returns:
    If all inputs have the same schema, the resulting bag will have that schema, else it will have a null schema; if the parameters are tuples, all schemas must have the same field names in addition to types

Since version:
    0.8

map TOMAP(...)

Parameter:
    Variable

Returns:
    Input parameters are paired up and placed in a map as key/value, key/value; all keys must be chararrays; an odd number of arguments will result in an error

Since version:
    0.9

bag TOP(int *numRecords*, int *field*, bag *source*)

Parameters:
    numRecords: the number of records to return

    field: the field to sort on

    source: the bag to return records from

Returns:
    A bag with *numRecords*

Since version:
    0.8

tuple TOTUPLE(...)

Parameter:
    Variable

Returns:
    A tuple with all of the fields passed in as arguments

Since version:
    0.8

Built-in filter functions

```
boolean IsEmpty(bag)
```

Parameter:
   input
Returns:
   Boolean
Since version:
   0.1

```
boolean IsEmpty(tuple)
```

Parameter:
   input
Returns:
   Boolean
Since version:
   0.1

Miscellaneous built-in UDF

```
double RANDOM()
```

Returns:
   A random double between 0 and 1
Since version:
   0.4

Piggybank

Piggybank is Pig's repository of user-contributed functions. Piggybank functions are distributed as part of the Pig distribution, but they are not built in. You must `regis ter` the Piggybank JAR to use them, which you can do in your distribution at *contrib/piggybank/java/piggybank.jar*.

At the time of writing, there is no central website or set of documentation for Piggybank. To find out what is in there, you will need to browse through the code. You can see all of the included functions by looking in your distribution under *contrib/piggybank/*. Piggybank does not yet include any Python functions, but it is set up to allow users to contribute functions in languages other than Java, so hopefully this will change in time.

Overview of Hadoop

This appendix gives a brief overview of Hadoop, focusing on elements that are of interest to Pig users. For a thorough discussion of Hadoop, see *Hadoop: The Definitive Guide*, by Tom White (O'Reilly). Hadoop's two main components are MapReduce and HDFS.

MapReduce

MapReduce is the framework for running jobs in Hadoop. It provides a simple and powerful paradigm for parallelizing data processing.

The *JobTracker* is the central coordinator of jobs in MapReduce. It controls which jobs are being run, which resources they are assigned, etc. On each node in the cluster there is a *TaskTracker* that is responsible for running the map or reduce tasks assigned to it by the JobTracker.

MapReduce views its input as a collection of records. When reading from HDFS, a record is usually a single line of text. Each record has a key and a value. There is no requirement that data be sorted by key or that the keys must be unique. Similarly, MapReduce produces a set of records, each with a key and value.

MapReduce operates on data in jobs. Every job has one input and one output.* MapReduce breaks each job into a series of tasks. These tasks are of two primary types: map and reduce.

---

* It is possible to bend this rule, as Pig and many other applications do. For example, the one input can be a concatenation of multiple input files, and files can be opened on the side in tasks and written to or read from. But, conceptually, each job has one primary input and one primary output.

Map Phase

In the map phase, MapReduce gives the user an opportunity to operate on every record in the data set individually. This phase is commonly used to project out unwanted fields, transform fields, or apply filters. Certain types of joins and grouping can also be done in the map (e.g., joins where the data is already sorted or hash-based aggregation). There is no requirement that for every input record there should be one output record. Maps can choose to remove records or explode one record into multiple records.

Every MapReduce job specifies an InputFormat. This class is responsible for determining how data is split across map tasks and for providing a RecordReader.

In order to specify how data is split across tasks, an InputFormat divides the input data into a set of InputSplits. Each InputSplit is given to an individual map. In addition to information on what to read, the InputSplit includes a list of nodes that should be used to read the data. In this way, when the data resides on HDFS, MapReduce is able to move the computation to the data.

The RecordReader provided by an InputFormat reads input data and produces key-value pairs to be passed into the map. This class controls how data is decompressed (if necessary), and how it is converted to Java types that MapReduce can work with.

Combiner Phase

The combiner gives applications a chance to apply their reducer logic early on. As the map phase writes output, it is serialized and placed into an in-memory buffer. When this buffer fills, MapReduce will sort the buffer and then run the combiner if the application has provided an implementation for it. The resulting output is then written to local disk, to be picked up by the shuffle phase and sent to the reducers. MapReduce might choose not to run the combiner if it determines it will be more efficient not to.

After the shuffle, each reducer will have one input for each map. The reducer needs to merge these inputs in order to begin processing. It is not efficient to merge too many inputs simultaneously. Thus, if the number of inputs exceeds a certain value, the data will be merged and rewritten to disk before being given to the reducer. During this merge, the combiner will be applied in an attempt to reduce the size of the input data. See Hadoop's documentation (*http://hadoop.apache.org/common/docs/r0.20.2/mapred _tutorial.html#Shuffle%2FReduce+Parameters*) for a discussion of how and when this prereduce merge is triggered.

Because the combine phase will be run zero, one, or multiple times, the input and output keys and values of the combiner must be of the same type.

Shuffle Phase

During the shuffle phase, MapReduce partitions data among the various reducers.

MapReduce uses a class called `Partitioner` to partition records to reducers during the shuffle phase. An implementation of `Partitioner` takes the key and value of the record, as well as the total number of reduce tasks, and returns the reduce task number that the record should go to. By default, MapReduce uses `HashPartitioner`, which calls `hashCode()` on the key and returns the result modulo of the number of reduce tasks. MapReduce users can override this default to use their own implementation of `Partitioner`. See the Hadoop documentation (*http://hadoop.apache.org/common/docs/ r0.20.0/api/org/apache/hadoop/mapreduce/Partitioner.html*) for more details on `Partitioner`s.

Data arriving on the reducer has been partitioned and sorted by the map, combine, and shuffle phases. By default, the data is sorted by the partition key. For example, if a user has a data set partitioned on user ID, in the reducer it will be sorted by user ID as well. Thus, MapReduce uses sorting to group like keys together. It is possible to specify additional sort keys beyond the partition key. So, for example, the user could choose to partition by user ID and also sort by timestamp. This feature is useful, as the user does not have to implement her own sorting on the reduce data.

Reduce Phase

The input to the reduce phase is each key from the shuffle plus all of the records associated with that key. Because all records with the same value for the key are now collected together, it is possible to do joins and aggregation operations such as counting. The MapReduce user explicitly controls parallelism in the reduce. MapReduce jobs that do not require a reduce phase can set the reduce count to zero. These are referred to as *map-only jobs*.

Output Phase

The reducer (or map in a map-only job) writes its output via an `OutputFormat`. `Output Format` is responsible for providing a `RecordWriter`, which takes the key-value pairs produced by the task and stores them. This includes serializing, possibly compressing, and writing them to HDFS, HBase, etc. The `OutputFormat` is also responsible for providing the `OutputCommitter`, which is used to do post-output operations such as cleaning up after failure and indicating to the storage medium that data is available (e.g., a database commit).

Distributed Cache

Sometimes all or many of the tasks in a MapReduce job will need to access a single file or a set of files. For example, when joining a large file with a small file, one approach is to open the small file as a side file (that is, open it directly in your map task rather than specify it as an input to your MapReduce job), load it into memory, and do the join in the map phase. When thousands of map or reduce tasks attempt to open the same HDFS file simultaneously, this puts a large strain on the NameNode and the DataNodes storing that file. To avoid this situation, MapReduce provides the *distributed cache*. The distributed cache allows users to specify—as part of their MapReduce job—any HDFS files they want every task to have access to. These files are then copied onto the local disk of the task nodes as part of the task initiation. Map or reduce tasks can then read these as local files.

Handling Failure

Part of the power of MapReduce is that it handles failure and retry for the user. If you have a MapReduce job that involves 10,000 map tasks (not an uncommon situation), the odds are reasonably high that at least one machine will fail during that job. Rather than trying to remove failure from the system, MapReduce is designed with the assumption that failure is common and must be coped with. When a given map or reduce task fails, MapReduce handles spawning a replacement task to do the work. Sometimes it does not even wait for tasks to fail. When a task is slow, it might spawn a duplicate to see if it can get the task done sooner. This is referred to as *speculative execution*. After a task fails a certain number of times (four by default), MapReduce gives up and declares the task and the job a failure.

Hadoop Distributed File System

The Hadoop Distributed File System (HDFS) stores files across all of the nodes in a Hadoop cluster. It handles breaking the files into large blocks and distributing them across different machines. It also makes multiple copies of each block so that if any one machine fails, no data is lost or unavailable. By default it makes three copies of each block, though this value is configurable. One copy is always written locally to the node where the write is executed. If your Hadoop cluster is spread across multiple racks, HDFS will write one copy of the block on the same rack as the machine where the write is happening, and one copy on a machine in a different rack. When a machine or disk dies or blocks are corrupted, HDFS will handle making another copy of the lost blocks to ensure that the proper number of replicas are maintained.

HDFS is designed specifically to support MapReduce. The block sizes are large, 64 MB by default. Many users set them higher, to 128 MB or even 256 MB. Storing data in large blocks works well for MapReduce's batch model, where it is assumed that every job will read all of the records in a file. Modern disks are much faster at sequential read than seek. Thus for large data sets, if you require more than a few records, sequentially reading the entire data set outperforms random reads. The three-way duplication of data, beyond obviously providing fault tolerance, also serves MapReduce because it gives the JobTracker more options for locating map tasks on the same machine as one of the blocks.

HDFS presents a POSIX-like interface to users and provides standard filesystem features such as file ownership and permissions, security, and quotas.

The brain of HDFS is the *NameNode*. It is responsible for maintaining the master list of files in HDFS, and it handles the mapping of filenames to blocks, knowing where each block is stored, and making sure each block is replicated the appropriate number of times. *DataNodes* are machines that store HDFS data. They store each block in a separate file. Each DataNode is colocated with a TaskTracker to allow moving of the computation to data.

Index

Symbols

!= inequality operator, 40
\# dereference operator for maps, 25
$ macro parameter, 79
$ parameter substitution target, 77
% modulo operator, 38
() tuple parentheses, 36
* all fields, 37
* multiplication operator, 37
* zero or more characters glob, 35
\+ addition operator, 37
\- subtraction operator, 37
\- unary negative operator, 38
\-- single line comment operator, 34
.. range of fields, 37
/ division operator, 37
/* */ multiline comment operator, 34
< inequality operator, 40
<= inequality operator, 40
== equality operator, 40
> inequality operator, 40
>= inequality operator, 40
? any character glob, 35
? bincond operator, 38
[] map brackets, 36
\ escape character, 35
{} bag braces, 36
{} macro operator, 79

A

ABS function, 172
accumulator interface, 139
ACID, 166
ACOS function, 172

AddForEach optimization, 96
algebraic calculations, 43, 135
algebraic interface, 135–138
aliases, 33, 53
Amazon Elastic MapReduce (EMR), 10, 17
Apache HBase, 166–168
Apache HCatalog, 169
Apache Hive, 165
Apache open source, 1, 11
arithmetic operators, 37
as clause (load function), 35, 40
as clause (stream command), 70
ASIN function, 172
ATAN function, 173
AVG functions, 176

B

bad records, handling, 109
bag data type, 25, 28, 123, 135, 142
bag DIFF function, 185
bag projection, 38
bag TOBAG function, 186
bag TOP function, 186
BagFactory class, 123
baseball examples
    base on balls and IBBs, 29
    batting average, 38
    data set, xii, 57
    players by position and team, 74
    slugging percentage, 52
behavior prediction models, 8
binary condition operator, 38
bind call, 113
bindings, multiple, 114, 116
boolean IsEmpty functions, 187

We'd like to hear your suggestions for improving our indexes. Send email to *index@oreilly.com*.

About the Author

Alan Gates is an original member of the engineering team that took Pig from a Yahoo! Labs research project to a successful Apache open source project. In that role, he oversaw the implementation of the language, including programming interfaces and the overall design. He has presented Pig at numerous conferences and user groups, universities, and companies. Alan is a member of the Apache Software Foundation and a cofounder of Hortonworks. He has a BS in Mathematics from Oregon State University and an MA in Theology from Fuller Theological Seminary.

Colophon

The animal on the cover of *Programming Pig* is a domestic pig (*Sus scrofa domesticus* or *Sus domesticus*). While the larger pig family is naturally distributed in Africa, Asia, and Europe, domesticated pigs can now be found in nearly every part of the world that people inhabit. In fact, some pigs have been specifically bred to best equip them for various climates; for example, heavily coated varieties have been bred in colder climates. People have brought pigs with them almost wherever they go for good reason: in addition to their primary use as a source of food, humans have been using the skin, bones, and hair of pigs to make various tools and implements for millennia.

Domestic pigs are directly descended from wild boars, and evidence suggests that there have been three distinct domestication events; the first took place in the Tigris River Basin as early as 13,000 BC, the second in China, and the third in Europe, though the last likely occurred after Europeans were introduced to domestic pigs from the Middle East. Despite the long history, however, taxonomists do not agree as to the proper classification for the domestic pig. Some believe that domestic pigs remain simply a subspecies of the larger pig group including the wild boar (*Sus scrofa*), while others insist that they belong to a species all their own. In either case, there are several hundred breeds of domestic pig, each with its own particular characteristics.

Perhaps because of their long history and prominent role in human society, and their tendency toward social behavior, domestic pigs have appeared in film, literature, and other cultural media with regularity. Examples include "The Three Little Pigs," Miss Piggy, and Porky the Pig. Additionally, domestic pigs have recently been recognized for their intelligence and their ability to be trained (similar to dogs), and have consequently begun to be treated as pets.

The cover image is from the Dover Pictorial Archive. The cover font is Adobe ITC Garamond. The text font is Linotype Birka; the heading font is Adobe Myriad Condensed; and the code font is LucasFont's TheSansMonoCondensed.

Get even more for your money.

Join the O'Reilly Community, and register the O'Reilly books you own. It's free, and you'll get:

- $4.99 ebook upgrade offer
- 40% upgrade offer on O'Reilly print books
- Membership discounts on books and events
- Free lifetime updates to ebooks and videos
- Multiple ebook formats, DRM FREE
- Participation in the O'Reilly community
- Newsletters
- Account management
- 100% Satisfaction Guarantee

Signing up is easy:

1. Go to: oreilly.com/go/register
2. Create an O'Reilly login.
3. Provide your address.
4. Register your books.

Note: English-language books only

To order books online:
oreilly.com/store

For questions about products or an order:
orders@oreilly.com

To sign up to get topic-specific email announcements and/or news about upcoming books, conferences, special offers, and new technologies:
elists@oreilly.com

For technical questions about book content:
booktech@oreilly.com

To submit new book proposals to our editors:
proposals@oreilly.com

O'Reilly books are available in multiple DRM-free ebook formats. For more information:
oreilly.com/ebooks

O'REILLY®

Spreading the knowledge of innovators   oreilly.com

Have it your way.

O'Reilly eBooks

- Lifetime access to the book when you buy through oreilly.com
- Provided in up to four DRM-free file formats, for use on the devices of your choice: PDF, .epub, Kindle-compatible .mobi, and Android .apk
- Fully searchable, with copy-and-paste and print functionality
- Alerts when files are updated with corrections and additions

oreilly.com/ebooks/

Safari Books Online

- Access the contents and quickly search over 7000 books on technology, business, and certification guides
- Learn from expert video tutorials, and explore thousands of hours of video on technology and design topics
- Download whole books or chapters in PDF format, at no extra cost, to print or read on the go
- Get early access to books as they're being written
- Interact directly with authors of upcoming books
- Save up to 35% on O'Reilly print books

See the complete Safari Library at safari.oreilly.com

Lightning Source UK Ltd.
Milton Keynes UK
UKOW05f1954030116

265653UK00002B/9/P